Finding a Fallen Hero

Anthony Joseph Korkuc
December 25, 1917–February 25, 1944

Finding a Fallen Hero

The Death of a Ball Turret Gunner

Bob Korkuc

Foreword by James M. McCaffrey

UNIVERSITY OF OKLAHOMA PRESS : NORMAN

Library of Congress Cataloging-in-Publication Data

Korkuc, Bob, 1962–
  Finding a fallen hero : the death of a ball turret gunner / Bob Korkuc ;
foreword by James M. McCaffrey.
       p. cm.
  Includes bibliographical references and index.
  ISBN 978-0-8061-3892-3 (hardcover : alk. paper)   1. Korkuc, Anthony,
1917–1944—Death and burial.   2. World War, 1939–1945—Aerial
operations, American.   3. Aircraft accidents—Investigation—United
States.   4. Aircraft accidents—Germany.   5. Aircraft accident victims—
United States.   6. United States. Army Air Forces. Bomb Squadron,
532nd—Biography.   7. United States. Army Air Forces—Biography.
8. United States. Army Air Forces—Aerial gunners—Biography.   I. Title.
  D790.263532nd .K67 2008
  940.54'4973092—dc22
  [B]   2007027662

The paper in this book meets the guidelines for permanence and
durability of the Committee on Production Guidelines for Book Longevity
of the Council on Library Resources, Inc. ∞

1 2 3 4 5 6 7 8 9 10

This book is respectfully dedicated to my parents, Dorothy and Edmund Korkuc, but especially to my father, who asked an innocent question that sent me on a seven-year quest to find the answer. It is also dedicated to the memory of my uncle, Anthony Korkuc, and his five crewmates—Thomas Hunnicutt, Anthony Bartolo, Dale Schilling, Boyd Burgess, and Earl Wonning—who paid the ultimate sacrifice on February 25, 1944, while on a B-17 bombing mission against Germany. Lastly, it is dedicated to the "Greatest Generation" of men and women, many of whom have helped me understand the events of so long ago.

Contents

Foreword

The very title of this book tells a story. It is a story that repeated itself thousands of times during World War II—the death in combat of a bomber crewman. Casualties among American bomber crewmen in Europe during World War II were high. Every time a heavy bomber— a B-17 or a B-24—failed to return from a mission, it meant the loss not only of an expensive piece of machinery but of its ten-man crew. Some men parachuted to safety and ultimately returned to their bases to fight again; others spent the rest of the war in German prison camps. Many died. Anthony Korkuc, from the small town of Seekonk, Massachusetts, was one of those killed in action.

Anthony Korkuc was one of millions of young men who served in the military when his nation needed him. He entered the army a couple of months before the Japanese attacked Pearl Harbor and wound up in the medical corps. He soon grew tired of the routine at a stateside psychiatric hospital and applied for transfer to the Army Air Forces, where he hoped to become a pilot. The Army trained him instead as an aerial gunner and assigned him to the crew of a B-17 bomber.

Designed by Boeing to be one of the nation's frontline strategic bombers, American B-17s saw combat on the first day of the war. Even as Japanese planes attacked the naval base at Pearl Harbor, they also attempted to destroy as many Army airplanes as they could, and these included a handful of B-17s. In the Philippines, likewise, B-17s on the ground at Clark Field made tempting targets for Japanese pilots. The B-17s' introduction into combat against Germany, however, was several months away. On August 17, 1942, a dozen B-17s attacked railroad yards in German-occupied France. They did not inflict significant damage, but it was a start, and all of the planes returned intact. It would not always be that easy. On the first American bombing raids against the German homeland, in August 1943, sixty bombers—along with six hundred crewmen—were lost.

Advocates believed that these bombers, with their ten (and later thirteen) machine guns, would be able to defend themselves against enemy fighters and would not, therefore, require American fighters as escorts. The number of bombers lost to the Luftwaffe soon disproved this idea. There was strength in numbers, however, and the bombers limited losses somewhat by flying in large compact formations so that the combined defensive firepower of every plane would defend the formation against attack.

Because of their heavy array of defensive firepower, the B-17s came to be known as Flying Fortresses. Their defenses included revolving, spherical machine gun mounts on the undersides of the bombers. Ball turrets were so small that only men of slight physical stature could occupy them, and even then the space was so crowded that men could not wear parachutes. If enemy action or mechanical difficulties necessitated abandoning the aircraft in flight, often one of the other gunners had to help the ball turret gunner climb out of his turret and into the airplane where he could then don his parachute and bail out. Ball turret gunners often spent hours in an almost fetal position as they rotated their turrets through full 360-degree lateral rotations, looking for attacking enemy fighters to engage before they could inflict damage on the bomber. In spite of later statistics to the contrary, bomber crewmen universally regarded the ball turret position as the most dangerous one on the aircraft. Anthony Korkuc, standing at just a shade over five and a half feet, was shorter than other gunners on his crew and wound up flying in the ball turret.

An air war against Germany was an essential first step toward ultimate victory. The Allies would have to inflict as much damage on the enemy's war-waging capabilities as possible before committing land forces to the continent. This required the destruction of more than just the military hardware that already existed. Factories that produced airplanes, tanks, and their components were, of course, primary targets. Road and railroad networks, oil storage facilities, and electrical generating plants had to be destroyed as well.

By early 1944, with the scheduled invasion of France only months away, it became imperative to destroy as much of the German air force as possible so that it could not disrupt the proposed landings. This meant not only defeating German pilots in air-to-air combat but destroying Germany's industrial capacity to produce more airplanes. With an eye toward such destruction, Allied planners launched Operation ARGU-MENT during a stretch of unseasonably good flying weather in the last week of February. It consisted of six successive days of heavy air raids against industrial targets in Germany, Austria, and Poland. American bombers of the Eighth Air Force flew from bases in England, and others from the Fifteenth Air Force took off from Italy to drop some ten thousand tons of bombs in daylight raids while Royal Air Force bombers conducted nighttime attacks on the same types of targets.

On Friday, February 25, the final day of what became known as "Big Week," almost twelve hundred American B-17 and B-24 bombers took to the skies. The first few days of the campaign saw the destruction of a significant percentage of factory buildings and set enemy production schedules back by several months, but there were still viable targets. The Messerschmitt plants at Regensburg and Augsburg were high on the target lists, as well as plants producing aircraft components at Fürth and Stuttgart. German defenders had already exacted a significant toll of Allied bombers, and on this day Luftwaffe fighters and anti-aircraft artillery knocked dozens more of the attacking planes out of the sky. The ball turret gunner on one of those ill-fated B-17s was Anthony Korkuc. His plane had already dropped its bombs on Augsburg and was headed for its base in England when it went down. The end of his life marked the beginning of the present story.

When Bob Korkuc visited his uncle's grave at Arlington National Cemetery in 1995, the former airman had been dead for more than a half century, and his nephew realized how little he knew of the circumstances of Anthony's death. Thus began a quest, a labor of love, a search for a sense of closure. The closure was not for Bob, who never met his uncle and in fact had not even been born when his uncle died. Closure was for Edmund Korkuc, Bob's father and Anthony's younger brother.

Bob Korkuc realized from the beginning that he lacked much of the basic information he needed if he were ever going to find out about his uncle's last moments. His father provided a few clues, but he would have to dig for the rest. The story of his dogged pursuit of information should serve as a guide for others looking for answers from history.

He learned a lot during his long quest, and he shares what he discovered—and how he discovered it—in this book. He learned, for example, something that police detectives have known for a long time:

that eyewitnesses to an event do not always agree on what transpired. Were there, for instance, three German fighters that attacked the crippled B-17 that day, or only one? Witnesses disagreed.

He learned that "official" information is not always what it seems. Why, for instance, did the official Individual Deceased Personnel File for his uncle have the wrong month, date, and even year of his death? And who was actually responsible for the downing of his uncle's plane? Was it a German fighter pilot, or was it German anti-aircraft artillerists? Each claimed the kill in official wartime reports.

He learned the value of networking. By attending reunions of Eighth Air Force veterans, he met men whose experiences had paralleled his uncle's. By corresponding with historians and journalists, both in the United States and in Europe, he found more pieces of the puzzle. By visiting Internet discussion forums of World War II enthusiasts, he learned what government documents to look for and where to find them.

And he learned what it was like to actually fly in a B-17.

Perhaps most of all, he learned what his uncle's last day of life was probably like, and he learned how German villagers saw to the decent burial of this enemy airman who only a short time before had been taking part in an attack on their homeland. And he learned of the circuitous route by which his uncle's remains moved from a churchyard in a small German village to the National Cemetery at Arlington, Virginia.

He came to appreciate even more the men of what Tom Brokaw has called the Greatest Generation, but he also learned something else about these men. He learned that even after more than sixty years, some of them find it painfully difficult to talk about their comrades who died in combat: men such as Anthony Korkuc who never had a chance to grow old.

Finding a Fallen Hero highlights one man's exhaustive efforts to learn the truth about an uncle he never met. It is a tribute both to a long-dead airman and to his nephew's drive and determination to find answers. It illustrates the value of perseverance—and of luck! Bob Korkuc's search for answers should serve as encouragement to others with similar quests.

James M. McCaffrey
University of Houston

Preface

Letter to Saint Peter

Let them in, Peter, they are very tired;
Give them the couches where the angels sleep.
Let them wake whole again to new dawns fired
With sun not war. And may their peace be deep.
Remember where the broken bodies lie . . .
And give them things they like. Let them make noise.
God knows how young they were to have to die!
Give swing bands, not gold harps, to these our boys.
Let them love, Peter,—they have had no time—
Girls sweet as meadow wind, with flowering hair . . .
They should have trees and bird song, hills to climb—
The taste of summer in a ripened pear.
Tell them how they are missed. Say not to fear;
It's going to be all right with us down here.

Elma Dean[1]

On February 25, 1944, Anthony Joseph Korkuc—my Uncle Tony, my father's oldest brother—was killed when his plane was shot down over Germany during World War II. He was only twenty-six years old. He and the other members of his aircrew who died in the crash were buried by the Germans in a small village cemetery, and for many years, no one in our family knew where his broken body lay. As far as we knew, Tony had been lost forever that day. It was not until 1995 that we found out that his remains had been recovered from his original burial site in Germany and re-interred in Arlington National Cemetery. In searching for answers about his final journey, I embarked on a seven-year quest that connected me with people and places I will never forget. It really is all right with us down here, Tony—but even all these years later, you are missed.

I would like to thank the following people who have helped make this book possible: the late Brian Pohanka, the late Ernest "Mo" Moriarty, Ted Darcy, Sigrid Kellenter, Don Caldwell, Tony Wood, Rabe Anton, John Manrho, Keith Poulter, Terry "TJ" Johnston, Jr., Gregory Urwin, the late Richard Brown, James Good Brown, Joe Waddell, Leonard Spivey, Elizabeth Yee, John Wood, Howard Van Hoozer, Al Suchy, Allen Webb, Edward Carr, Armour Bowen, John Howland, Dave Brophy, Dale McCrory, Frank Slomzenski, 381st Bomb Group historian Dave Osborne, Ron MacKay, Hermann Möck, Karl Heinz, Mrs. Anna Ulmer, Ulli Semmelrock, Uwe Kühnapfel, Günter Clemens, Hans Grimminger, Rudi Penker, Jochen Prien, Danny Lee, Lee and Eva Hunnicutt, Jennie Domiziano, the late Virginia Burgess Prescott, Norman Wonning, Dianne DeRose Stansell, Harley and Dee Foos, Charles Korkuc, Johnny Korkuc, and Sophie Connors.

Without the help of my friend Michael D. Smith, I would not have been able to decipher the German texts that I encountered in the course of my research.

I was so pleased to be able to correspond with the three crew survivors who were alive when this research began—Don Henderson, Nick DeRose, and Raoul Ramos. Their thoughtful and candid responses to all of my questions were greatly appreciated. With the passing of Raoul Ramos in 2003 and Nick DeRose in 2004, the entire crew of February 25, 1944, is now reunited once again.

I would also like to thank the entire staff of the University of Oklahoma Press, who helped me polish this book into shape. I want to particularly thank copyeditor Jane Lyle, and Editor-in-Chief Chuck Rankin for encouraging me throughout the process.

I am especially grateful to Marcus "Moc" Mockler, his wife, Susanne, and their entire family for being the perfect hosts during my trip to Germany.

Lastly, I want to thank my wife, Martha Jean, who took care of our two children, Jennifer and Ryan, while I put the finishing touches on this book.

I am hopeful that this book will act as a blueprint for readers who are interested in attempting similar research into the circumstances surrounding the wartime death of a family member. When I first set out to research my Uncle Tony's story in 1995, little help was available, and the path seemed difficult. Much has changed in the last decade, and the available resources are now plentiful. To assist the reader, I have included a "Web Resources" section at the back of the book that should prove helpful in getting others started. I encourage those who are so inclined to make the journey, because the rewards are many.

Amherst, New Hampshire
April 29, 2007

Finding a Fallen Hero

CHAPTER 1

Mourning a Hero

My father and I awoke at dawn on July 15, 1995, in Manassas, Virginia. We were nearing the end of a ten-day tour of the American Civil War battlefield sites. Our Toyota van, nicknamed the "Gray Ghost," had no air conditioning, and we were suffering from the heat of the Virginia summer. Nevertheless, this was the trip of a lifetime—father and son sharing each other's company as we learned about the bloody Civil War battles of 1861–65.

I wanted to see the mansion that Robert E. Lee lived in prior to taking up arms against his country—now home to Arlington National Cemetery—and visit the graves of those who had fallen in its defense throughout the years. One of those was my father's oldest brother, Anthony Korkuc. On this day we would be paying our respects to my Uncle Tony, who volunteered his service to the United States Army Air Forces during World War II. From a photograph that my father had, we knew that Tony's name and the date of his death—February 25, 1944—were etched on a memorial at Arlington.

We entered the cemetery via Patton Avenue and drove aimlessly through the silent gardens of stone. We soon realized that it would be futile to look for Tony's memorial without help from the cemetery staff, so we made our way to the Visitors' Center, where we asked for directions. An attendant searched through several file cabinets, then told us that Uncle Tony's gravesite was located in section 34 at plot 1631.

My dad was dumbfounded. The attendant had located not his brother's memorial, but his *gravesite!* How was this possible? Tony Korkuc had been lost forever while on a bombing mission to Augsburg, Germany. His airplane had been shot down, and his body was never recovered. How could this be his gravesite? All the attendant could

Arlington National Cemetery memorial to Anthony Korkuc, September 1993.
Photo courtesy of the Korkuc family.

tell us was that the remains were returned under the World War II Dead
Program, and Anthony Korkuc was buried in plot 1631.

I asked the attendant for directions to the site. She produced a map
of the cemetery and marked the route with a yellow pen. We returned
to the "Gray Ghost" and followed the path toward Tony Korkuc's
gravesite. I pulled the van to the curb as we reached the "X" on the
map. As we got out, I caught sight of a gravestone that looked to be
the one in my father's photo. I paused and let Dad approach the stone
by himself. After reading his brother's name, he hung his head in
silence for a minute or so before turning away. I then approached the
stone and paid my own respects to an uncle I had never known.

Once back in the van, we drove in silence as we continued our tour
of the historic grounds. Finally my father broke the quiet mood: "I
wonder how Tony's remains got from Germany to Arlington."

It took me seven years to be able to answer the innocent question
that my father asked on that hot July afternoon. How was it that
Arlington became my Uncle Tony's final resting place, given that he
had been lost over Germany in February 1944? The search for the

answer has taken me across America and to Europe, and along the way I have been privileged to meet many honorable men of the World War II generation. I have traveled across time to piece together the last moments of my uncle's life. This is the story of my search, and of Tony Korkuc's last combat mission.

THE SEARCH FOR ANSWERS BEGINS

After returning from Virginia, I wrote to Arlington National Cemetery to see whether anyone there could shed some light on the mystery. Six weeks elapsed before I received a response. It was disappointingly brief. The letter reiterated that Tony's remains had been returned under the World War II Dead Program, and recommended that I forward any questions I might have to two other government agencies—the American Battle Monuments Commission (ABMC) and the National Personnel Records Center (NPRC) in St. Louis, Missouri. Other than Tony's Army serial number—31036784—it provided no new information.

Feeling a bit demoralized, I did not take the next step until the following spring. In May 1996, I sent letters to both the ABMC and the NPRC. A month later, I received a response from the NPRC. It said that the records of Anthony J. Korkuc had been lost in a fire at their facility in 1973. The fire had destroyed about 80 percent of the records for Army personnel discharged between 1912 and 1960. It was hard to determine exactly what was lost, because there were no indexes to the blocks of records involved. Since no copies had been made of the originals, they could offer no further help. I was already beginning to realize that my research would require resilience in the face of disappointments and patience with the slowness of responses.

Several weeks later, the ABMC wrote to tell me that the records I was seeking were not stored at their facility, but the Department of the Army's U.S. Total Army Personnel Command (TAPC) in Alexandria, Virginia, might maintain the data. To the ABMC's credit, they saved me some effort and forwarded my letter to the TAPC. In early July, I received a letter from the command in response to my Freedom of Information Act (FOIA) request for World War II casualty information pertaining to my uncle. I was informed that their command maintains Individual Deceased Personnel Files (IDPF) on all Army personnel who were killed while overseas during World War II and Korea. They thought that Tony's IDPF, also known as a "293 File," would help me, as it contained the death and burial information that I was seeking. I was pleased to finally be making some headway, but I was disappointed to learn that the command was in the process of handling more than one thousand FOIA requests for IDPF information. Further, I was told that I should expect a delay of approximately a year before receiving a response from them!

My options were clearly limited at this point. My best course of action seemed to be to go in person to Washington, D.C., to get the information that I was now committed to obtaining. However, my job as an engineer in southern New Hampshire kept me busy, and I took no further action on the mystery until nine months later—when an envelope arrived in the mail.

A ST. PATRICK'S DAY GIFT

The envelope that arrived on March 17, 1997, was from the U.S. Total Army Personnel Command. Enclosed was a letter from the Freedom of Information and Privacy Act officer, informing me that my request for Tony's Individual Deceased Personnel File had been fulfilled. The paper file contained all the pertinent information on the burial of my uncle. As I was soon to learn, the IDPF would be the gateway through which I would gain an understanding of what really happened to my Uncle Tony. As I eagerly pored over the seventeen-page file, I began to learn more about him.

Tony Korkuc was born on Christmas Day, 1917. At the time of his death, he was twenty-six years old. The identification data form indicated that Tony had blue eyes and brown hair. He was five feet six and a half inches tall and weighed 155 pounds, and he wore a size 9D shoe. Had he been fortunate enough to grow to maturity, I would have towered over him by more than eight inches and outweighed him by almost eighty pounds. The basic facts were listed on the form in such a way that they could be used to identify his remains. I used them to get a mental image of what my uncle looked like.

Tony's rank was listed as staff sergeant, and he had served with the 532nd Bomb Squadron of the 381st Bomb Group (H). According to the form, he had been "Lost on bomb mission to Augsburg, Germany."

The bomb group and bomb squadron numbers meant little at the time, but I knew that the information might be useful, so I made a note of it.

Another sheet in the IDPF revealed that in February 1950, Tony and the three other men whose names were listed on the Arlington gravestone—Boyd Burgess, Dale Schilling, and Earl Wonning—had all been interred in the United States Military Cemetery in Saint-Avold, France. The men were listed as unknowns X-6643, X-6644, X-6644-A, and X-6644-B. The remains had been identified as a group burial, and thus individual identity could not be established. Who were these men who were laid to rest together at Arlington? Were they all members of the same crew who had shared the same fate on that winter day in 1944?

As I read through the information, new questions were forming as my original ones were being answered. Why had these men been buried in France after they were lost on a mission to Germany? On another page in the file, Tony Korkuc's date of death was given as May 11, 1945. Why was his death dated a year after he was shot down, and why was it different from the date etched on his gravestone? In faint pencil next to a box labeled "Place of Death or Place Last Seen If MIA" were the words "28 Mi. SO of Stuttgart, Willmandingen, Ger." Where was this place called Willmandingen, Germany, and why were the men buried so far from it in Saint-Avold? So many questions were coming to mind!

According to the paperwork, Tony had served in a number of places in the United States. He had actually seen a lot of the country in his short life, having spent time in Massachusetts, Virginia, Mississippi, Nevada, Texas, Louisiana, Utah, and Illinois.

On another sheet, Tony's home address was listed as 187 West Avenue, Seekonk, Massachusetts. This was the birthplace of my father and the place I fondly remember as my grandparents' home. The names of my grandparents were listed as Anna and Michael Korkuc. In my youth, I knew them simply as Batcha and Pop.[1]

On the "Flying Personnel Dental Identification Form" filled out by Station 167's dental surgeon on November 12, 1943, I learned that Tony's aeronautical rating was "ball turret gunner."

The next page stopped me in my tracks. It included a copy of some text that had been sent to my grandmother in the form of a Western

Union telegram. On Friday, March 10, 1944, she received these simple but unforgettable words: "The Secretary of War desires me to
express his deep regret that your son Staff Sergeant Anthony J. Korkuc
has been reported missing in action since twenty five February over
Augsburg Germany." My grandmother, a Polish immigrant, never
learned how to read English very well, so one of her children must
have read those words to her.

After reading the IDPF, I was deeply frustrated. Despite all of the
information contained in the file, I was no closer to learning when
Tony had been buried at Arlington National Cemetery. All I knew for
sure was that as late as February 1950, six years after he had been lost
in action, France was still his home.

My mind was racing as new questions continued to surface. That
night, I searched for answers on the Internet. How far was Saint-Avold
from Willmandingen? What exactly was a ball turret gunner? Who
were the men of the 381st Bomb Group, and what role did they play
in helping the Allies win World War II? Who were those men who
shared a plot of earth with Tony at America's most hallowed cemetery? What was the significance of the date of May 11, 1945, as com-
pared to February 25, 1944?

I had so many questions, but now I felt confident that the answers
lay solely with my desire to answer them.

THE FIRST PUZZLE PIECES

I spent the next few weeks combing the Internet for answers to my
questions. My very first web search led me to http://www.381st.org/,
a website dedicated to the men of the 381st Bomb Group. I e-mailed
the secretary, Joe Waddell, asking whether he had any information
about my uncle and the fate of his plane, and whether he could explain
the circumstances surrounding Tony's burial at Arlington or Saint-
Avold.

A day later, Joe responded. He told me that the 532nd Bomb
Squadron and the 381st Bomb Group were formed in December 1942
and trained at Pyote, Texas, before being sent to Ridgewell
Aerodrome, Station 167, in Essex, England, as part of the Eighth Air
Force in June 1943. The 381st Bomb Group consisted of the 532nd,
533rd, 534th, and 535th bomb squadrons. They flew B-17 heavy

bombers, and participated in 297 missions before the war ended. He recommended that I buy two books. The first was *The Mighty Men of the 381st: Heroes All* by James Good Brown, a history of the 381st Bomb Group as told through the perspective of its chaplain. Brown was with the group from its beginning to its end. The other book was *Triumphant We Fly: A 381st Bomb Group Anthology, 1943–1945*, a history of the 381st as told by selected members.

Joe's e-mail also listed the names of the crew of my uncle's plane on its final mission:

Pilot: Donald Henderson
Co-pilot: Jack Fournier
Navigator: Earl Wonning (KIA)
Bombardier: Nicholas DeRose
Engineer and Top Turret Gunner: Raoul Ramos
Radio Operator Gunner: Boyd Burgess (KIA)
Right Waist Gunner: Anthony Bartolo
Left Waist Gunner: Thomas Hunnicutt
Ball Turret Gunner: Anthony Korkuc (KIA)
Tail Gunner: Dale Schilling (KIA)

Although only four were listed as killed in action (KIA), Joe believed that all had been killed. I now knew the identities of the men with whom Tony was buried at Arlington. He had been buried with his navigator, his radio operator, and his tail gunner.

Joe noted that after the war, many bodies were disinterred and brought back to the United States or were reburied in military cemeteries in England and the Netherlands. The official war history written by the 532nd Bomb Squadron did not contain the final status of the downed airmen, since the Germans did not notify units about the deaths of individuals during the war. After the war, the Army Graves Registration Service, part of the Quartermaster Corps, located the bodies of Americans and arranged for their final burial.

While looking at the 381st Bomb Group's website, I learned that the airmen often personalized their airplanes with cartoons and names such as *The Joker, Tinkertoy, Shoo Shoo Baby,* and *Mizpah.* I asked Joe Waddell whether my uncle's plane had a name. He told me that the aircraft had no name, but that the tail number was 42–37787, and it had the squadron markings of VE-B—the "VE" designating that it was part of the 532nd Bomb Squadron, and the "B" identifying the particular aircraft within the squadron. The plane's tail markings consisted of the letter "L" inside a triangle, the triangle denoting the Eighth Air Force's First Air Division, and the "L" the 381st Bomb Group. Joe added that 42–37787 was the only aircraft lost by the 381st Bomb Group on the February 25, 1944, mission. The plane had arrived in England on November 21, 1943, but he had no record of how many missions it flew before it was downed.

Joe related that the information had been obtained from microfilm at the Air Force Historical Records Agency at Maxwell Air Force Base. He and fellow group historians David Osborne and Ron MacKay were in the process of extracting data from the microfilm reels and compiling the information. A major goal was to develop a database on all the Americans who had served at Ridgewell. Joe could not tell me the exact dates that my uncle served, but he asked me to be patient, because the project had not yet been completed. I was elated: in less than a week, I had learned more about the outfit my uncle served with than I had been able to find in the previous two years.

In February 1950, Tony Korkuc's body lay in a single cemetery plot at the United States Military Cemetery in Saint-Avold, France. How had he come to be buried there, more than a hundred miles from the German village of Willmandingen? Had he made it there of his own accord, after struggling with wounds suffered during the Augsburg bombing mission? I sought help from a co-worker who had served as a tail gunner with a heavy bombardment group in World War II. At his suggestion, I called the Mortuary Affairs and Casualty Support Division in Washington, D.C. I asked the woman who answered how I could obtain the burial information for a World War II casualty named Anthony J. Korkuc. She responded that the name was very familiar to her, as she was the person who had recently made the copies of his IDPF! She told me that she had unintentionally omitted two letters from the file she had sent me—letters that were written to my grandfather in 1950 and 1952. The first informed my grandfather of the upcoming burial of his son at Arlington National Cemetery, the second that a stone was being placed on his son's grave. She promised to mail me copies of the letters, and she advised me to write to the Air Force Historical Records Agency for further information.

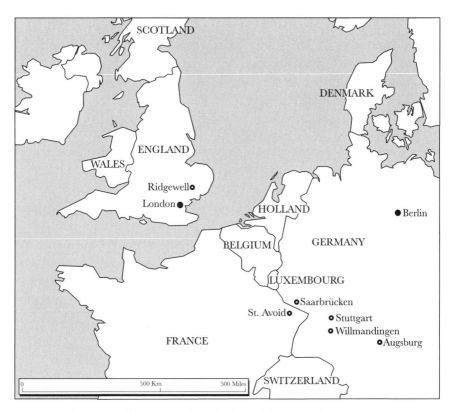

England, France, and Germany. Map by David Wasserboehr.

The leads were coming in so fast, I felt like a cub newspaper reporter on a breaking story. A couple of days after my conversation with the woman at the Mortuary Affairs Division, an envelope arrived containing the missing Arlington letters. The first letter, dated February 8, 1950, read:

Dear Mr. Korkuc:

The Department of the Army desires that you be given the most recent information concerning your son, the late Staff Sergeant Anthony J. Korkuc, ASN 31 036 784.

The American Graves Registration Service in their search for deceased American personnel recovered certain remains from the area in which your son and others of his comrades met their death. As identifications could not be established at the time of the recovery, unknown designations were assigned pending further investigation, and temporary interments were made in a United States Military Cemetery overseas. The investigation has now been completed, and although the circumstances rendered individual identifications impossible, sufficient evidence was present to determine that they were those of your son and three comrades and to warrant a group identification of the remains. The remains are now casketed, and being held overseas, pending return to the United States for interment in Arlington National Cemetery, located at Fort Myer, Virginia.

The second letter, dated October 28, 1952, was much shorter and to the point:

Reference is made to the interment of your son, the late Staff Sergeant Anthony J. Korkuc, and his comrades, which was made in Grave 1631, Section 34, Arlington National Cemetery. It is regretted that because of the fact it was impossible to identify individually the remains of your son, you were deprived of the comfort and consolation which you might have been afforded by interring his remains at home.

It is felt that you might like to have the enclosed photographs of the stone which has been placed at his grave.

You are assured that the grave will always be cared for in a manner fully commensurate with the sacrifice your son has made for his country. Any desired information concerning the grave or the cemetery will be furnished upon request.

THE MIGHTY MEN OF THE 381st BOMB GROUP

It turned out that Chaplain Brown, the author of *The Mighty Men of the 381st*, lived just north of me in Haverhill, New Hampshire. I called him the same day I heard about him from Joe Waddell. Brown told me that my uncle's name was listed on page 335 of his book, as part of the Don Henderson crew, and that he would be glad to send me a copy. When it arrived, it was accompanied by a short letter:

I am pleased to send this book to you. I know that you will enjoy reading it. The book is a sad and tragic book because it tells a vivid and true story of a bomb group in World War II. Day after day, week after week, month after month, and year after year, the war took our men from us. The pain was terrible. Your uncle, Anthony J. Korkuc was one of those great men whom we lost in combat on February 25, 1944. He sacrificed his life for his country. He gave everything that he had—his life. I mourned his loss on that day in 1944. I still mourn his loss. Best wishes to you.

Dr. James Good Brown
Chaplain

Tony Korkuc arrived in England in the middle of November 1943; he was part of a replacement crew assigned to the 381st Bomb Group. By that time, the original group, having been in England since June 1943, had already experienced five bloody months of air combat. The 381st was in dire need of aircrews so that they could continue the relentless pace required to inflict daily bomb damage on Germany.

According to Chaplain Brown, the men of the 381st were renowned for their ability to fly their B-17s in tight combat formations. He attributed the success of the bomb group to its original commander, Colonel Joseph J. Nazzaro, a senior pilot who had experience with both fighter planes and bombers. When the heavy bombardment group was formed, Nazzaro handpicked many of its original officers. Colonel Nazzaro accepted James Good Brown as the chaplain of the 381st Bomb Group, and with that appointment, the unit would forever live on in the sensitive observations of its chaplain.

When administering to the spiritual needs of the men, Chaplain Brown represented no particular denomination, creed, or faith. He characterized himself simply as "the Chaplain of the 381st Bomb Group."[2] In the book, he described his official duties:

Sermon preparation each week was of primary importance. I vowed that I would preach with the same high quality that I had set for myself in a civilian pulpit. The men in the service deserved more than a chitchat talk from the pulpit. Another important duty was the ever demanding task of writing hundreds of letters to the families whose sons (or husbands) were missing in action; then followed by a second letter if it were known that the men were killed in action. There were also official Air Force communications and reports to be sent out. And the daily writing of the "Life of the 381st in War." My typewriter was kept very busy. (29)

Between June 22, 1943, when the 381st Bomb Group underwent its baptism of fire, and February 25, 1944, forty-eight Flying Fortresses went missing in action or suffered casualties. On June 23, 1943, only the second full operational day for the bomb group, an explosion occurred while one of the B-17s was being outfitted with its bomb load. Twenty-three men were killed. Three days later, Chaplain Brown conducted the funerals for all of the men. "There were too many caskets to be placed inside the little chapel," he wrote. "The funeral, therefore, was held at the graves. All caskets were covered with American flags. . . . At the close of the service, the color guard fired the gun salute, and taps was sounded. I returned to the base to continue working. It was not easy" (52–53). I was struck by the simple phrase "It was not easy." Chaplain Brown had great respect for the airmen.

The daily toll of lost men must have been mind-numbing. As the losses mounted, Chaplain Brown became introspective about the men's odds of survival.

> [W]e have so many days before the war ends or before the flier's stated number of missions are completed. That marks an end for him. Does he have enough "life" to last that long? . . . Here are men, each one of them looking at that quantity of life which is his. Will there be enough to go round? Will there be enough of that life to go around to all the men over several months? What if the quantity is exhausted? But there is the rub. There is not enough to go around. All the laws of statistics prove this. . . . All this may seem like silly reasoning. But it is not silly to a man in combat facing death. (75)

I wonder whether Tony Korkuc ever speculated on his own odds of survival.

Chaplain Brown also reflected upon the learning process that the airmen underwent as they became aware of what being in war really meant:

> Isn't it to be regretted that it takes a war with killing to cause men to become serious, and by this I mean the desire to grasp and understand life? We have had enough raids now to remove all the glamour of war. Men now know the value of life. They are now beginning to love life. Oh, how each one cherishes it! Often a man says to me, "I don't mind

if I never go back into combat." But he will go. That is what he came
here to do. He will not go back on his word. He is every inch a man.
That is why he is a flier. He would not be a flier if he were not a man.
The more I look at these fellows, the more I know why they are here.
(85–86)

After reading Brown's words, I felt intense pride about the choices
that my uncle made in volunteering to fly on each and every combat
mission from December 1943 until his death, and gratitude for the
chaplain's expression of admiration for the men he served with. I am
proud of all the men who did their duty for the 381st Bomb Group.
They may have been young from the standpoint of their earthly age,
but in the eyes of that forty-two-year-old clergyman, they were men who
had earned his respect.

The 381st Bomb Group suffered greatly in its first five months of
combat. But by the 20th of November, it was a seasoned outfit. New
men, including Tony Korkuc, arrived to fill the gaps in the ranks, and
Chaplain Brown was glad they had the veterans to help them understand the nature of their missions. The new crews were well trained,
but they lacked an understanding of the realities of combat. They all
expected to complete their required twenty-five missions and go home,
but Brown knew only too well that many of them would never make
it back to the States. "As for the '25 missions'—that has turned out to
be quite a myth. . . . 'Quality of character' in men had nothing to do
with the safety of men in combat. The finest men in the Group 'blew
up,' and the best of men went down. . . . The best of fliers were hit by
flak. And the best-trained fliers were hit by enemy fighters" (225–26).

Four crews were lost on December 1, but then it seemed that the
luck of the 381st had changed. The men all returned safely from the
next four missions, as new crews continued to fill the ranks. But on
December 20, "Lightning struck again. Four planes and 40 men
lost. . . . Twenty days without a loss gave us a kind of reprieve and lifted
our spirits, as we approached the Christmas season. Today's losses convince us that this war is grim business. I do not welcome the task of
writing letters of condolence to all those families announcing this sad
news five days before Christmas" (252).

The 381st flew a mission on Christmas Eve, but not on Christmas
Day—my uncle's twenty-sixth birthday. The men were served a

Christmas dinner that Brown described as "a feast fit for a king. Ah, it tasted good! And there was plenty of turkey for all. I heard the enlisted men say that they could reach out on the platter as they passed by, taking all the turkey they wanted. As for the officers, we were served our plates, but each plate had on it all we could eat" (256).

On December 30, thirteen members of the 381st Bomb Group returned from Ludwigshaven, Germany, having completed their twenty-fifth mission. They had felt a mix of emotions as that milestone neared. Lieutenant Richard J. Niederriter, a pilot with the 534th Bomb Squadron, confessed that before his last couple of missions, "he was unable to sleep at nights without tablets from the doctor. Without these, he just dreamed of everything that he had gone through. All the old raids came back to him. The flak was hitting him, and the fighters were coming in at him." Chaplain Brown was well aware of the suffering that his men were experiencing. "The fliers may not believe this: When I entered their Nissen huts at night when they were sleeping, it was like going into a madhouse, hearing them talking in their sleep." Now, however, with their final bombing run behind them, the men allowed themselves to feel joy. "They had everything against them according to the statistics of the early part of the war. Today, they received something that they hardly expected—life. Yes, the answer to their happiness was simple—one word—LIFE. That is what these fellows were smiling about. Here it was, given to them as a gift, right out of a clear sky—rich, full and beautiful. . . . This shows that these fellows do not love killing. They are not eager for battle" (275).

On January 11, 1944, the 381st Bomb Group flew to Oschersleben, Germany, where they were credited "with the destruction of twenty-eight German fighters" (299). Between the flak and the German fighters, however, eight 381st Bomb Group planes went down. Eighty men were lost to the group, a figure second only to the losses in the tragic raid to Schweinfurt on August 17, 1943, when the 381st had lost ten planes and one hundred men.

At the time of the Oschersleben raid, Tony Korkuc had been on the base less than two months, and he was seeing firsthand the high attrition rate of flying combat missions against the German Luftwaffe. On January 30, 1944, the group lost three Flying Fortresses and thirty more men during the Brunswick raid. Reflecting on the loss and the attitude of the aircrew survivors toward the war, Brown wrote, "If an attitude of 'glory' is attached to war, it comes from those who are not in the war. . . . And we must guard against the danger that the glory of war develops after the war is over. No glory is experienced by the men who are fighting" (308).

Just three days prior to Tony's death in battle, on February 22, six more planes were lost to the group on a mission to Bunde. All told, during Tony's stay with the 381st, he suffered through the loss of thirty-three Flying Fortresses and 330 of his fellow fliers. His crew would suffer the thirty-fourth Flying Fortress loss on February 25, 1944.

On the very next mission after Tony's death, with the departure of Colonel Nazzaro and the arrival of the new commander, Colonel Harry Leber, Chaplain Brown was finally able to convince a 381st Bomb Group commander to let him fly in a B-17 and experience what his men did. After returning from the mission, he wrote,

> What of myself? I am a different person. Before going into combat, I felt guilty. I felt ashamed of myself for sitting safely back in England or talking to the ground personnel while the fliers were in combat. I felt ashamed of myself and dreaded to look the men in the face. I hung around them all the time but felt like a heel—one who avoided the tough spots. . . . I know this: when I got out of the plane, I was a changed individual. I took a good deep breath of air and felt that I had a right to it. I now knew first hand how all my fliers feel when they step out of the plane on their return from combat and breathe that good fresh air, bequeathed to them by Divine Nature. (355)

Chaplain Brown would go on to fly in a total of five missions, and even though he never fired a gun at the enemy, he received the air medal for his courage in accompanying his men in combat.

In March 1997, when I had first embarked on my journey to find war's true meaning, I was but a babe in the woods. As my understanding evolved, I was beginning to comprehend the inglorious truths of what it was like to fight for the Army Air Forces in World War II.

CHAPTER 2

The Loss of a Flying Fortress

In the spring of 1997, I posted my story to a website dedicated to perpetuating the memory of Air Force personnel. I included what I had learned to date, in the hope that someone would be able to add new information. I also found a website sponsored by the Military History Group, which had an online form that I could use to obtain the S-2 Summary of Eyewitness Accounts for Tony's plane. For a charge of ten dollars, they promised to locate all relevant information concerning the downing of any B-17 aircraft during World War II. My confidence growing, I posted my story on just about every website that I thought could help me in my research.

About a week later, I received an e-mail from someone named Ted Darcy: "I believe the serial number for your uncle's aircraft should be 42–37786 vice the number you are showing. Any further problems e-mail me." My ten-dollar investment was starting to pay dividends. I responded that I had received the tail number from Joe Waddell, the secretary of the 381st Bomb Group. I told Ted that I had no way to validate the number, and it was possible that Joe had inadvertently mistyped it. Believing that Ted was from the Military History Group, I asked him whether he was the person investigating my case.

A day later, Ted responded that there was "not much left to investigate. The company is almost finished with its complete accounting of B-17's and their crews. I talk with Mo Moriarty on a regular basis and he had asked me to check this one out. That's how I found the [tail number] error. What may be of further interest to you is the fact that Bartolo is buried in Connecticut and Hunnicutt is buried in Texas. If you have any more questions let me know." I was pleased to be learning more about the fate of two more members of my uncle's crew—

Anthony Bartolo and Thomas Hunnicutt. I was puzzled, however, over Ted's reference to Mo Moriarty. I had no idea who he was.

I sent Ted another e-mail. "With the information on the known burial sites of Bartolo and Hunnicutt, along with my uncle, Anthony Korkuc, Burgess, Schilling, and Wonning, do you know where the rest of the crew are buried? Also, do you know where Bartolo is buried in Connecticut? Are you close to being able to get me the S-2 Eyewitness file?" Ted responded, "All I can tell you about Bartolo is that he is buried in a private cemetery. We wouldn't take it any further than that unless we were doing a profile case. As for Henderson, Fournier, DeRose and Ramos, you don't bury survivors. They were all taken as POW's."

Ted had just changed the course of my research. Joe Waddell had inadvertently misled me again. This time it was not simply a typo; his assertion that there were no survivors from the mission was incorrect.

Filled with excitement, I realized that I might be able to talk to some of Tony's crewmembers from his last mission. I might be able to talk to men who knew exactly what happened on that dreadful day so many years ago. My father's belief that his brother's plane had been blown to bits was one hundred percent wrong. There was much more that could be learned.

FIRST CONNECTIONS

I placed a call to Ted Darcy, and the phone was answered within a few rings. In the first couple of minutes, I learned that Ted was not affiliated with the Military History Group, as I had thought; he was with a private organization known as the WFI Research Group of Fall River, Massachusetts. Ted noted that the WFI had more than twenty-five years of experience in military research, and their data was now being made available to the public. Their extensive databases covered a wide variety of fields, from aircraft accidents to unit histories. Ted said that his interest had been piqued by my posting on a website called the Air Force Memories Guest Book, which was authored by Ernest T. "Mo" Moriarty. Moriarty had contacted Ted Darcy on my behalf. Mo himself had flown with the Eighth Air Force as a B-17 waist gunner with the 306th Bomb Group during World War II.

The WFI Research Group maintains an electronic database of all Missing Air Crew Reports (MACRs) filed for World War II. According to Ted, a total of 16,708 MACRs were filed through 1947. His database also contains information on the 400,000 men who lost their lives in the war. Additionally, the group has documented the final fates of the 12,731 Flying Fortresses produced by the Boeing, Douglas, and Vega (Lockheed) aircraft companies from 1943 to 1945. Given the extensive resources of the WFI, Mo knew that Ted could easily answer my posted questions.

I asked Ted how he knew that there were four survivors from my uncle's last mission. He replied that the loss of Tony's B-17 was documented in Missing Air Crew Report #02933. According to his database, pilot Don Henderson, engineer and top turret gunner Raoul Ramos, bombardier Nicholas DeRose, and co-pilot Jack Fournier were each listed as having been taken prisoner. He could not tell me whether the four men were alive as of 1997, but it was certain that they had survived the Augsburg bombing mission.

Thanks to the help of Mo Moriarty and Ted Darcy, I had made a major breakthrough in my research. The next step was obvious—I had to find out whether any of Uncle Tony's fellow crewmembers were still alive. Ted suggested that I use an Internet people-search engine to locate them. He recommended the one called Switchboard, at www.switchboard.com; I could enter each crewmember's name in the search box, and thereby obtain the address of everyone with that name in the United States. He admitted that this approach could be tedious, but it was an effective method of finding people whose location you did not know.

As soon as I hung up the phone, I logged on to my computer and went to switchboard.com. I decided to start with the man on the list with the most unusual surname, DeRose. I typed in his full name and hit the "search" button. Switchboard supplied me with only two names from the entire country—one from Grand Ledge, Michigan, and the other from Le Mars, Iowa. In addition to the addresses, phone numbers were provided.

I picked up the phone and called the DeRose who lived in Grand Ledge. After a couple of rings, a woman answered. Not knowing exactly what to say, I asked whether Nicholas DeRose resided there, and if so, had he been a bombardier in World War II? The woman answered "Yes," then called for him to pick up the phone. I could not believe my luck—I was actually going to speak with someone who had known Uncle Tony and who knew the circumstances surrounding the loss of the B-17 on February 25, 1944!

A few moments later, a man came to the phone and said that he was Nicholas DeRose. His voice sounded old and raspy. With my heart pounding, I asked him whether he had flown with my uncle, Anthony J. Korkuc, during World War II. Nicholas, as I respectfully would call him throughout that first conversation, told me that he did not recognize the name. Puzzled, I asked whether he had flown as part of the 532nd Bomb Squadron and the 381st Bomb Group on a B-17 bombing mission to Augsburg, Germany, on February 25, 1944. "Yes," he replied. I then asked him whether Don Henderson had been his crew pilot. Once again, he answered "Yes." Now very puzzled, I asked whether his plane had been shot down on the mission. Yet again, he answered in the affirmative.

I then repeated my uncle's last name, and again Nicholas denied having flown with him. I told him that Tony was listed as having flown the ball turret on that mission, and that he had been killed in action. Nicholas told me that as bombardier, he entered his crew position by going through the nose hatch in the front of the plane. He concluded that my uncle must have been a replacement gunner, and since the ball turret gunner entered the B-17 via the waist gun door in the rear of the plane, he had never met him.

As we both became more comfortable with the conversation, I asked Nicholas his age. He told me that he was seventy-nine, having been born in 1917, and that he had been known as the "Old Man" of his aircrew—a status that was given to the oldest man on each ten-man crew. As he continued to recall the distant past, it was as if I were talking to the twenty-six-year-old man he had been back in 1944. His voice came alive, and I could no longer hear the raspy old man who had originally picked up the phone. I asked Nicholas on what day he was born, and he told me December 30. I then burst his bubble by telling him that my uncle was five days older than he was, and thus Tony was the rightful and deserving owner of the title "Old Man" of the crew. Nicholas got a chuckle out of this revelation.

I then asked whether he could share with me the circumstances surrounding the plane's downing. He told me that the B-17 had lost two engines, and enemy fighters had attacked from the rear. Don Henderson had ordered the men to bail out, and Nicholas was one of the last men out of the plane—having jumped at an altitude of about 500 feet. The Germans captured him immediately, and he served out the remainder of the war as a prisoner of war in Barth, Germany, at Stalag Luft I on the Baltic Sea.

As we continued to talk, I told Nicholas that I was researching my Uncle Tony's story so that I could tell my father, Tony's younger brother, exactly what happened on February 25, 1944. I then shared what I knew about the fate of his crew on that day. Nicholas had known about their loss, but he was surprised to hear that "his boys" had all eventually been buried in the States.

According to Nicholas, Don Henderson was not the crew's regular pilot, and he was flying on his twenty-fifth and final mission. The co-pilot, Jack Fournier, had not been promoted to crew commander after his original crew pilot had stepped down. DeRose was glad that Henderson had piloted his ship on that last day, because he was a very good pilot. He added that even though they had fallen prey to the fighters on that last mission, he much preferred Henderson's piloting skills to Fournier's. Nicholas added that Henderson, who was from Nebraska, had also been taken to Stalag Luft I after being captured.

Nicholas told me that he had trained as a bombardier and as a gunner at the Las Vegas Army Gunnery School. I told him that my uncle had also trained as a gunner in Las Vegas. According to DeRose, his crew arrived in England in November 1943 and flew their first combat bombing mission sometime in December. He believed that the mission to Augsburg was his twelfth combat mission.

As we continued to talk, Nicholas told me something very unexpected. Several years earlier, his wife had brought home a book on the Eighth Air Force called *The Mighty Eighth War Diary*. It was a day-by-day recounting of all the missions flown by the Eighth Air Force during World War II. Interested in learning what the book had to say about his last mission, Nicholas had gone directly to the page listing for February 25, 1944. Near the top of the page was a photograph showing the crash site of a B-17 that had a tail marking of a black "L" in a white triangle. The accompanying caption said that the aircraft pictured was the only one lost to the 381st Bomb Group on the mission, and that it had been dispatched by a fighter plane and crashed in Willmandingen, Germany. Nicholas told me that he could hardly believe his eyes—he was actually staring at a photo of the crash site of the Flying Fortress that he had flown into battle so many years ago! He told me that someone who was standing on the ground in front of the plane had photographed the scene, and the caption said that the bomber had been shot down by an ME-109.

Nicholas and I talked for about an hour that night. Before I ended the call, I thanked him for being so candid with me. Even though he had not known Tony, it was satisfying to know the circumstances surrounding the loss of the B-17. Not only had I spoken with a survivor of the mission, I had learned that a photo existed of the crash site. I knew that I had to get a copy of that book.

After hanging up with Nicholas, I immediately dialed my father's number. I told him that I had just spoken with the bombardier on Tony's crew, and I now knew what really happened on that last mission. I excitedly shared the details I had learned. I also told him about the photograph of the downed plane, and said that I would try to find a copy of *The Mighty Eighth War Diary* so that we both could see what the crash site looked like.

When I finished, my father sighed and said that what had happened to his brother was really sad and ironic. Tony had caught a bad break on his last mission. Of all the crews he could have been substituted into, he was assigned to one that was shot down. I was calmer by then, and as I listened to him talk, I realized that I had failed to recognize the tragedy of the news I had just given him. His brother had not been a regular crewmember. In fact, Nicholas DeRose had not even known Tony. In my rush to share the details of my conversation with Nicholas, I had been oblivious to the insensitive way I was informing my father about the fate of his older brother. Nonetheless, he was glad to at least know the circumstances of his brother's death. After so many years, he was starting to get some answers.

Needless to say, that was a pivotal day in my research. Hoping to repeat my success, I went back to switchboard.com the next evening to attempt to locate another crewmember. The next most logical candidate to search for was Raoul Ramos, the crew's engineer and top turret gunner. When I ran a search on his name, I was rewarded with just one response. A Raoul Ramos was listed in Long Beach, California. Had I found yet another member of the crew?

I dialed the number, and after a few rings, a woman answered. I told her my name and asked if I had reached the residence of the Raoul

Ramos who had flown in World War II as a top turret gunner. She, like Mrs. DeRose, answered "Yes." I had found two crewmates in my first two calls! As luck would have it, Raoul was home, and he came to the phone. I explained who I was, and that the previous night I had spoken with Nicholas DeRose, his bombardier, and had learned that my uncle was a substitute gunner on the crew's last mission. Raoul quickly responded that Nicholas had spoken in error. Tony Korkuc had been a regular member of his crew. In fact, Ramos told me that he had trained with "Korky" in Alexandria, Louisiana, while they were with the 797th Bomb Squadron as part of the Lundell Provisional Training Group. I told Raoul that my closest friends also called me "Korky"— an interesting coincidence. In defense of Nicholas DeRose, I said that I had referred to Tony by his formal name, and most likely DeRose had known him only by his nickname.

I asked Raoul what he remembered about my uncle. He replied that Tony was always smiling and joking around, and he loved to drink beer. He added that he knew Tony to be a good Catholic boy, and they often went to Catholic Mass together. He recalled that "Korky" had grown up on a family farm, and he laughed as he told me that Tony would always say he was glad he wasn't home, or he would be having to help dig up those damn potatoes. I told Raoul that my father would be relieved to hear that Tony was a regular crewmember, because it had pained him to know that his brother had flown as a substitute gunner on his last mission. Raoul responded that the crew did have a substitute on that last mission, but it was the tail gunner, Dale Schilling, not Tony.

I asked whether he could share any memories of the last mission. He told me that their plane was headed for Switzerland, because their superchargers had given out. They were also experiencing engine trouble. The loss of the superchargers caused the B-17 to lose power, and it had to leave the safety of the bomb group. The plane was then heavily attacked by fighters. The tail gunner, Schilling, was the first of the gunners to be shot. Ramos believed that Tony was killed in his ball turret position. The men were ordered to bail out. Ramos was the second-to-last man out of the plane, followed by his pilot, Henderson. Both bailed out at an altitude of about 250 feet. After landing, the two men were captured and taken to the Dulag Luft interrogation center; afterward, Raoul was confined at the Stalag Luft III POW camp.

I told Raoul about my conversation with Nicholas DeRose and that Nicholas thought the crew had flown about twelve missions. Raoul agreed that the total seemed correct. I also mentioned that the B-17 had been photographed after the crash, and I confidently told him that I would obtain the photo and get a copy for him. According to the information that I had seen in Tony's IDPF, their plane had crashed twenty-eight miles south of Stuttgart. Raoul said he thought they were closer to Switzerland.

As I continued to pepper Raoul with questions about the crew, I was impressed with his memory. He told me that Don Henderson was from Red Cloud, Minnesota, and that he was a replacement pilot; the original pilot had stood down after becoming overly tense from flying in combat. He seemed to recall that the man's name was Covington, but he wasn't certain. He recalled that his co-pilot, Jack Fournier, was from Columbus, Ohio, and his navigator, Earl Wonning, had lived in Indiana. Wanting to share the information I had found, I told Raoul where the other members of the crew were buried. He had not been aware of that information. He told me that the youngest crewmember was Thomas Hunnicutt, and he remembered that Thomas's father had been a colonel in the Army. He also recalled that Dale Schilling hailed from Illinois. Eventually I ran out of questions. I thanked Raoul for his answers and told him that I would fill my father in on our conversation.

MISSING AIR CREW REPORT #02933

A couple of weeks after I'd found Nicholas DeRose and Raoul Ramos, a piece of the research puzzle arrived at my house. The National Archives had sent me the Missing Air Crew Report that I had requested through the help of Ted Darcy.[1] What would the microfiche reveal about the loss of the B-17 with tail number 42–37786? I immediately jumped into my car and drove to the Merrimack Public Library in hopes of finding a microfiche reader/printer. Luck was with me. I sat down and began to read the MACR. Sheet one indicated that on March 16, 1948, the report had been reclassified from confidential to restricted. Aside from the number 2933 in the top left-hand corner and some numbers of no apparent significance on the right-hand side, the only other markings on the sheet were the faint names of Wonning, Burgess, Korkuc, Bartolo, and Schilling. Each of those men had been killed during the mission. For some reason, Thomas Hunnicutt's name was omitted.

On the next sheet there were notes on the four men who had survived the mission, just as Ted Darcy had told me. The sheet indicated the date of the incident—February 25, 1944—and the fact that the plane was a Fortress. Just to the left of this information, on the same line, was the underlined notation "KU 1022."

The third sheet was a loading list of the men who flew on the mission. Beside each name, the next of kin was noted, including his or her relationship to the crewmember, along with an address. The first name on the list was Sergeant Dale E. Schilling, who gave as his next of kin his mother, Mrs. George W. Schilling of Lowell, Indiana. Next was the pilot, Donald G. Henderson, who had listed his wife, Mrs. Yolanda N. Henderson of Red Cloud, Nebraska (not Minnesota, as Ramos had told me). The navigator, Second Lieutenant Earl H. Wonning, was from Seymour, Indiana, and the next of kin he had listed was his mother, Esther E. Wonning. Second Lieutenant Jack H. Fournier, the crew's co-pilot, and his mother, Mrs. Gertrude A. Fournier, were from Cleveland, Ohio—not Columbus, as Raoul Ramos had said. Bombardier Second Lieutenant Nicholas J. DeRose listed his wife, Mrs. Charlotte A. DeRose of San Bernardino, California, as the loved one he wanted the Army Air Forces to notify if he should be lost in combat. The radio operator, Technical Sergeant Boyd E. Burgess, the last of the crew's married men, listed his wife, whose name appears only as Mrs. Boyd E. Burgess of Kershaw, South Carolina. My uncle's name was listed next on the sheet. Staff Sergeant Anthony J. Korkuc wanted his mother, my grandmother, Anna Korkuc of Seekonk, Massachusetts, to be notified in case of an emergency. Mr. Philip A. Bartolo, the father of Anthony J. Bartolo of Wilshire Farm in Greenwich, Connecticut, was listed as the right waist gunner's next of kin. The left waist gunner, Staff Sergeant Thomas R. Hunnicutt, named his mother, Mrs. Eleanor J. Hunnicutt of Dallas, Texas. Lastly, the engineer and top turret gunner, Technical Sergeant Raoul B. Ramos, listed his mother, Delores B. Ramos, as his closest contact. Like Henderson, Ramos was from Nebraska—Alliance, to be exact.

The next sheet of the MACR contained a copy of a report marked "KU 1022." The names of DeRose, Fournier, and Ramos had been typed in, with check marks near their names, following which someone had written in by hand that the men were all POWs. Another hand-written note indicated that there were six KIAs, with a further reference to "SD case 1457." The last name in the typed list was Thomas Hunnicutt. Next to it, someone had written "KIA." Still faintly visible underneath that notation were the letters "POW," as if Hunnicutt had once been thought to be a prisoner of war and his status was later changed to "killed in action." Typed to the right of Hunnicutt's name were the words "Cemetery of Willmandingen."

Below the four typewritten names, the KU-1022 report revealed that "6 dead and 4 POW are mentioned in the report, regarding shot down Fortress II on 25 Feb. 1944 at Willmandingen. However, DeRose, Fournier, and Ramos are not stated weather [sic] they are dead or alive." When this version of the report was prepared, it obviously was not known that DeRose, Fournier, and Ramos had survived the mission.

Each of the next six sheets was headed "Individual Casualty Questionnaire." There was one sheet for each airman killed on the mission, listing his name, rank, serial number, and bomber crew position.

The eleventh sheet was a form titled "Casualty Questionnaire." The first question on the page was "Your Name?" Hand-printed to the right was "Henderson, Donald Guy." An American must have interviewed Don Henderson after he was released from the POW camp. Apparently none of the other survivors—Ramos, Fournier, or DeRose—had filled out one of these questionnaires. Henderson was asked whether Tony had bailed out, and he responded no, that he was killed in his gun position by enemy aircraft gunfire. The last verbal contact occurred when Tony was calling in fighters on his interphone. To the best of Henderson's knowledge, Tony had flown thirteen missions.

Henderson's casualty questionnaire included more interesting facts. The target of the mission had been Augsburg's aircraft plant, and the estimated altitude of the mission was 19,000 feet. According to Henderson, the plane had left the safety of its bombing formation at Augsburg. Having recorded that he had bailed out, Henderson was asked: "Did other members of the crew bail out?" Henderson's answer was "six killed at guns positions in air and went down with ship." He was then asked when and how the other surviving crew had bailed out of the plane. Henderson answered, "Engineer Ramos—out Bomb Bay; Bombardier DeRose—nose hatch; Co Pilot Fournier—Bomb Bay; myself Henderson—out Bomb Bay. [When?] After I had rung alarm bell and given order to bail over interphone. [Where?] S.W. of Stuttguard [*sic*], exact position unknown." Asked to name the crewmembers who went down with the plane, Henderson responded, "Wonning, E.H.; Burgess, B.E.; Korkuc, A.J.; Bartolo, A.J.; Hunnicutt, T.R; Schilling, D.E." He also stated that when the plane struck the ground, each man was dead in his gun position. When asked when he last saw his surviving crewmembers, Henderson responded, "saw other three members in good condition in Camp Lucky Strike in France—May 1945."[2]

The remaining four sheets of the report were filed shortly after the plane went down. They constituted the first official filing on the loss of the aircraft. Lieutenant Dale McCrory, a pilot from the 381st Bomb Group, 532nd Bombardment Squadron, filed a three-page report entitled "Missing Airplane on Combat Mission" on February 27, 1944. Among other things, it said:

> Over the target, Lt. Fastrup, Lt. Genther, and Lt. Henderson fell back and were left behind for about five minutes. Lt. Genther and Lt. Fastrup pulled back into formation, but Lt. Henderson was lagging behind. Gradually he got back into formation. Almost immediately he started falling back again, then started down. He was then observed to fly under the formation for about ten minutes by the ball-turret gunner. From then on it seemed that he couldn't stay with the formation. The ball-turret gunner and navigator saw him hit the deck and parallel our course across the French border. At this point, the plane was over a large forest and blended in with the trees to such an extent that we were unable to distinguish Lt. Henderson's plane any longer. The weather was clear and visibility unlimited over the entire enemy territory.

McCrory's report did not mention that German fighters had been attacking the B-17. Also, it appears that Henderson's plane was experiencing trouble independent of the harassment by the fighters. The Fortress was having problems keeping up with the formation within five minutes of passing near the target of Augsburg. McCrory's ball turret gunner and navigator kept watch on the B-17 for upwards of ten minutes after it left the formation. Clearly, the presence of fighters was not the only factor that contributed to the loss of the aircraft that day. But what was happening inside the plane that caused it to leave formation? The more information I learned, the more questions I had.

The last, but certainly not the least, of the information contained in the report was a map that revealed the course of the bombing mission, showing the route from Ridgewell to the target and portions of the return leg. Of particular note were hand notations indicating the time whenever the plane changed course on its way to and from the target. According to the map, the bomb group left Ridgewell Aerodrome, Army Air Forces Station 167, and assembled into formation at 0954 hours. The planes passed just west of London at 1030. After flying over Portsmouth at 1046, they passed over the Isle of Wight and started across the English Channel. The Channel flight took approximately forty minutes, and the bombers made landfall in German-occupied France at 1127. Landfall occurred at approximately 50.00 degrees north latitude and 1.25 degrees east longitude, near the town of Le Treport, about sixty statute miles northeast of Le Havre. The group then changed course again and flew on for approximately one hour, until another course change near Bar-le-Duc at 1223 hours.

Continuing in a southeasterly direction, the planes flew just thirty-five statute miles north of Stuttgart as they continued on to the target. At 1316, the B-17 formation was approximately sixty miles northwest of Augsburg. Forty minutes later, just north of Munich, the Flying Fortresses of the 381st headed due south as they started to make their bomb run. At 1404 they changed course for the last time, heading west toward Augsburg's aircraft factories. At 1409 the bombers released their lethal cargo. The formation then headed southwest toward the city of Mindelheim, and at 1417 the planes changed course again, heading in a northwesterly direction. The map indicated that Don Henderson's Flying Fortress was last seen at 1530, about ten statute miles southwest of Luxembourg.

A review of the map's last sighting of my Uncle Tony's B-17 and the position of its crash site indicates that the report filed by Dale McCrory was incorrect. The plane could not have crossed the French border with the formation and still have crashed in Willmandingen. Based on the times noted on the map, the B-17 flown by Don Henderson must have left the formation shortly after 1417 hours. It may have crashed within twenty to thirty minutes after changing course at Mindelheim. Given when and where it came down, there is no way it could have last been sighted at 1530. The information contained in the official report could not be correct.

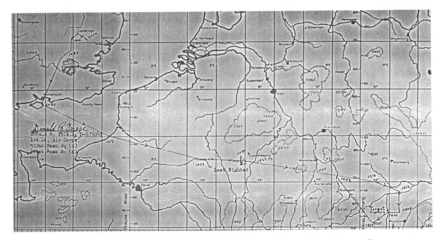

Flight route of the 381st Bomb Group for the mission to Augsburg, Germany, on February 25, 1944. Missing Air Crew Report 02933, Record Group 92, Microfiche 988, National Archives and Records Administration II [hereafter NARA II], College Park, Maryland, 14.

Fighters must have jumped the plane, and Henderson presumably made every effort to head in a southwesterly direction, and eventually due south, so that he could get his crew safely to Switzerland. However, instead of being welcomed at Ridgewell Aerodrome with a party to celebrate his twenty-fifth and final mission, Don Henderson had to settle for an interrogation at the Dulag Luft, the Nazi Luftwaffe interrogation center in Frankfurt.

So what exactly had happened to the Don Henderson crew? Why did they leave the safety of the formation? Apparently there were no fighter planes in the vicinity of Henderson's B-17 when it first left formation. Given McCrory's curious belief that the plane was last seen near the French border at 1530 hours, he may have been unaware that it was attacked by German fighters. After all, he had been inaccurate about the time and place of the last sighting, so he may simply not have known the true fate of my uncle and the rest of the Henderson crew.

THE PILOT REMEMBERS

The Missing Air Crew Report had shed some light on Tony's last mission. Unfortunately, it also suggested that further questions needed to be answered before I could be satisfied as to the true fate of my uncle's crew. Despite having spoken to both Raoul Ramos and Nicholas DeRose, I knew that I needed the stories of the co-pilot and the pilot in order to better understand the events of February 25, 1944. I now had to locate either Don Henderson or Jack Fournier. Surely the men flying the plane would be able to explain what had actually happened.

Switchboard yielded only one man by the name of Jack Howard Fournier in the entire country. Unfortunately, he was not the co-pilot of my uncle's plane. I feared that my next search, for crew pilot Donald Henderson, would be a difficult one, because Henderson is such a common surname. In fact, Switchboard came up with more than twenty matches from all across the country. Unfortunately, none of them resided in Red Cloud, Nebraska. Over the next couple of weeks, I talked to a lot of men named Donald G. Henderson, but none had ever taken the helm of a B-17 during World War II.

I decided to try another route—searching for everyone with the last name of Henderson who lived in Red Cloud. The first few calls got me nowhere, but on my fifth attempt, I spoke to a Hazel Henderson. I explained that I was looking for a man named Donald Henderson who had flown with my uncle in 1944, and I wondered whether she knew him. Hazel responded that she did, and that after his return from POW camp he had worked as a rural postal carrier. I finally was making headway, but unfortunately, Hazel did not know Donald's present whereabouts. She told me that she would ask around, and if I called her back in a couple of days, perhaps she would able to provide me with a mailing address for him.

I then considered another option. If Red Cloud was a small farming community, maybe someone at the police station could put me in touch with Donald Henderson. Perhaps the Red Cloud police chief was like Mayberry's Andy Griffith, and would know everything about everyone in his town. I placed a call to the Red Cloud Police Department, and as luck would have it, the man who answered the phone was indeed the chief of police. Concerned that he might think me mad, I cautioned him to hear me out, as I was about to make a very strange request. The chief listened patiently as I spoke. After a pause, he answered that he did indeed know Donald Henderson. In fact, Henderson's son had been a close friend of his. My hunch had paid off! He told me that to the best of his recollection, Don had moved to Wichita, Kansas, some time ago.

Now that I knew that Donald Henderson had relocated to Wichita, I returned to switchboard.com and renewed my search. Switchboard came back with a list of eight names, the seventh of which was Don G. Henderson. Hastily, I dialed the number. I explained to the woman who answered the phone that I was looking for the Donald Henderson who had been a World War II Flying Fortress pilot and who had once lived in Red Cloud, Nebraska. A few seconds later, Don Henderson himself came to the phone to talk with the nephew of his ball turret gunner from World War II.

Don was preparing to have hip surgery the next day—his third such procedure. Little did he know that the night would be memorable for other reasons. I introduced myself and asked him about his twenty-fifth mission and his memory of Tony and his crew. He explained that he had flown his first fifteen missions as a co-pilot with the Bernard Beckman crew, also of the 532nd Bomb Squadron. In early February 1944, he was assigned to lead my uncle's crew. His allegiance and his close friendships, however, were still with the Beckman crew, with whom he continued to bunk.

Don said that just prior to his issuance of the bailout command on February 25, he instructed his engineer, Raoul Ramos, to check the status of the men in the back of the plane. Ramos reported that radio operator Boyd Burgess had been killed, and that each of the gunners was either dead or too severely wounded to bail out. Co-pilot Jack Fournier was the first man out of the aircraft, followed by DeRose, then Ramos. Henderson recalled seeing the navigator, Earl Wonning, huddled at the nose hatch staring out. Wonning appeared to be unhurt at the time, and Henderson did not know that he had ended up being killed during the mission. I told Henderson that according to the Missing Air Crew Report, Wonning was killed in his position by enemy gunfire, and that apparently Henderson was the witness who had provided this information. Henderson said again that at the time of the order to bail out, Wonning was unhurt.

Although I thought I should perhaps refrain from pursuing this line of questioning, I persisted. I was asking about that day so many years ago without any regard for Don Henderson's feelings. Had he falsified Earl Wonning's Individual Casualty Questionnaire in order to protect Wonning's family from the truth of what really happened? Wonning was not killed by enemy gunfire, but met his death in some other way. Henderson said simply that he did not know whether Wonning ever got out of the plane.

Henderson went on to say that his plane had been badly damaged by German fighters that attacked from the rear, and it had also suffered damage from German anti-aircraft fire. One engine was on fire, and he was also having trouble with another engine. He explained that when an engine could no longer be controlled, the propeller blades needed to be feathered—rotated into a position where they would not cause unnecessary drag on the plane—but he was having trouble feathering the propeller blades on the damaged engines. He detailed the damage that had been inflicted on his ship: the co-pilot's right front cockpit window was broken, as was the pilot's left side window, and the left wing was so badly shot up that it looked like a "tin can after being hit with a shotgun shell." He recalled that he disengaged the autopilot, pulled back the stick, and then bailed out of the plane at an altitude of approximately 500 feet.

Henderson said that he landed in two or three feet of snow, and its cushioning effect probably saved his life. As it was, he badly damaged his kidneys when he hit the ground. He recalled seeing the B-17 crash and then burst into flames. He was so close to the plane that his trailing parachute actually tangled with its burning parts. He was captured by about fifteen to twenty Germans, some of them carrying deer rifles. This was the fifth consecutive mission that Don Henderson had flown in combat, and it was his twenty-fifth and last planned combat mission.

Don told me that in 1945, after he had returned to the States, he was contacted by Colonel Lee Hunnicutt, the father of left waist gunner Thomas Hunnicutt. Colonel Hunnicutt told Henderson that in trying to understand how his son was killed in action, he had made some inquiries about Henderson's flying record. Hunnicutt said that the men of the 381st Bomb Group had defended Don's record. The colonel had most likely spoken with Henderson's first aircrew—the Bernard Beckman crew. As I reflect on that night's conversation, I realize that Henderson was defending his piloting skills to me.

Don also described another mission he had flown. Several missions before that of February 25, the Beckman crew had experienced some trouble and were forced to leave the protection of the formation. Henderson was flying as Beckman's wingman on that mission. Distressed to see his former crew drop out of position, Don decided to leave his spot in the formation in order to help them out. Shortly thereafter, another crippled plane linked up with the two B-17s, and the three planes, flying in a three-element formation, managed to get back to Ridgewell unharmed. Beckman's bombardier later sent a letter to Henderson's wife telling her of her husband's heroic act to save his crew's life. The Red Cloud newspaper printed the letter so that everyone in the town could learn of Don Henderson's heroism on that day. In telling me about the incident, Don promised to send me the newspaper clipping so that I could see it for myself.

Don told me that when he returned to the base after that mission, his commanders were furious that he had taken his plane out of formation in order to help another one. He was reprimanded for having unnecessarily put his B-17 and his crew into harm's way. The Bernard Beckman crew felt differently; they believed that Henderson deserved the Distinguished Flying Cross for his actions that day. Because of his reprimand, Henderson never received any award decorations for the mission. He did, however, earn the eternal admiration of the Beckman crew.

Colonel Hunnicutt told Henderson that he felt better knowing that everything possible had been done to bring his son back alive. Henderson said that the conversation with the colonel was a very special experience for him. Although the colonel had lost his son, he was still able to express his appreciation for Don's professionalism as a pilot and the actions he had taken to try to save his crew.

After Don was captured, he was taken to the Willmandingen town hall. He told me that he was led into the Burgermeister's office, where he was interrogated by a woman who spoke perfect English. He responded to each of her questions with only his name, rank, and serial number. Henderson admitted that he had always regretted not talking to this woman who could have told him more about where he had crashed.

After leaving the small village, Henderson was sent by boxcar to Frankfurt. He was taken to the interrogation center known as Dulag Luft, where he was left in solitary confinement for ten days. He described his interrogation as rather humane, and said that he was impressed with the techniques used by the Germans to obtain information from the downed airmen. On the third or fourth day of his confinement, the English-speaking German interrogators brought out a photo album of his base and told him everything they knew about his crew and the missions of the 381st Bomb Group. Henderson was amazed at what his captors knew. The interrogation technique was very effective—just when a flier thought that he could add no more to the interrogator's vast store of knowledge, he would inadvertently say something that the interrogator knew nothing about. After a stay at Dulag Luft, Henderson was sent to Barth, where he sat out the remainder of the war at Stalag Luft I.

I asked Don what he had done before the war. He told me that he was a rural postal carrier in Red Cloud. In fact, after he came home from Germany, he returned to Red Cloud and went back to carrying the mail. I asked him whether he had ever piloted a plane again after his February 1944 flight, and he told me that he had flown for the last time twelve years earlier, at the controls of his own Cessna 172. After the war, he had promised his wife that he would not fly anymore. But years later, after his children were grown and had been put through college, she allowed him to take to the skies again.

As it turns out, Henderson was also deserving of the title "Old Man of the Crew" along with either DeRose or my Uncle Tony. At the time of his last mission, he, too, was twenty-six years old.

I asked Don what, in retrospect, had been worse—his combat missions or his stay in the POW camp? He responded that the missions were much worse than his days in confinement. Being a POW was not all that bad, he said—although he added that without the food provided by the Red Cross, he was convinced that he might have starved to death.

One of his last thoughts as we wrapped up the conversation was that his last mission had disappointed him greatly. He had always regretted the loss of so many men that day. During those ten days of solitary confinement, he had thought of nothing else.

With that last thought, I wished Don Henderson good luck with his surgery and thanked him for his honesty. He had shed much light on my uncle's last mission.

CHAPTER 3

Revelations from Willmandingen

At the same time that I was finding and interviewing the surviving crewmembers, I was starting to pull on another thread of my research. After talking with bombardier Nick DeRose in April 1997, I wanted to find *The Mighty Eighth War Diary* and view the crash site photo that he had said was in it. I learned that the book was written by Roger A. Freeman, along with Alan Crouchman and Vic Maslen, and that it had been published by Arms and Armour in 1981. Unfortunately, it was now out of print. In early May, I conducted a web search for the book and was fortunate to be able to purchase a copy from a bookseller in Woking, Surrey, England.

Knowing that I would soon be viewing the crash site photograph, I began to wonder about the circumstances surrounding its existence. Nick had told me that the photo was taken at ground level. Who had taken it? How had the author of *The Mighty Eighth War Diary* obtained a copy of it? Since the book had been published so long ago, would I be able to locate the photographer? I decided that the logical next step was to try to locate a villager in Willmandingen who remembered the crash of the Flying Fortress in World War II.

My first move was to attempt to find the village on a map. Where exactly was Willmandingen? All I knew was that it was approximately twenty-eight miles south of Stuttgart. I went to the travel section in my local Barnes & Noble bookstore and found a map of Germany. With the map opened to its full size of four by five feet, I sprawled on the floor and began looking for the village. I easily found the city of Stuttgart in southwestern Germany on the outskirts of the Black Forest region. Despite the detail of the map, however, Willmandingen was nowhere to be found.

Once again I turned to the Internet. A search on the term "Willmandingen" led me quickly to several websites. Unfortunately, however, all of them were written in German. Fearing that my lack of language skills might bring me to a screeching halt in my venture down this new research avenue, I decided that I needed an interpreter to help me over my language hurdle. Perhaps a web search for German clubs would connect me with someone who could help me communicate with the villagers of Willmandingen. With this new idea, hope resurfaced.

I sent out several e-mails to German clubs in the United States, concentrating on colleges and universities in hopes that I might be able to interest a student or professor in undertaking an interesting research project. One of those messages went to Sigrid Kellenter, professor of German and chair of the Department of Modern Languages and Literatures at Union College in Schenectady, New York. Her homepage biography gave me hope that she might be willing to help me, as it expressed her enthusiasm about teaching the German language and her pride in her German heritage. In the e-mail, I asked whether she would consider helping me locate the town and communicate with the villagers. Only a week later, an e-mail arrived in my inbox from Professor Kellenter. She was coming to the aid of a perfect stranger. "Thank you for your interesting inquiry," she wrote. "I do not know the town Willmandingen, but will send out for some information. A colleague of mine in Germany might help and I will try the Web too. Hopefully, I will be successful."

Professor Kellenter was true to her word. About three weeks later, she sent me an e-mail that answered my questions and gave me some guidance in pursuing my goals. It said, "My colleague in Germany finally responded with the following addresses. I think you could write your letter of inquiry to them in English. There are plenty of people who understand English in Germany, particularly at a [news]paper like these, and they will be able to respond to you. I hope this will bring you closer to an answer to your questions. Let me know the outcome!" According to the colleague, Willmandingen was "indeed a very small place perhaps a dozen kilometers south of Reutlingen, and lying in the postal code area for Sonnenbühl: 72820." The message included references to several newspapers in the area—the *Reutlinger General-Anzeiger,* the *Reutlinger Wochenblatt,* and the *Reutlinger Nachrichten*—complete with postal addresses and phone numbers.

Rather than send each newspaper a letter, I ran a web search for sites that mentioned the town of Reutlingen. I e-mailed the webmaster of each relevant site in hopes that someone would aid me in the same way that Sigrid Kellenter, Mo Moriarty, Joe Waddell, and Ted Darcy had. In my message, I requested information about the B-17 Flying Fortress that had crashed in Willmandingen in 1944. I wrote, "I would appreciate any help [you] could provide in getting me in touch with someone who could converse in English and help me understand more about the events surrounding the February 25, 1944 plane crash."

One of my inquiries paid dividends. Less than a week later, I received a response from Jens Boysen, the webmaster for a company based in Reutlingen. Germany also had its share of good Samaritans! Oddly enough, Boysen was affiliated with one of the newspapers that Sigrid Kellenter's colleague had recommended that I contact. He wrote,

> Indeed, my Englisch is crazy bad, but I for the first shall try to help you as good as I can. I am journalist at the Reutlinger General-Anzeiger, the newspaper which is also spread in the [Schwäbische] Alb, where Willmandingen is situatet. We have correspondents in Willmandingen and, sure, contacts to the local administration. I soon, may be already tomorrow, shall try to look for the rekords at my newspaper and further at the local archives at Willmandingen—allthough the problem about your uncle Anthony J. Korkuc seems to be very complicated. I never heard anything about war-affairs at Willmandingen nor what happened with the downed airplane or the dead soldiers. We'll find it out! And tell you if there is anything remembered.

Less than an hour after receiving the e-mail, I responded to Boysen, telling him, "Your English is not crazy bad as I understood it perfectly!" Despite his broken English, his message had come through loud and clear. Sigrid Kellenter was correct; I could find assistance in Germany by conversing in English. I also told Jens about the Willmandingen Flying Fortress crash scene photo that had appeared in the book *The Mighty Eighth War Diary,* and that I hoped more pictures might be available.

On June 10, 1997, I received an amazing message from one of Boysen's colleagues, a man named Marcus Mockler:

On behalf of Jens Boysen I answer your e-mail dated 04 June 97. Like Mr Boysen I am member of the staff of the "Reutlinger General-Anzeiger," a daily newspaper which covers not only the city of Reutlingen but also the surrounding communities. One of the communities I write about is Willmandingen.

When I had read your mail I called a man in Willmandingen who is an eye-witness of the B-17 crash. His name is Hermann Möck. He was the second person who came to the crashed plane. As he recalls, the date of the crash was Febr. 23rd (not 25th!). The 15-year-old Möck took a photograph of the airplane the day after. This photo has been published in a regional calendar (I will try to get a copy).

His information is: The 4-engine "Super-Flying-Fortress" B-17 had bombed the German city of Augsburg. The squadron was pursued by German airplanes. The Germans succeeded to separate one airplane from the squadron. Possibly the German defender gave the crew some time to leave the B-17 which they didn't do. When the B-17 lost height and threatened to hit the village, it was shot down.

The B-17 crashed between 1330 and 1400 about 300 meters southeast of Willmandingen near the house of a man called Otto Flad. Immediately, the airplane burnt out. Four members of the crew survived, the others—among them your uncle—lost their lives.

It must have been a difficult situation for the people of the village: What should they do with the corpses? A cemetery is an honorable place—and these were the bodies of enemies! The local leader of the NSDAP (the Nazi-party) wanted to bury them somewhere outside of Willmandingen. But the public opinion argued that they should be given a more respectable place. The other day the corpses were buried at the cemetery of the village which was on the backside of the church. They were given no coffins. But ironically the place of the burial itself was very honorable—behind the graves of two ministers who had served in the local Lutheran congregation before. (Today, there are no graves beside the church anymore, but Mr. Möck is still able to show precisely the place where the grave was.) Instead of a cross, a part of the B-17 (a door?) was put on the grave. It said "Hier ruhen 6 amerikanische Soldaten" (Six American soldiers rest here).

Unfortunately, I have not been able to find any documents about the incident yet. There is no information about names, for example.

Möck remembers that he had read the name Lt. DR Rose on a cap. The other five are unknown.

Two years later . . . a team of Americans came to exhume the corpses and bring them to France. It was a very hot day. They forced German men to help to dig out the bodies. Because of the special conditions in the soil of that place, the corpses were much less decayed than expected. Möck remembers the little anecdote that the pockets of the leather flying suits were searched through—and about 7,000 dollars were found in one of them! Obviously, none of the inhabitants of Willmandingen had raided the dead American soldiers.

That's all I could find out about this incident. I think about writing an article for our newspaper about the B-17 and the story of its crew. Can you mail information? What happened to the corpses when they had left Willmandingen? What was the profession of your uncle before he had to fight in WW II? Do you intend to visit the historical places? As I wrote, Mr. Möck is able to show the place where the airplane crashed as well as the place where the corpses were buried.

Please contact me.

The story is exciting, and after 50 years many people are interested to collect the reminiscences of a time they first tried to forget.

Best wishes,
Marcus Mockler

I replied to Marcus, thanking him for his help. I was excited at the prospect of talking to Hermann Möck so that I could better understand what had happened after the plane went down. I assured Marcus that I would gladly help him write the story of the B-17 crash. I told him that although I would love to visit Willmandingen someday, I hoped that in the meantime he would be willing to interview Hermann on videotape. I also wanted to see in color what the crash area and the cemetery looked liked. Curious about the circumstances of the Willmandingen burial, I requested that Marcus ask Möck a question for me. I wanted to know why Thomas Hunnicutt and Anthony Bartolo, the two men who had been buried separately in their hometowns, had been buried apart from the other four men.

On June 12, I received an unforgettable message from Marcus Mockler. That morning, he had met with Hermann Möck and a local historian named Wilhelm Speidel, and they had discussed the events

Crash site of Flying Fortress 42–37786 in Willmandingen, Germany. This photo was taken just days after the plane was shot down. Hermann Möck, the eyewitness who gave the photo to Marcus, is barely noticeable just to the right and behind the B-17's tail. Photo courtesy of Hermann Möck.

of 1944. During the meeting, Möck had given Marcus a black and white photograph that was taken at the crash site. Marcus assured me that after he was finished with his newspaper article, he would send me the photo, and meanwhile he would have it scanned and uploaded to a website so that I could see it.

Marcus was true to his word. A couple of days later, an e-mail arrived with a web link to the scanned photo. I clicked on the link with great anticipation, and within seconds, I was looking at the crash site of 1944. It was a remarkable image. The only portion of the aircraft that looked remotely like its former self was the tail. The 381st Bomb Group's tail insignia was clearly visible. Located just under the black "L" in the white triangle, I could discern a portion of the tail number— 37786—as well as the top of the letter "B." There was no doubt about it: this was the B-17 that had taken my uncle into battle on February 25, 1944!

On top of the wreckage stood six children from Willmandingen, looking out at me from the past. I would later learn their identities:

Willi Betz, Karl Maier, Willi Maier, Hermann Möck, Willi Heinz, and
Karl Heinz. According to Möck, his father's camera was used to take
the picture. Hermann, who was fifteen years old at the time, had taken
the camera with him to the crash site and convinced one of the armed
soldiers guarding the debris to snap a picture of the friends as they
posed atop the American bomber.

At the time the photograph was taken, my uncle and his five crewmates had already been removed from the plane and were buried in
the Willmandingen town cemetery. Möck and Speidel had answered
one of my questions: they were certain that the six men were placed
in a single grave. The fact that the bodies were separated later in the
United States obviously had nothing to do with the way they were initially buried in the churchyard in Willmandingen.

Marcus asked me for some specific help with his article. He wanted
to know how he could contact the two survivors I had found. He was
interested in learning what they remembered about the mission. Why
had they bailed out of the plane but the others had not? Were they
arrested immediately? How were they treated by their German captors? Mockler asked whether he could e-mail me his questions, so that
I could then phone DeRose and Ramos to ask them what he wanted
to know. I agreed, since I too wanted to reopen communications with
Nick and Raoul. When I told Mockler that I would be glad to interview them for him, I made it clear that I would not release their names
or any of their information unless they gave me permission. At that
time, I was still about three weeks away from locating Don Henderson.

As usual, the first person I talked to was my father. I read him
Mockler's message, eager to hear what he had to say. Dad was comforted
to know that his brother had been given a respectful burial in enemy
soil. A couple of days later, I made a Father's Day visit and gave him a
printout of the picture of Tony's plane. We talked for a while, and then,
with his consent, I e-mailed Mockler and asked him to tell Hermann
Möck that the Korkuc family wanted to extend our heartfelt thanks to
the people of Willmandingen for burying Tony in their town cemetery.

RECONNECTIONS

I placed another phone call to Nick DeRose, explaining that I wanted
his help so that a German newspaper reporter could write an article

about his crew. He paused, then said that he did not want to participate. He could see no good in remembering the past. I told him that
it was important to remember, and in fact it had offered some solace
to my father. With that, he decided that no harm would be done, and
he agreed to help with the article.

I told him about my interview with Raoul Ramos, and explained that
my uncle had not been a substitute crewmember. I said that most likely
Nick had known him only by his nickname, "Korky." Light dawned, as
DeRose finally remembered Tony. Feeling bad about misleading my
father initially, he told me to tell him that the crew had been very close.
He then laughed and said that officers and enlisted men often went
into town together. He seemed especially proud of that.

Feeling a need to atone for not remembering Tony, Nick told me
that his sister in Hillsboro, Michigan, had a picture of him with his
crew, and he had asked her to find it and have a copy of it made for
me. The photo had been taken in the summer of 1943 while they were
stationed in Alexandria, Louisiana. Nick added that he would be
proud to be able to show me what my uncle looked like as part of his
crew. I thanked him for his kindness.

I then asked Nick whether he could recall any more details of his
last mission, and he mentioned that *The Mighty Eighth War Diary* indicated that the lead bombardier had released his bomb load prema-
turely and the bombs had fallen short of the target. Despite being
trained as a bombardier, Nick had not used his Norden bombsight but
had simply released his bombs when the lead plane did. He told me
that a Messerschmitt 109 had jumped the plane, and that engine trouble was already causing a drag on the aircraft. The pilot could not
feather the propellers of the engine, and they also suffered damage
from flak. It was a terrible feeling, knowing he was going to have to
bail, but he did so from the nose hatch at an altitude of about 500 feet.

DeRose then made a confession. "I don't think I should be telling
you this," he said, and then after a short pause he proceeded to tell
me something that had weighed heavily on his mind all those years.
After the bailout order was given, the navigator, Earl Wonning, was supposed to jump out of the nose hatch first, followed by the bombardier.
But Wonning, although unhurt, would not jump. He looked really
scared, and DeRose pleaded with him, but to no avail. "I did all I could
to make Wonning jump out of the plane," he told me. DeRose said he

thought about his wife and unborn baby and bailed out, leaving Wonning behind. I told DeRose that even though I could not relieve him of his sense of guilt, I knew that he was not the only one who had been in a position to get Wonning out of the plane. Raoul Ramos had also seen Wonning huddled at the nose hatch. In my interview with Don Henderson a few weeks later, I would learn that he also recalled seeing Wonning in the plane.

DeRose said that when his parachute opened, he lost his cap and his boots. Instead of his normal flight boots, he was wearing a special fur-lined pair. Since they did not fit that tightly, they came off when he hit the B-17's slipstream. When his German captors approached him, they were armed with guns, clubs, and pitchforks. Nick was carrying an escape kit that contained a .45-caliber handgun, and as he squared off against the townsfolk, the weapon accidentally fell to the ground. Guns were aimed at him, and it was an extremely tense moment. But soon the tension eased, and he surrendered to them without anyone getting hurt. The Germans took him to a bakery in town. He described the situation as surreal: one moment he was in a fight with ME-109 fighters, and the next he was breathing in the sweet smells of a bakery. He was obviously shaken, and his captors tried to reassure him. DeRose remained in the bakery until the Gestapo came to take him away.

Before the conversation ended, Nick shared with me a story about his crew. While they were on R & R in London, several of the enlisted men got into trouble and ended up in jail, and the officers came to their rescue and bailed them out. Nick could not recall the exact details of the arrest, but he chuckled and said that his crew were as close as brothers.

Ten days later, I made another call to Nick DeRose. He told me that he had received the package I sent him, containing an enlarged printout of the Hermann Möck crash site photo. He confirmed that it was the same photo that was featured in *The Mighty Eighth War Diary*. He also said that his sister had not yet located the crew picture he had told me about, but she was still looking for it.

I asked Nick whether he had any lasting memories of his earlier raids to share with me. He recalled the time a German Ju-88 fighter fired a rocket at his formation and blew one of the 381st Bomb Group planes out of the sky. He feared the Ju-88, because it could fly out of range of the Fortresses' .50-caliber guns, yet still launch its rockets at the bombers. Another distinct memory was the intensity of the German flak. On one mission, flak fragments had come through his plane. Flak was a difficult problem because the B-17s had little in the way of protection against it. The crews had some success initially with dropping small pieces of metal out of the planes in an attempt to confuse the flak units' radar stations. Once the Germans caught on, however, that countermeasure lost its effectiveness.

I next asked Nick if he would comment on his experiences as a prisoner of war. He said that after his capture, some German ham radio operators sent messages to their counterparts in the United States, letting them know what had happened to him. People on the East Coast received the messages, and in turn sent postcards to Nick's family about his POW status. In Nick's opinion, the German ham radio operators showed a lot of class in relaying the information.

Nick recalled that Stalag Luft I was run by the Luftwaffe, and the prisoners were not treated badly. However, the adjoining camp housed political prisoners, and its occupants were all poorly fed and looked like skeletons. Nick described prison life as boring. The barracks were freezing, he said, with only small stoves to provide heat. (On reflection, he noted that the POW camp was probably no colder than his quarters in Ridgewell!) The men passed the time playing cards— mostly bridge and cribbage—and during the warmer months they played softball. The Germans let the men dig escape tunnels—tunnels that they easily found and destroyed.

I asked whether he was ever afraid while in captivity, and he told me that he was at first, but as he got used to the place, he lost his fear. When he first arrived at Stalag Luft I, the guards were young SS men, but later on they were replaced by old men who gave the prisoners little trouble. He was proud of the Americans' bravado. The U.S. servicemen often razzed the guards, forcing them to raise their guns. But he couldn't recall any shooting that ever resulted.

Nick had both good and bad war memories. He wanted to talk, and I was eager to listen. My relationship with him had become special, and his information added much to my understanding of life as a POW.

My experience with Raoul Ramos was very different. On June 12, I called Raoul, but he was not there. His twenty-four-year-old grandson Robert answered the phone and told me that Raoul and his wife were celebrating their fiftieth wedding anniversary in New Orleans. He suggested that I call back the next day. In our short conversation, Robert told me that he knew little about Raoul's wartime experiences. He had accompanied his grandfather to a POW convention, but Raoul was unhappy about the behavior of some of the other attendees; he was ashamed of the men who boasted to the crowds about their time as prisoners. Raoul's own memories were darker. For years, he had kept a spoon he used in the camp. Robert did not personally understand the spoon's significance, but he knew that his grandfather valued it greatly.

The next day, I spoke with Raoul Ramos and told him about my contact with the Willmandingen eyewitness. I asked whether he would be willing to assist me in learning more about his last mission so that I could share the information with the German journalist Marcus Mockler. Raoul replied that he did not want his name or address revealed, but he would help anonymously. I asked whether he could offer any more memories of Tony, and he told me that Tony had a lot of guts to fly as the ball turret gunner of his crew. He recalled an incident on one mission when Tony's guns had frozen, preventing him from firing. When Tony crawled out of the ball turret, he was "pretty pale," according to Ramos, but he still had a big smile on his face.

I told Raoul that Nick had believed he was the only one who knew that Wonning refused to bail from the plane, and that he had drawn some comfort from the fact that he was not alone in that knowledge. Ramos said that Wonning's face was "as red as a cherry," and he knew he wouldn't jump. I told Raoul that I had sent him a package containing a picture of my uncle's gravesite at Arlington, as well as a photo of the crash site. I had included a brief account of Tony's last mission, including a summary of my interviews with Nick and him as well as the accounts of the German eyewitness. I asked Raoul whether I could read my account to him and get his comments, and he agreed. I read an excerpt from Mockler's e-mail. He responded that it was "a crock" that the plane was shot down only after it appeared to threaten the town. Ramos made it clear that the actions of the ME-109 pilot had nothing to do with how close they were to Willmandingen.

When I mentioned Hermann Möck's and Marcus Mockler's assertion that $7,000 had been found on the body of one of the dead airmen, Raoul was equally dismissive. He said that none of his crewmates would have been carrying that much cash on them. He was also taken aback by the claim that the Germans had shown respect for the Americans' bodies by not stealing from them. He told me that when the villagers captured him, he was led into town. He emphasized that many of the people in the crowd did not like him or what he stood for. With that last statement, Raoul and I ended our call.

Ironically, Raoul's and Nick's memories of the war differed drastically. Nick could easily talk about his experiences, while Raoul seemed disgusted by the war and his memories of it. And while Raoul had deeply respected Tony, Nick could offer me little in the way of memories of my uncle, except for his vague recollection of the trouble the crew had gotten into in London.

THE MIRACLE OF THE NET

After my initial contact with journalist Marcus Mockler in June 1997, our exchange of information proceeded at a snail's pace. To speed things up, and to gain more control over the communication, I proposed to "Moc" that we meet in an Internet chat room. Hoping that he would be receptive, I sent him an e-mail invitation to meet me in a chat room at 10:00 P.M. German time on June 18. When I signed in at 4:11 P.M. U.S. Eastern Standard Time, I posted "Korky here." A minute later, I was ecstatic to receive the reply "Hi Korky. Just popped into the room—Moc." It was exciting that a real-time electronic communication was about to take place between the United States and Germany about a B-17 crash that had occurred fifty-three years earlier.

One of the many questions I had been asking Moc concerned the fate of Nick DeRose's cap. I wanted to know whether Hermann Möck still had it in his possession. Mockler had not answered this particular question via e-mail, but now that I had his full attention in the chat room, I was hoping to get an answer. He told me that Möck had a few things from the B-17, but no personal items belonging to the aircrew. He added that Hermann still had a motor that he'd taken from the plane in 1944.

Moc was confident that his newspaper article would soon be completed, and said that it would probably appear in July. I posted four more questions: What specific items had Hermann Möck taken from the plane? How many people in Willmandingen still remembered the

crash of 1944? Did Möck recall the condition of the bodies at their initial burial? Would Marcus be able to videotape the Hermann Möck
interview and the Willmandingen sites for me?

Moc wasn't sure what items Hermann had removed from the plane,
and said that he seemed sensitive about revealing exactly what he had.
The newspaper sold about fifty thousand copies each day, but the population of Willmandingen was only about fifteen hundred, and he suspected there were few who remembered the B-17 crash. He also told
me that he did not own a camcorder, so he would not be able to provide me with a videotape of any of his interviews. I asked whether he
knew of the existence of any other crash site photos, and he responded
that to the best of his knowledge, the Möck photo was the only one
ever taken.

Learning from my rapid-fire method of asking questions, Marcus
came back with some questions of his own. He asked me to provide
more information on who I was, and to share with him the crewmembers' memories of their time in captivity. I told him that I was preparing an airmail package for him in which I would include a brief
biography of myself along with a biography of Tony and the portrait
of him that had appeared in the *Seekonk Sentinel.* I would also be sending him a profile picture of a B-17 and a close-up of the B-17 ball turret gunner's position. Lastly, I told him to expect a photo of my father
that I was hoping he would publish in the paper.

Moc returned to his question about the men's experiences as POWs.
I assumed that he wanted to explore that particular subject in his article. I told him that one of the survivors wanted to remain anonymous,
and that neither man was comfortable speaking about his time in captivity. I told him that the fifteen months in POW camp were not pleasant for either of the survivors. After fifty-two years, both men wanted
to forget their last mission; after all, they had lost six of their crewmates.
I was hesitant to reveal the full conversation I had had with Nick
DeRose about his memories of life as a POW. Moc responded that he
could understand perfectly how difficult it was to talk to the men about
their time in captivity. But wasn't it part of the story? His readers would
want to know how the survivors were treated.

I asked Marcus a new question of my own: How did Germans
remember World War II? Now that fifty years had passed, how did they
feel about the war? I speculated that Germany was still about thirty

years away from being able to look back objectively at those traumatic times. Marcus responded that my thoughts about historical objectivity were certainly interesting, but he had some problems with them. That conversation, however, would have to wait for another day. We had been "talking" for about forty-five minutes, and it was nearing 11 P.M. for him. Marcus told me that he wanted to "meet" again in a couple of days, then communicate further by e-mail. He said that he had greatly enjoyed his first active participation in an online chat room. I felt good. We had exchanged some key information and were also in the process of forming a friendship.

A couple of weeks later, the day before his interview with Hermann Möck, Marcus and I had our last late-night chat-room discussion. A lot had happened in the interim. First and foremost, I had located Don Henderson. True to form, Moc posted at 10:49 P.M. German time. He immediately answered one of my recent questions: the reason I had been unable to locate Willmandingen on a map was that in 1975 it had been combined with three other small communities to form the town of Sonnenbühl.

Moc wanted to know more about the Americans' retrieval of men who had been reported missing or killed in action. Were there teams traveling around Germany whose goal was to transport the remains to France and then to Arlington? I told him that the teams were part of the American Graves Registration Service, and their job was to locate and provide a final resting place for all of the fallen sons of America. The six crewmembers had been removed to the American Military Cemetery in Saint-Avold so that the AGRS could begin the process of identification. I explained to Moc that four of the six men were buried together in Arlington because they could not be individually identified.

I requested that Marcus ask Hermann Möck about the condition of the bodies after the crash. Also, I wondered whether the Nazi officials had removed the dog tags from the dead men, thus making it more difficult to identify them later. In addition, I wanted to know whether Hermann recalled seeing Don Henderson near the burning plane. I asked whether the names of the ME-109 fighter pilots who had shot down the B-17 were known. Marcus admitted that he did not even know where to begin looking for that sort of information. He emphasized that his interest and expertise lay only in the Willmandingen event; after all, his was only a local newspaper.

I was indebted to Marcus for his help, and thankful that we were able to communicate so easily because his English was so good. He told me that he had learned English while living in South Africa as a child. He had even traveled to the United States as a student. "The fact that I studied history and English," he added, "is just an 'accident'—or let's say Providence." During the course of my research, I have sensed the hand of Providence many times.

With this last exchange, the chat ended, and I awaited the news from his interview with Hermann Möck.

Could the German fighter pilots be found? I wondered. Given the difficulty I was having researching the American side of the story, was it foolish even to try to find out about the incident from the Luftwaffe point of view? Perhaps I should wait before I tugged on that research thread.

GLIMPSES OF A WINTER'S DAY

On July 9, 1997, Marcus Mockler met with Hermann Möck and Wilhelm Speidel in Willmandingen. They spent two and a half hours discussing the events of February 25, 1944. After the interview, Marcus sent me an informative e-mail in which he reconstructed the events:

> On that winter day Hermann Möck was standing in front of his home when the B-17 approached. It looked as if the plane wanted to pass the village, flying northeast to southwest, but then it turned west and came down on the nearby hill. A few meters higher it would have missed the hill and come down in Willmandingen.
>
> Möck ran up to the hill. The machine was burning, two Americans [Don Henderson and Raoul Ramos] were walking around. One airman was dead at the side of the plane. As he had tried to bail out, his parachute had got tangled up with the plane. A little stream of blood ran out of his mouth, Möck recalled.
>
> One ME-109 flew over the place a few times, then returned to its base in Nellingen near Böblingen. The pilot came a few days later to look at the crashed B-17, but nobody today remembers his name.
>
> The crowd of villagers coming from Willmandingen and Undingen kept their distance, for when the plane had caught fire, ammunition

Willmandingen historian Wilhelm Speidel (left) and eyewitness Hermann Möck on the hill where Flying Fortress 42–37786 struck the ground on February 25, 1944. Photo courtesy of Marcus Mockler.

went off. Two hours after the crash, two soldiers from the military camp (about six miles away) came and guarded the plane.

Two local soldiers who were at home on vacation arrested the surviving Americans, and they were taken to the town hall. A third American [Jack Fournier] who had jumped off a mile before and had already packed his parachute in his bag, was also picked up. It was reported later that a fourth flyer [Nick DeRose] was arrested in another village.

Möck emphasized that unlike in the heavily bombed cities, there was no hatred against the Americans in Willmandingen. Boys like Möck even felt a sort of admiration, seeing the crew of such an impressive airplane!

The corpses in the plane, among them Tony Korkuc, were recovered about two days later. Möck wasn't there when this was done, but it is likely they were heavily burnt.

The local people discussed where the Americans should be buried, and the World War I veterans demanded that the men be given an honorable burial. Möck didn't know whether there was any kind of ceremony.

Spring came and the snow melted. In late April or early May it was
the inhabitants' job to tidy up the crash site and get the metal to the
railway station in nearby Mössingen. During the clean-up operation, little Hermann Möck discovered a small electric motor. He hid it in a
bush and came back in the evening to get this "treasure" and take it to
his home (what he did was forbidden, of course).

In July 1946 the Americans came to exhume the six corpses. A team
of Willmandingen inhabitants had to do the digging.

The story about the soldier's uniform with several thousand dollars
in a pocket stems from this time. If true, it is most likely the money was
in the pocket of the soldier who died outside the plane because the
other corpses were burnt so heavily.

I now had another question: Who was the airman whose body Herman
Möck had seen near the plane?

On July 16, Mockler's story about Uncle Tony and the Flying Fortress
appeared in the *Reutlinger General-Anzeiger*, occupying a full page. A
week later, I received four copies in the mail. My uncle's photo was
prominently displayed just to the left of the photo of his crashed B-17,
and in the same column was a picture of me. As a result of my inquiries,
the Willmandingen villagers were beginning to understand more
about the 1944 crash of the B-17 just south of their town.

FIVE BAIL, BUT ONLY FOUR SURVIVE

On arrival in Willmandingen in May 1946, the men from the American
Graves Registration Service obtained statements from eyewitnesses.
They learned that a total of six fliers had been buried in the local cemetery. They had the bodies exhumed and moved to the American
Military Cemetery in Saint-Avold, France, where they began trying to
identify them. The AGRS examined the dental records and other
forensic information collected for each of the six. The process took a
total of three and a half years, and in the end they were able to individually identify only Anthony Bartolo and Thomas Hunnicutt.
Nevertheless, the records contained some very interesting information. Among the documents was an eyewitness statement from the
mayor of Willmandingen, Burgermeister Heinz, about the plane crash
of the American Heavy Number L 37786:

Together with some men from here I was working on the road to Melchingen removing snow when a formation of enemy planes was flying very high over this town in a western direction. We looked at these planes when suddenly one man said there is still another plane coming by itself. I then saw also that a big plane flying very low came from the same direction while a German fighter plane was steadily approaching it. All of a sudden, you could see a man bailing out of the airplane; the fighter attacked again, then another man bailed out. The fighter attacked again, and at this point the plane had caught fire. At this moment, three more man bailed out but only two of them safely. The third man's parachute got caught on the plane. The plane itself, as it was burning, turned to the right and slid over the right wing and crashed.

We men hurried to the crash site in case we could save some lives. When we came up on top of the hill we saw that it was behind the next hill. You couldn't have actually gotten to the plane itself though, without putting your life in grave danger, because there were many explosions.

Civilians brought three men from the crew to the town hall. At the same moment medical Dr. W. Fischer from Undingen and a staff officer—a lieutenant colonel—from the ammunition dump Haid arrived with their car. The doctor examined the men to see if they had been injured in any way. One of the men had been slightly injured due to the low altitude; his parachute hadn't opened much.

A half-hour later, a fourth man was brought in. I heard him say at the crash site as the lieutenant colonel interrogated him that they had come from Augsburg and that they were ten, that is to say that there were ten men in the plane.

The place of the plane crash was blocked and guarded by soldiers who arrived in the meantime from the ammunition dump Haid.

The following day an officer from Nellingen arrived who ordered the salvage of the bodies. They were buried in the civilian cemetery in a common grave. The plane was shot down on February [25], 1944 at about 1430 hrs.[1]

The mayor's statement that five men, not four, had bailed out of the doomed bomber was consistent with Hermann Möck's claim to have seen an unburned body near the downed aircraft. Further confirmation that a fifth man had jumped came from a statement from the men in Willmandingen who witnessed the burial:

On February 26, 1944 . . . the [deceased soldiers] were removed from
the wreckage. The identification tags which were then found were taken
away by the [German] officers. On sleds these men were brought to the
civilian cemetery. To look at these bodies was dreadful because there
were only charred remains left with the exception of one man that could
have been identified.[2]

With this new bit of information, I had yet another question to answer.
Of the six men who were killed, which one had jumped to his death?

CHAPTER 4

Flying Machines and Memories

I had learned from Mo Moriarty that the Hanscom Air Force Base in Bedford, Massachusetts, would be hosting an air show on June 21, 1997, to honor the fiftieth anniversary of the United States Air Force, and would be featuring an exhibit on vintage World War II aircraft. I was hopeful that a B-17 would be one of the planes on display; I very badly wanted to see and touch a Flying Fortress for myself. I was also hopeful that I would cross paths with Mo. But how would we find each other? "I will be dressed in boots, and my pants will be tucked into the boots," he said. "We'll find each other somehow."

When I arrived at Hanscom, the field was filled with people, food vendors, and airplanes. After traversing a good portion of the airfield, I looked to my left and spotted an aircraft in the distance, one with four engines and a Plexiglas nose. Immediately I knew that I had seen my first B-17 Flying Fortress! I walked over for a closer look, but was stopped by a barrier of yellow rope. The plane was being kept off limits to everyone until it had flown in the air show, and even then, no one would be allowed to board and see the interior of the aircraft. I was disappointed, but I was nonetheless thrilled to be so close to it. The profile of the plane clearly revealed the ball turret gunner's position.

A crew fueled the plane in preparation for its flight, and as a crowd collected, the four engines were turned over. The roar of the propellers was deafening, but I was enjoying myself. I felt closer to Uncle Tony as I tried to imagine what his first reaction to the plane must have been. The B-17 taxied off the hardstand and rolled down the runway. It took to the air majestically and within seconds was just a small speck on the horizon. About a half-hour later, it returned.

Profile of the flying tribute to the B-17F model *Memphis Belle* at the 1997 Hanscom Air Show. Photo by author.

As time passed, two men wearing red "Distinguished Visitor" tags took their place in line nearby. Not yet having found Mo Moriarty, and wanting to share my excitement with anyone who would stand still long enough to listen, I started to talk to the men. I explained why I was so excited to see the Flying Fortress, and I told them about my research and the details of my interviews with Tony's surviving crewmates. The men were interested in my story, and they asked me some questions: What position had my uncle flown? When was his last mission?

I asked the men who they were. The older of the two looked down at his tag and told me that he had seen it on the ground and simply put it on—he was an ordinary visitor just like me. I sensed that my new friends were putting me on. These two men were indeed distinguished visitors, but who were they? Finally they owned up. The older man told me that he was a former fighter pilot and a former Blue Angel pilot. He had flown many different types of fighter aircraft, but he had never flown a bomber. He then introduced me to the younger man, who had also been a fighter pilot; during his service days he had shot down two Russian MiGs. The three of us started to talk about the air war in World War II. The two marveled at the bravery of the men who

Exterior view of the ball turret of David Tallichet's *Memphis Belle* at the 1997 Hanscom Air Show. Photo by author.

had manned those heavy bombers, and I knew that this respect had been reciprocated.

Within a few minutes, an air show official walked over to the barrier rope, unhooked a portion of it, and announced that it was time for the distinguished visitors' private showing of the *Memphis Belle*. In disbelief, I learned that the tour party was to consist of the two fighter pilots—and me! My new friend had designated me as an honorary distinguished visitor. I was deeply touched by his generosity.

I followed the two men toward the waist gunner's hatch at the rear of the Boeing Flying Fortress. Before I entered, however, there was something I had to do. I walked slowly to the ball turret. I sighed as I thought about my Uncle Tony. He had taken his last breath while curled up in this small space. I snapped a picture of the ball turret so that my father could see where his older brother sat on his last mission. Then I too entered the rear hatch and made my way toward the front of the plane.

When negotiating the waist gunner's hatch, I could see the open windows on either side of the plane, and I tried to imagine Tony's crewmates manning the .50-caliber machine gun posts. Thomas Hunnicutt would have stood on the left, and Anthony Bartolo on the right. I pictured Tony's crewmates as they valiantly battled the ME-109 fighters on that last mission. I crawled into the nose of the plane, where I viewed the navigator's table and looked at the bombardier's chair, which sat just in front of the clear Plexiglas window that separated the bombardier from the outside world. I noticed the famous Norden bombsight perched in front of the window.

An air show official signaled for us to leave the aircraft. My companions and I hastily snapped a few more pictures and exited the rear hatch. Leaving my images of 1944 behind me, I stepped back into the warmth of the sun and the reality of 1997. When I exited, I noticed a man wearing blue jeans tucked into a pair of brown boots. I walked up to him and asked if he was Mo Moriarty. He gave me a big smile and told me yes. I thanked him for the generous help he had given me. We chatted for a while; I told him about the thrill I had just had in boarding the B-17, while he talked about his website and the joy he drew from helping people like me understand the past.

As I told him more about my research and my recent encounter with the German eyewitness, he told me about a similar experience of his own more than two decades earlier. As a twenty-one-year-old kid in 1943, he had been shot down on a bombing mission and had parachuted to the ground in German-occupied France. With the help of the French Resistance, he had managed to evade the Germans and return to his base just twenty-three days later. In 1981 he had begun searching for the French people who helped him escape, and he had been successful in finding all but two of them. Sadly, Mo passed away a couple of years ago. I am glad we met, and that I had the opportunity to thank him in person for his help.

In early July, just days before the release of Marcus Mockler's story in the *Reutlinger General-Anzeiger,* I received a letter from bombardier Nick DeRose. He had finally located the crew picture! I was struck by how "cool" Tony looked in his leather flight jacket—like James Dean ready to take on the world. I was thrilled to be staring back in time at my uncle and his B-17 crew. Seven of the nine pictured took part in the mission on February 25, 1944, and four of them lost their lives that day. Unfortunately, the photo did not include Don Henderson, Dale Schilling, or Thomas Hunnicutt. A couple of days after receiving the crew photo, I made a computer scan of it and presented it to my father. The only wartime image he had previously seen of his brother

The Bill Herrington crew at Alexandria Army Air Force Base, Louisiana, in August 1943. Standing, left to right: Raoul Ramos (top turret gunner), Anthony Korkuc (ball turret gunner), Boyd Burgess (radio operator), Harvey Reeves (tail gunner), and Anthony Bartolo (right waist gunner). Front row, left to right: Bill Herrington (pilot), Jack Fournier (co-pilot), Earl Wonning (navigator), and Nick DeRose (bombardier). Photo courtesy of Nick DeRose.

was one of him in his dress uniform; now he was seeing him with his crewmates, part of a B-17 crew.

The puzzle that had presented itself to me in Arlington National Cemetery was starting to come together. I had made some incredible connections in the course of my research, and those connections were helping me put the pieces into place. But I was about to have the chance to connect much more personally with Tony. I was about to learn about my uncle from his own words, and the words of those who had known him.

AN INTIMATE PORTRAIT OF TONY KORKUC

During 1997, I visited my father in Rhode Island many times, to keep him abreast of my research. We would go off on our own and sometimes talk for hours, speculating about what more could be learned and what really happened. On one visit, I showed him Tony's Individual Deceased Personnel File. It revealed that my grandmother had received a package from the Army in February 1945, which contained Tony's personal belongings. Among the items were a set of rosary beads, Tony's gunner's wings and his military decorations, some books, and a bundle of letters. When I visited Dad again over Father's Day weekend, he surprised me with the letters that had been returned to my grandmother. He had discovered them after my grandparents passed away, and he had taken them home with him in order to preserve his brother's memory. He had never been able to bring himself to read them, but now he wanted me to do so.

Tony was the second child born to Polish immigrants Anna and Michael Korkuc. Ironically, his parents had both departed European soil via ports in Germany. The couple met and married in 1915. Anna and Michael had eight children: five boys—Anthony, John, Stanley, Edmund, and Charles; and three girls—Josephine, Helen, and Sophie. Tony, born in 1917, was the oldest son, and my father, Edmund Thomas Korkuc, the fourth-oldest boy, was almost ten years younger.

In the bundle were twenty-six letters that Tony had written home during his stateside training with the U.S. Army. Each began "Dear Family." The first letter was postmarked from Camp Lee, Virginia, and dated October 25, 1941, just ten days after he joined the Army. It said that Tony had been assigned to the Medical Corps. For a while it looked as though this would be his permanent assignment, and he might well sit out the war in the States.

Tony's letters are full of expressions of affection for family members, and reveal his wry sense of humor. In one he bewails the fact that he is still a private:

> They have passed out a lot of ratings around here. Don't be surprised about me still being a measly ol' yard bird private. The ones that got the ratings had to suck too many asses to get them. That's just the way this Army (our camp) is being run. So if things are run the same down here I'll be a yard bird 5 years from now because I'm not going to kiss nobody's ass to get my stripes.

My Polish-speaking grandmother had difficulty reading English, so her children most likely censored Tony's letters when they read them

The Korkuc boys, at home on West Avenue in Seekonk, Massachusetts, 1934. Front row, left to right: Edmund (my father), Charles, and Stanley. Back row, left to right: Johnny and Tony. Photo courtesy of the Korkuc family.

to her. In one letter, Tony talks about an unannounced phone call he had received from the family. Although he was excited to hear from them, he was perturbed that the call had shaken him up so much. "I was going to write right after the telephone call," he wrote, "but time sure flies. I just got your letter. I was half shaved when I was told of the call and it had me scared a little while I was walking over to the office. I have a couple of pals who got calls the same way but it was because of a death in the family. So, if you're going to call again, let me know ahead of time." In the same letter, he apologized for something he had said during that phone call: "Excuse me for calling Air Corps guys sissies, but at this camp, it's just loaded with sissies and gold-bricks. I hope all other air corps camps are better than this one. (For the good of Uncle Sam). When I said sissy, it meant no reflection on Tom." He must have remembered that his future brother-in-law Tom Connors, his sister Sophie's boyfriend, was in the Air Corps.

In late March 1942, Tony was reassigned to the psychiatric ward at Keesler Air Field in Biloxi, Mississippi, where he worked the graveyard shift. In one of his letters, he said that many of his patients were "battier than bed bugs but still I get along with them O.K." One of them even tried to commit suicide, but Tony and his fellow ward nurses were able to save the poor soul. I got another glimpse of his sense of humor in his description of administering vaccines at Keesler: "I'm still working at the laboratory and I like it. I throw a needle at the Air Corp rookies and I sure scare hell out of them. The best part is making them 'come to' after they faint. I don't blame them for fainting after they get one look at my polack puss."

After working for some months in the psychiatric ward without a furlough, Tony decided to apply to the Air Corps. He requested three letters of recommendation. "I know y'all will be wondering what it's all about," he wrote, "but all I want to do is get out of this damn medical corps. and take a shot at something else where I can get ahead instead of being a *buck private* all my life. Try to have these letters make me look good in the eyes of an officer. (Ya' know, let them write some kind of bull-shit to build me up.) If I don't get out of the nut-house soon, they'll be putting me in a room (cell) all by myself."

There are no known letters from the fall until December of 1942. It is possible that the letters from that period were lost, but it is more likely that Tony was given an extended furlough to Seekonk. At the end of the year, he was accepted by the Army Air Corps. His dream of becoming a pilot was not to be, but he looked toward the future knowing that he would be trained as an aerial gunner. A letter dated Christmas Day 1942 is postmarked from the Las Vegas Army Gunnery School.

As 1943 rolled in, Tony found himself in a classroom for the first time since his graduation from Hope High School in Providence, Rhode Island, six years before. With no farm chores to do, he could now apply himself fully to the subject of aerial gunnery, and apply himself he did. Although he had been an average student in school, he maintained a 90 percent grade average in his gunnery training, while many of the other candidates washed out. He wrote home, "That's what I like about the place, it proves to yourself whether you know anything or not." The course got tougher, and Tony had to focus on his studies. But not everything in Las Vegas was work; at one point the students got to attend a

Tony Korkuc (right) with his friend Joe Fabianski in Amarillo, Texas, April 17, 1943. Photo courtesy of Edmund Korkuc.

special show that Bob Hope put on for the troops, earning this accolade from Tony: "he's the hottest shit I've seen in years."

In a letter postmarked March 18, 1943, from Amarillo, Texas, where Tony had been transferred to the Army Air Forces Technical School to train to become be a B-17 flight engineer, he comments, "School isn't too bad and I'm afraid if I keep at it I'll know something about an airplane. That's the only thing that bothers me, I didn't think anybody could teach me anything." A month later, after learning that a friend from Seekonk had been listed as missing in action, he wrote, "Read about MacDougal being missing and it doesn't sound real. They say this war business is serious and I imagine a guy can get hurt if he doesn't watch his step."

The last letter in the bundle was mailed in September 1943 from Alexandria, Louisiana, where Tony was training with his B-17 aircrew while preparing for combat duty. "Thought I'd drop a line and let you know about those papers I sent home two days ago," he wrote. "I imagine you have the Insurance papers. I sent the Allotment and power of

Attorney, they are to be read over carefully and put in a safe deposit box or some other safe place for safe keeping. I'm getting along O.K., and will call-up if it isn't against regulations. Hope y'all are getting along alright and tell Pa 'I wish I were home to help him dig the spuds right now.' Not that I mean it."

The parcel also contained some letters that were sent to Tony by family and friends. Like all soldiers, he must have treasured the letters he received from the "real world," letters that brought his hometown and loved ones magically close. Of the sixteen letters that he received between 1942 and February 1944, ten were sent to him while he was at Ridgewell, flying with the 381st Bomb Group. Two of those were from my father, both written in January 1944. Another was from his sister Helen. Postmarked December 23, 1943, it undoubtedly brought him comfort:

Dear Tone,

I got your second letter yesterday and was indeed glad to get it. How are things in England? In your letter you said that you hadn't received the "addresses" you asked for. I sent that letter about 3 weeks ago, I hope by now you have them and meet at least one of them for a bit of Christmas spirits.

We are all well at home and do hope you are the same. It's a mad house around here, trying to keep one another's presents a secret. Glad you had turkey for Thanksgiving. We did too. Pa bought two a few weeks before Thanksgiving so we could have one for each holiday but a great tragedy arose—the second turkey died one day. So I guess we'll have to have a good old rooster for Christmas.

Pa and Edo have been papering the kitchen this past week. I usually lock myself in the parlor every time they start mainly because I'm not used to that sort of language and another reason, I don't want to learn any new words. While Pa was painting the ceiling, the can of paint tipped and spilled all over our dear old Dad. My! My! Such grammar. I thought Edo, Cozu & myself would split our sides.

We have our tree up & it sure looks good. . . . We sure will miss you boys this Christmas. Ma keeps saying, "I wonder where Tony is now?" We tell her you're OK though. I don't know whether or not that's a lie just hope it isn't. . . .

What's it like there or aren't you supposed to say? How about meals? Can you get enough smokes? . . . Edo is still on the hockey team, he must be kinda good if they haven't kicked him off yet. . . . Well that's all the dirt for now. Write soon & Love from all. I hope you *had* a "Merry Christmas" & *have* a good "New Year."

Your little sister,
Helen

Along with the letters, the bundle contained a newspaper article that had been published in the *Seekonk Sentinel* on Memorial Day in 1974. It was written at the time of the dedication of a memorial marker in Tony's honor. The marker was placed on the corner of West Avenue and Newman Avenue in Seekonk. Tony had grown up on West Avenue, and the town saw to it that the street would be forever linked to the memory of its fallen son.

My father drew my attention to a paragraph that quoted a letter written by Raoul Ramos to my grandparents, in which he mentioned that Tony had been buried at Arlington. Dad had obviously never read the article, or he would have known where Uncle Tony was buried and, more important, that there had been at least one survivor from Tony's last mission.

Accompanying the article were two pictures. One was captioned "MEMORIAL MARKER commemorates Sgt. Korkuc and three other crew members at a site in Arlington National Cemetery." The second was the more interesting to me—it was a photo of my Uncle Tony in uniform. But the caption stated that he was "presumed killed."[1] How one can be buried at Arlington but only "presumed killed," I do not know! I was more determined than ever to set the record straight .

ANSWERS FROM THE 1940s

I decided to find out whether anyone on my father's side of the family could add to my knowledge of Tony. Unfortunately, my grandparents both passed away in the 1980s, as did my Uncle Starsh, followed by my Aunt Helen in 1993. However, my father's other four siblings were still alive—Uncles Cardo and Johnny and Aunts Sophie and Josephine. At Dad's suggestion, I contacted Aunt Sophie first. She confirmed that if anyone had had information about Tony, it would have been my Aunt Helen. Unfortunately, Helen's husband Ed had also passed away, but Sophie was confident that her sister's possessions were still intact and being held by Ed's brother Henry. She contacted Henry, who assembled a box of family papers for me. It included a series of letters from 1944 and 1945 that helped to explain why the Korkuc family had remained uncertain about Tony's fate for so long, and why my father had refused to believe that Tony was actually buried at Arlington National Cemetery. The first of the letters was from the 381st Bomb Group chaplain, dated March 5, 1944:

> I am writing you this letter in regard to your son, S.Sgt. Anthony J. Korkuc, 31036784, who is missing in action. The uncertainty of his present state is grave reason for worry and anxiety, but we hope that the time is not far distant when more comforting news comes your way. The majority of the missing are later reported to be safe and well, so we are hoping you hear similar good news soon about your son. We would appreciate your forwarding any additional information which you may receive as we depend largely upon you for that. . . . May God soon see fit to grant us peaceful times again reunited with our loving ones.
>
> Respectfully,
> Martin J. Collet, Chaplain, (Capt.)

Almost eight weeks later, having heard nothing from the War Department since the original telegram, Aunt Helen, writing on behalf of my grandmother, responded to Chaplain Collet. Undoubtedly frustrated by the lack of information and by the chaplain's request for information from them, Helen wrote, "We deeply appreciate your letter concerning Anthony J. Korkuc and wish to thank you for the interest you have shown on his behalf. As soon as we receive any additional information, we will communicate with you."

A letter dated May 20, 1944, from Major E. A. Bradunas, Casualty Branch Chief, Headquarters Army Air Forces, Washington, D.C., offered more information. It conveyed the contents of the February 27, 1944, Missing Air Crew Report:

> Further information has been received indicating that Sergeant Korkuc was a crewmember of a B-17 (Flying Fortress), which departed from

England on a bombardment mission to Augsburg, Germany on February 25th. Details are not available, the report stating that, after having difficulty in remaining with the flight, your son's bomber was seen to leave the formation near the French-German Border. The report further states that this occurred about 3:30 p.m., and that at that time his craft appeared to be under control. The crew members of other planes were unable to make further observation of your son's Fortress, therefore there is no other information available at this time. For your information I am enclosing a list of those who were in the plane and the names and addresses of their next of kin.

Why it took two months to get to the Korkuc family, who were thirsting for any news about Tony, I will never know.

Just four days later, Aunt Helen opted to make contact with those on the list. Each family received a similar request: "Further information as to the eventual landing of the craft is not yet available. If you have any information concerning our boys, I would deeply appreciate hearing from you." On May 26, the wife of radio operator Boyd Burgess responded. She had no information, she wrote, but she remained hopeful: "I feel sure, and have all the time, that we will hear from the boys in the near future. Or they may come home without us having heard from them at all, that has happened you know."

The next day, a letter arrived from the wife of the crew's pilot, and it provided the positive boost the Korkuc family was seeking:

I received a telegram April 7th that Don is a prisoner of War of the German Gov't. Yesterday I received a card from him written March 8th; he was not in a permanent camp so he could not send me his address. He did not mention any names but said he was uninjured in any way. Try not to worry too much as your son might have got with the underground and will get back to his base in England. When that happens it takes months to hear from them. I feel sure that he made it to the ground O.K. If I receive any news from Don regarding your son I will immediately inform you.

Sincerely,
Mrs. Don Henderson,
Red Cloud, Nebraska

Mrs. Burgess sent another ray of hope just over a week later. After receiving a letter from the co-pilot's mother, she wrote:

> I received a letter from Mrs. Gertrude Fournier saying that she has heard from her son, Lt. Jack Fournier. I imagine she has already written you but just in case she hasn't I thought I would write and tell you. I am so happy for her. Now that one of the boys have been heard from I feel sure we will hear from the others soon. Don't you think they must have bailed out? In so doing they must have gotten separated from each other. I hope that Lt. Fournier can soon tell his mother what really happened to the other boys. The letters are censored so strictly though it will be hard for him to tell very much. He is in a German prison camp and told her that as soon as he got his address he would let her know. First she heard from the Red Cross in April. It does seem hard to understand why God doesn't let all of us hear from our loved ones, doesn't it? But I believe He will answer our prayers in His own way. If you have any further information be sure and let me know.
>
> Sincerely,
> Virginia Burgess

The Korkuc family now knew that at least two of the ten men were alive and being held captive by the Germans. But if the letters from the crew's families offered hope, three letters from the War Department over the next seven months kept them on an emotional roller coaster. Three months after receiving Mrs. Henderson's letter, my grandmother received the following from Major General J. A. Ulio:

> I am again writing you concerning your son, Staff Sergeant Anthony J. Korkuc, 31, 036, 784, who was previously reported missing in action since February 25, 1944. It distresses me to have to inform you that no report of any change in his status has yet been received. . . . The War Department is mindful of the anguish you have so long endured and you may rest assured that, without any further request on your part, you will be advised promptly if any additional information concerning your loved one is received. . . . You have my heartfelt sympathy in your sorrow and it is my earnest hope that the fortitude which has sustained you in the past will continue through this distressing period of uncertainty.

Exactly one day after the anniversary of Tony's last combat mission, another letter came from Major General Ulio: "All information concerning your son has been carefully reviewed and considered and an official determination has been made as of February 26, 1945, continuing him in the status of missing in action." This was the first official letter that truly offered the Korkuc family hope. Although it was not the definitive information they were seeking, the War Department had officially determined that Tony might still be alive.

The last of the three letters to arrive from the War Department must have been difficult for the family. For the first time, an official letter used the salutation "Mr. and Mrs. Michael Korkuc" rather than the familiar "Dear Mrs. Korkuc." This fact alone should have been reason for caution. The letter said:

> Since no information has been received which would support a presumption of his continued survival the War Department must now terminate your son's absence by a presumptive finding of death. Accordingly, an official finding of death has been recorded. The finding does not establish an actual or probable date of death; however as required by law, it includes a presumptive date of death for the purpose of determination of pay and allowances, settlement of accounts and payment of death gratuities. In the case of your son, this date has been set as May 11, 1945.

I now knew why the date of death in Tony's personnel file did not match the date on his gravestone.

That should have been the end of the matter. But a month later, a letter from Jack Fournier's mother conveyed a small glimmer of hope that Tony might still be alive. She wrote, "As yet Jack is not home. We don't even know where he is or how he is. We had one Telegram from War Dept. and one from Red Cross telling us he was liberated and that is all. They said it may be weeks before he gets here but when he does I will surely ask him to tell you what he knows. But do not give up as there have been quite a number listed as dead that have been alive. I sincerely hope you hear from him soon." In the light of this correspondence, it is easy to understand why the Korkuc family continued to hold on to a thread of hope that Tony had survived.

Reaching into the box, Aunt Sophie gave me the last of the information that my Aunt Helen had held on to throughout the years. After being liberated from their POW camps, pilot Don Henderson, bombardier Nick DeRose, and engineer and top turret gunner Raoul Ramos each wrote to Anna Korkuc, sharing the sad news that Tony had perished in battle. With all the conflicting information being received from the crew families and the War Department, did these three letters finally convince the Korkuc family that all hope was lost? Don Henderson wrote from Red Cloud on July 2, 1945:

I knew your son for only a short time—but in that time we became fast friends and I can assure you he was as good a soldier as he was a son—always pleasant courteous and efficient.

It is my duty and privilege to tell you about your son—my duty because he was killed in action—a privilege because he died a hero at his gun position—fighting an enemy that tried to conquer the world—giving his all for you, me and his country.

I feel you want to know just what happened so I will do my best to explain.

Our mission that day as you know was near Augsburg, Germany—no different from any other, except perhaps just a little longer—everything went well until just before the target—when we had internal engine failure on No. 4, the propeller would not feather—this causing an additional drag on the already overworked three remaining engines—we managed to stay with the formation pretty well until our bombs were dropped on the target, then kept falling back, being unable to maintain speed to keep up with the formation. Our fighter escort at that point failed to meet us and the enemy planes flying below us, afraid to battle with a large formation, came up to pick on the "cripple."

We were many miles from England, on three engines and fighters coming up on us, we had been told under circumstances such as these to head for neutral territory—so I headed for the Swiss border, only a few minutes flying time to safety for my crew.

I started losing altitude and taking evasive action as we had been trained to do, with my crew battling it out with three enemy fighters—fate must have ruled it that this was not our time to win—for we were riddled with holes and finally had our controls shot out—during which time six of "my boys" had been killed at their gun positions—but they had made the enemy pay—for two of those enemy planes had gone down.

As soon as my controls were shot out, I gave the orders over the interphone to "bail out" and at the same time giving the "bail out" signal on the ship's alarm bell. I bailed out close to the ground and landed very close to the ship—which burst into flames when it hit—I was captured immediately by the Germans and taken away.

I do not know the name of the village near where the ship crashed—only that it was southeast of Stuttgard [*sic*]and close to the Swiss border.

I extend to you my deepest sympathies and want you to know I have prayed many, many times for your son and the loved ones he left behind.

Nick DeRose's letter, written on the same day as Henderson's, said:

It grieves me very much to have to write you a letter like this, but I know that you want to know about your son Anthony. I know that the War Department has listed him as dead and I'm sorry to have to say that this is true. He was killed while we were under fighter attack on our last mission. I want you to know that everything possible was done but it seemed that everything was against us and Anthony died in the plane.

Unfortunately, Nick could provide little comfort on the final disposition of the bodies: "When the four of us that were unhurt were taken prisoners we asked the Germans to take us to the plane so that we could have the boys buried but they would not do this saying that they would see to it that the boys were properly buried. I can not say if this was done or not but I certainly hope so." In closing, Nick attempted to comfort Anna:

I want you to know that Anthony was a good soldier and that I thought a great deal of him. I want you to know that while we were together in England he was a very good boy. Being a Catholic myself, I saw to it that he did go to Mass on Sunday that we were not flying on missions. I want you to know that this is the hardest thing I've ever had to do and I want you to feel free to write me at any time if there is anything that I can do. If I'm ever in Seekonk I will certainly come to see you. I'll be in the Army for awhile but you can always contact me through my wife at 116 N. Broad St., Hillsdale, Michigan.

Sincerely yours,

Lt. N. J. DeRose

The last of the crewmembers' letters arrived that same week. It was sent by the only surviving enlisted man on the crew, Technical Sergeant Raoul Ramos.

Please forgive me for not writing to you at an earlier date. I regressed a few weeks before my Commanding Officers. I thought it best to wait so they could be first to inform you about Tony.

I take it for granted that they are now in the States and have written to you. This is a very serious matter and difficult for me to explain our mishap.

We were scheduled to fly to Augsburg. We dropped the bomb load and then had to leave the formation. Our Superchargers played out and we had a few flak wounds; one of the engines was smoking. The Pilot and Co-pilot fought quite a bit with the controls but to no avail. Fighters also jumped us. We put up a very good resistance. A few minutes before our order to bail was given, Korky had some kind of trouble in the ball turret. I was pretty busy at my position, the top turret. I don't know if he was wounded or what. A little later the phone system was inaudible from the radio room back. The ship was battered up pretty bad. The pilot and I bailed out at approximately three hundred feet. Everyone had sufficient time to bail out; I had trouble opening the bomb bay doors. In view of this I believe the boys were dead or badly wounded and couldn't bail out.

Korky and I were the engineers on the crew. We usually attended the same classes and practiced out in the line together. He was a good companion to work with. Full of fun and serious in his work.

I was one of the youngest of the crew. He used to kid me because I was in charge of the enlisted men—One day we were sitting under the plane and Korky playfully described himself to me that he was the guy whom the mothers pointed out at the Polish Hop. They would congregate their youngsters and say, "We want you to be like him when you grow up." Although he joked about this I admired him. He was very honest when performing his duties. I can't think of an incident in the air when Korky and I had trouble fixing or making a quick repair.

On one mission practically all the electrical system was out. We had to crank up all the gears with the Bomb Bay doors open. We were the life of the party with the other engineers on the Squadron after that mission. We certainly had fun at the pub that night.

I'm having a wonderful time at home, it's a luxury to eat three times a day again.

I'm not very good at describing our last mission nor in providing all the information you desire. If there is anything you wish to know please let me help you or if I don't make anything clear I'll do my best whenever I write again.

As commander of the ship, Don Henderson provided a detailed account of the circumstances that had led to the downing of his Flying Fortress. DeRose questioned whether the boys were buried properly. Raoul's letter was less technical, but probably gave more comfort to the grieving parents. And by saying "I believe the boys were dead or badly wounded," he may have allowed the family to hold on to the slim possibility that Tony had somehow survived the crash.

The letters from Tony's crewmates brought several new questions to my mind. In my discussions with the three survivors, I had been led to believe that there was only one ME-109 enemy attacker. Had there actually been three enemy pursuers, and had Tony helped to down two of them prior to his death? What had caused the B-17 to lose the number four engine and the superchargers before it was attacked by the German fighters? Had the plane also been damaged by anti-aircraft fire? I was troubled by Ramos's use of the word "mishap." Was he implying that there was a mishap that could have been prevented? Was there more to the story of what happened to the plane on that fateful day in February 1944?

CHAPTER 5

On the Road to Find Out

While the letters from the crewmembers and their families from 1944–45 offered explanations and led to additional exchanges of information, the upcoming months of my research would indicate that not all of my questions were welcome.

THE PILOT WISHES TO BE LEFT ALONE

In August 1997, I sent Don Henderson a letter to bring him up to date on my research. I included a signed copy of Chaplain Brown's book and a copy of the *Reutlinger General-Anzeiger* article. I followed up with a phone call to see how he was doing, and mentioned that I would be attending the annual 381st Bomb Group Reunion, to be held over the Labor Day weekend in Maryland. Don thanked me for the material I had sent him. In response to my requests in the previous month's phone call, he had found the article about the crash site in Willmandingen interesting. I asked him whether he would send me a copy of the newspaper article written by bombardier Bill Lofton, describing how Henderson had left formation in order to protect his former commanding pilot, Bernard Beckman, from enemy harm. Henderson recalled the incident again, saying that he thought he was going to get the Distinguished Flying Cross for the mission, or perhaps the Silver Star for his bravery, but instead his commanding officers had reprimanded him for his unauthorized use of the B-17 to save another crew.

As I look back at my notes from that phone call, I regret that I did not ask Henderson why Ramos had characterized their last mission as a mishap. I was at an early stage in my conversations with all three men, and my understanding of that last mission had not yet reached the level where I could formulate those types of questions. I was still amazed that I was even talking with any of them. My questions had no real focus, and I wish now that I had asked about certain things when they could have answered candidly and without reservation.

A couple of days later, I received a letter from Don, accompanied by four pictures and a newspaper clipping. "I guess this will give you a rough idea of what we looked like," he wrote. "There was a two inch piece of the newspaper article that the copy machine ate up anyhow I couldn't find it—it just detailed the fact that *Baby Dumplin* was hit bad and that I picked up Beckman and another cripple and got them safely back to England."[1] First Lieutenant Bill Lofton used the newspaper article to let the people of Red Cloud know about Don Henderson's wartime valor. He described Don as "one of the unsung heroes of this war."

[On February 11, 1944, Henderson] and his crew decided to stay back with us and see us home, you can't realize what a heroic deed this was. Absolutely forbidden by regulations to stay behind with anyone, Don had authorities to meet, even if we successfully beat off the enemy. Well, the enemy was around. They looked us over a dozen times but failed to make a pass. We were three Forts strong and a formidable sight to any one. The propeller on number three engine was still wind-milling. The cowling had ripped off, the engine head had cracked and fallen apart, the nuts and bolts were knocking holes in Don's cockpit window. . . . Therefore Don had to take the lead and guide us home. He did not falter. . . . Don came up for number twenty-five. It was a long mission. . . . We had planned a celebration for Don's return and made it a point to be at his dispersal area upon completion of the mission. We are still waiting and praying for his return as we feel we owe our safety to this magnificent man, our friend, and co-pilot.[2]

Along with the clipping, there was a photo of Don taken during his cadet days.

I went to the 381st Bomb Group reunion in September, but I did not run into any of Don's former crewmates. When I got home, I found another letter waiting for me from Don:

Don Henderson at age 24.
Henderson was the pilot of
Flying Fortress 42–37786 for
the Augsburg mission. Photo
courtesy of Don Henderson.

I hope you understand why I feel I must write this letter—I was real
pleased to be able to answer some of the questions you asked in the first
phone call—I answered them to the best of my recollection—honestly
and freely. I appreciate what you have done and know you firmly believe
in your pursuit of the information, but I don't believe you are aware of
the cost to others. I have never talked much about my experience—
not even to my family—any more than necessary. I feel old wounds and
memories should not be disturbed—perhaps this is why you did not get
a positive response from the other two crewmembers. I must ask you
not to contact me in the future.

I was shocked and hurt by his words. What had I done to warrant this
response? Our previous conversation had been pleasant, and I had
thought that our relationship would continue to grow. Had he taken
offense at something I said? I was stung by Don's accusation that I was
becoming a nuisance to the other crewmembers, and the implication

that this was why they were not talking to me. In our last conversation, I had expressed my frustration that my recent phone calls to both Ramos and DeRose had not been returned. Don had probably inferred that they too were uncomfortable with my in-depth questions.

I began to understand that I was waging a war with the past. The three men had answered all of my initial questions honestly, but I wanted more. I was not yet satisfied that I had learned everything there was to know about the events of February 25, 1944. My father and I wanted to understand what happened that day, and the crewmates wanted to forget. None of the men had ever talked about that last mission much after the war, and now I was asking them to relive it so that I could "see" it through their memories.

I understand that I was trying to take them someplace they did not want to go. However, I do not think they had ever really thought about the pain that was inflicted on the families of the men who were killed in the mission. I know they all prayed for the fallen men and for their loved ones back home. But if Don Henderson had seen my father's reaction to the sight of his brother's gravestone at Arlington, if he had been there when Dad asked what happened to Tony, I think he might have understood why I needed to understand what occurred on that last mission.

Does the family of a man killed in war have the right to ask the survivors for an explanation of what really happened? Do the families of the fallen have the right to invade the painful memories of those who were fortunate enough to survive the terror of war? Is there a statute of limitations that prevents the families of the fallen from probing the past? After much soul searching, on October 3, 1997, I sent Don Henderson a letter reassuring him that I would ask him no more questions.[3]

But now I was even more curious about the "mishap" that had apparently occurred on the last mission. Was that why Henderson had stopped talking to me? I was determined to proceed with caution in my future dealings with Raoul Ramos and Nick DeRose. If I alienated them, too, I might never learn what really happened to Tony.

A VISIT WITH THE BOMBARDIER

In late June 1997, my copy of Roger Freeman's *The Mighty Eighth War Diary* arrived from England. Beneath the photograph of the downed

B-17 that had been taken by Herman Möck was the following caption: "The broken machines of vanquished enemies were always an attraction for children. An Me 109 dispatched the 381 BG's only loss on 25 February, the Fortress crashing at Willmandingen near Stuttgart. Six of the crew perished. (H. Grimminger)"[4] I immediately had some questions. How did Roger Freeman know that an ME-109 fighter had downed Tony's plane? And who was H. Grimminger? I traced Freeman, the author of a number of books on the Eighth Air Force, to an address in England, and wrote to him. He responded immediately, but was unable to shed any light on my questions, except to say that he had obtained the photograph from someone named Hans Grimminger.

In November, I traveled to Indianapolis on business. After a year of research, I was well aware of the contribution that the Norden bombsight had made to the American air offensive of World War II, so I was struck by the irony when I learned that not only had the building I was visiting at the corner of 21st and Arlington been a naval ordnance plant from 1942 to 1946, but it had been built exclusively for manufacturing the Norden bombsight, the tool of the B-17's bombardier. During those years, the plant had built more than 14,000 bombsights.

Prior to my November trip, I called Nick DeRose, who lived just 250 miles from Indianapolis, and asked whether we could meet. He invited me to the home in Grand Ledge, Michigan, that he shared with his wife, Liz. Nick and I talked for hours during that visit, a conversation that I recorded on audiotape. I was in awe of the fact that I was actually sitting with the bombardier from Tony's last mission. We discussed his memories of February 25, 1944, and he talked some about the battle:

> That was the only time we were ever attacked from the rear. I had the whole front on everything. But it wasn't until the very last that this one 109 came out the front. When he came to the front, I thought he was going to shoot. I let out a machine gun burst. I remember that. He just laid back. He knew we were out of it. He wasn't one of those "blood and guts" guys or we would probably never have gotten out. He could have got us all, those of us that were left.

Perhaps recalling how his gunners had fought the attackers, he added:

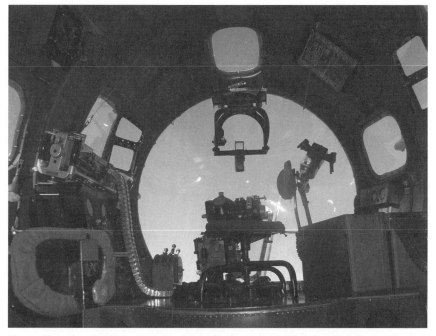

View of bombardier's position showing the famous Norden bombsight in the nose section of the Collings Foundation's B-17G model *Nine-O-Nine*. Photo by author.

You know they never gave the bomber gunners enough credit during the war when it came to downing German fighters. I don't know why they didn't. Everybody hated Doolittle, because when he took command, it was his policy that he left us uncovered fifteen minutes before the target and fifteen minutes after the target. That was to get the German fighters up. More German fighters were shot down by bomber gunners than there were in dogfights with the American fighters.

He spoke about the absence of the fighters on the last mission:

So it's just like that day [February 25, 1944] when all that flak came up and got us. If we hadn't been hit by flak, we probably would have never met those fighters. We might have, but it seems like on that particular day, they must have been busy somewhere else. Cause we didn't see any fighters at all until we fell back along the way.

I asked him for his memory of what happened after Henderson issued the order to bail out:

> When you mentioned that Henderson thought that he was last out of the plane—well, he could've easily been killed. I mean, he got tangled up with the plane. He got beat up pretty badly. I could have been killed as well. That guardian angel was just sitting on my shoulder, that's all. I was trying my damnedest to get Wonning to go. He would get up there at the nose hatch and he would get scared. Wonning told me that "I'm going out through the bomb bay." About that time, I said to myself, I've got to bail out now or never. And then you told me that Raoul saw him, or Henderson saw him, come up to the bomb bay? So I saw Wonning go through, and he was out of my sight. He was up there intent on going out of the bomb bay. He either didn't make it, or else Henderson or somebody else told him to go back and bail out the nose hatch.

He said that as he bailed out,

> I just kept worrying about my wife, my folks, and my unborn child. I never expected to be a prisoner. I figured I would get home in one piece or crash. I never figured I'd be a prisoner of war. But then knowing my folks and me being missing, they must have cried a lot of tears.... The ham radio operators in Germany tipped off the American operators, getting word to families about prisoners. They did that for everybody.

Nick's family first learned that Nick was alive through the actions of the German ham radio operators, and later from a postcard.

I asked Nick to comment on Don Henderson's skills as a crew pilot. "Well," he said,

> all I can tell you about Henderson for what length of time I knew him, he was cool. He was a cool cucumber, and I'm glad that they didn't give the crew to Fournier. I was surprised to hear you tell me that Henderson felt that Fournier was a little jealous that he got command of the crew [after Herrington left it]. But Fournier was just a totally different kind of a guy. Fournier did have a lot of training in fighters, and he was really mad when they put him back in the bombers. But anyway, when we were

Charlotte Lane and Nick DeRose on their wedding day, August 20, 1943. Nick was stationed at Alexandria Army Air Force Base in Louisiana for final crew training. Photo courtesy of Dianne DeRose Stansell.

still in the States training, whenever Fournier would get behind [the controls of the B-17], he would think that it was a damn fighter. I mean, we did some crazy things; we used to buzz them damn cattle down there in Louisiana. And that was always when Jack Fournier was at the wheel.

He said that they all "caught hell" after Henderson left formation to save Beckman's crew. "We weren't supposed to leave the formation, as that was a no-no. We were lucky that we didn't get hurt; everyone got back to the base safely. Henderson told us what he was going to do before he took the plane out of formation. If he had asked us, we would've said just go. In those days, you didn't think ahead to the next week."

Nick reminisced about life at the base in England:

I bunked next to Wonning. Funny thing, you know it's like going out in the wilds, and you find out how dumb some guys are. Wonning and I were the only guys who could build a fire. It was cold, and we went out

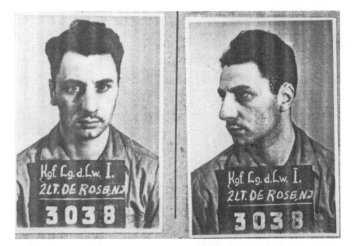

Mug shots of captured American flier Nick DeRose, February 29, 1944. Courtesy of Dianne DeRose Stansell.

and got wood and all that sort of stuff. We had one stove in England there. It was as bad as being in prison camp. The Brits had a big sign: "Don't cut down Her Majesty's growing trees." Wonning and I would go out and say, "That damn thing doesn't look like it's growing." We used to go down and get all the used oil, and we fixed up a little drip can on the stove and we had an oil burner. When you haven't got something, all the great minds start thinking. You should see some of the things that the guys did in prison camp.

When I asked Nick what he remembered about being held as a prisoner of war, he said, "Well, most of us who didn't get caught [by the prison guards], we used to write things down. I got a little diary that I gave my daughter Dianne. It doesn't really amount to much. We got the pictures; I look like a prisoner, with the beard and the number that the Germans took of us."

Nick talked some about his role in defeating Germany as a bombardier:

My crew, we were on the first eight hundred and thousand plane raids. This is the thing. The British bomb at night, and they go home and go to bed. And then we come in the daytime. The Englishman would come up to you and say, "You fellows have bags of guts flying in the daytime."

Boy, well, we used to think they had the bags of guts flying at night. Getting into those lights, and as much trouble as a lot of our navigators had in the daytime, all of us had in the daytime. Just think about coming back at night in those days.

He said that when a mission was scrubbed and they were unable to hit the intended target, he was instructed by his superiors to drop bombs anywhere in Germany. Nick was ashamed of having to follow those orders. I asked whether he had any lingering animosity toward the Germans. "No," he said. "If I fought the Japanese I would probably feel different. But the Germans, I met some good Germans. Really the bad Germans were the young men, the SS troop boys; they didn't want any part of going to Russia."

Nick reflected on why he had survived the mission and Tony had not. "I have lain sometimes when I couldn't sleep, I think of things that have happened to me. I don't know. I haven't done what I am supposed to do yet, I guess. But I have been in a lot of scrapes where I could have been killed. Going through the war, I mean, you know it just wasn't my time, that's all. That's all I can say." I told him about how difficult it was for Henderson and Ramos to talk about the war. "I can understand not wanting to talk about the war," he responded. "You talk some and say that's enough. I understand that. When I think of the other things that the war caused me to do—to be at certain places, the service in the war, where I was, how I got drafted, what I did before I went in the cadets, with the things that happened to me— hey, I'm tickled to death I got through all that."

Some months later, I had the opportunity to visit Nick's daughter, Dianne, in Carlsbad, California. She showed me his wartime letters and POW diary, which had been given to her after her mother's death in 1987. After his last mission, he had written in his diary: "Downed by German Fighters Feb. 25, 1944 at Augsburg, Germany. Arrived at Dulag Luft Feb. 27, 1944. Sent to Frankfurt-on-Main Feb. 28, 1944. Left Frankfurt Transit camp on March 1, 1944 and traveled by Boxcar to Barth, Germany arriving on March 4, 1944." Nick had also sketched a picture of himself bailing out of the B-17. I had a pleasant visit with Dianne and her husband, and I found Nick's wartime letters very interesting. But they shed little light on Tony, and none, of course, on their last mission.

Nick DeRose, age 79, at his home in Grand Ledge, Michigan, reading Roger Freeman's *The Mighty Eighth War Diary*. Photo by author.

PAYING MY RESPECTS

By the fall of 1997, my enthusiasm toward my research project had reached a new high. Over the previous eight months, I had obtained an extraordinary amount of information that had helped me better understand what happened to the Don Henderson crew. I now knew how and why my uncle's remains were returned to the United States after his initial burial in Germany and France. I had located three of the four surviving crewmembers, as well as an eyewitness to the crash in Willmandingen. And Tony's story had been printed in the *Reutlinger General-Anzeiger*. I now had confidence in my research skills—but what else might I be able to discover?

One possibility was to try and locate the families of the other crewmembers who died with Tony. They deserved to learn the information I had obtained. In particular, I wanted to see what Thomas Hunnicutt and Dale Schilling looked like. Hunnicutt had not been present on the day the crew photo was taken in 1943, and Schilling had been a last-minute replacement, so no picture was available for

Sketch from prisoner of war Nick DeRose's Stalag Luft I diary, depicting his B-17 bailout. Courtesy of Dianne DeRose Stansell.

Kriegsgefangenenlager

Datum FEB. 29, 1944

DEAR FOLKS: JUST TO LET YOU KNOW THAT I AM A PRISONER OF WAR IN GERMANY. I AM UNHURT AND OK. PLEASE LET CHARLOTTE KNOW THAT I AM OK. DO NOT WRITE TO THIS ADDRESS. I WILL LET YOU KNOW WHERE TO WRITE LATER. LOVE TO ALL—NICK

Postcard sent to Nick DeRose's family on February 29, 1944. Courtesy of Dianne DeRose Stansell.

Gravesite of Anthony Bartolo, St. Mary's Cemetery, Greenwich, Connecticut. Photo by author.

him, either. Could I locate Tony's remaining crewmates, Butch Reeves, Jack Fournier, and former pilot Bill Herrington?

In September, on my way to Maryland to attend the 381st Bomb Group's annual reunion, I made a stop in Greenwich, Connecticut. In the previous month, I had used the Internet to find the gravesite of Anthony Bartolo, who flew as the right waist gunner on the last bombing mission of aircraft 42–37786. Bartolo had been laid to rest at Willmandingen and then Saint-Avold in close proximity to Tony, but in 1950 the two crewmates had been forever separated. I paid my respects to Anthony Bartolo at St. Mary's Cemetery.

Later that same month, I contacted Ted Darcy and made use of his resources to obtain the Individual Deceased Personnel Files for the other deceased crewmates. In December, the much-awaited package of IDPFs arrived in the mail. The file for left waist gunner Thomas Hunnicutt indicated that he was buried at Sunset Memorial Park in his hometown of San Antonio, Texas. I did not visit San Antonio, but I did contact Sunset Memorial by phone; they had no information to give me about Hunnicutt's family, but they sent me a photo of his gravesite.

Gravesite of Thomas Hunnicutt, Sunset Memorial Park, San Antonio, Texas. Photo courtesy of Sunset Memorial Park.

THE NAVIGATOR'S BROTHER

In July 1997, I had tracked down a phone number for Norman Wonning, the younger brother of navigator Earl Wonning. I was hesitant to contact him, given DeRose's concern that the Wonning family would learn the true circumstances behind Earl's death, but I finally did so on December 29. During our conversation, I briefed him on what I had learned.

Early in 1998, a business trip took me back to Indianapolis, within twenty minutes of Norman's home. We agreed to meet. Norman picked me up at my hotel and took me to a local restaurant. Over dinner, he revealed that he had done some research of his own, in the course of which he had come up with an in-flight photograph of the aircraft. Feeling that we were kindred spirits, I was eager to share my own finds with him. I pulled out a copy of the crash site photo, only to learn that he already had one. I was pleased that Norman had done some significant work on his own. I told him that Earl's crew may have flown as many as sixteen combat missions together. They were certainly a well-seasoned group. At that point Norman eagerly added that Earl had once told him that he was part of a great B-17 crew.

Feeling more comfortable with Norman, I decided to share with him what I had learned about Earl's death. I told him that Earl had not been injured during the air battle with the enemy fighters, and that Raoul Ramos, Don Henderson, and Nick DeRose had each seen him alive and unharmed when the order to bail was issued. I did not reveal what the surviving crewmembers thought about Earl's state of mind that day. I simply stated that he was alive and unhurt when they last saw him.

I told Norman that one of the six men who were killed had died while parachuting out of the plane, and I believed that man was his brother. Norman's first reaction was that this would have been typical of Earl. It would have been Earl's instinct to make certain that everyone else was safely out of the plane before he bailed. As I concluded my analysis of Earl's last few minutes, I admitted to Norman that I had wrestled with my conscience about whether to tell him what I had learned. In the end, I decided that it was the right thing to do. "That's all right," Norman responded. "I would just like to really know what happened. I'd rather face the truth than face a lie. There's nothing I can do about it after fifty years."

Norman reminisced about Earl. Despite the ten-year gap in their ages, they had hung around together. He fondly recalled how Earl had allowed him to drive the family truck, even when he was still too small to reach the pedals. On one trip, Earl let him drive from their home in Seymour, Indiana, all the way to Cincinnati while transporting some produce from their farm to the farmers' market. While Norman drove, Earl was sprawled out in the flatbed, catching some sleep. Norman laughed while remembering the incident.

Even Norman's career path had been influenced by his brother. Earl had a real talent when it came to fixing all things electrical. Seymour

Earl (left) and Norman Wonning during Earl's last visit home to Seymour, Indiana, in the summer of 1943. Photo courtesy of Norman Wonning.

was part of the rural grid, and Earl was constantly being asked to fix his neighbors' appliances and radios. Norman often tagged along, learning from his brother. When he himself reached maturity, he opened his own television repair shop.

As our meeting drew to a close, Norman admitted that over the years, he had never really believed that Earl was dead. He continued to believe that Earl had somehow survived the mission and would someday return home. He was always on the alert for anyone who looked like Earl. Not until the late 1980s had he finally abandoned his hope that his brother would eventually come back.

Several weeks after our meeting, Norman sent me Earl's wartime letters from England to give me more insight into the crew. They contained the usual complaints about the lack of heating in the barracks and yearnings for home. There was nothing about Tony. There were, however, some interesting letters that the Wonning family had received from the surviving crew. In the span of three weeks, Earl's mother, Esther, received four letters. Raoul Ramos's letter arrived first, in June, while Don Henderson's and Nick DeRose's letters arrived within a day of each other in early July. It was another week before Esther heard from Jack Fournier. Ramos's letter to Mrs. Wonning was dated June 19, 1945. The letter that he wrote my grandmother was written two weeks later. Why, I wondered, had Raoul waited those two weeks before telling my grandmother what he knew?

Knowing that Earl was unhurt just seconds before the plane crashed, I was curious about what the men had been willing to reveal to the Wonning family. In his letter to my grandmother, Ramos was unable to be specific about how Tony died. All he could say was that Korky was either dead or badly wounded before the crash. In Earl's case, however, he believed that Earl had ridden the plane to the ground. How would he handle this when writing to Earl's mother? In the letter, Raoul said:

> I want to tell you how proud we were of Earl. He was the "big brother" to the enlisted men. If we needed money or advice he was the boy we'd see. Not only that but he was the best navigator in the squadron. He was slated for "Pathfinder School," in England which would have prob-ably given Earl a jump in rank. Earl was also the neatest and the clean-est friend I've ever known. He was beginning to teach me navigation. I confided in him very much. I told him it was my ambition to attend Pilot training upon completion of our tour. He didn't waste a minute; Had me studying every night.

Unfortunately, the letter ended there, as the Wonning family had lost the rest of it.

Ramos had wasted no time in telling my grandmother what hap-pened on that last mission. In contrast, the first page of Mrs. Wonning's letter revealed nothing about the mission. True to form, Raoul told Esther only good things about her son. Earl had been a "big brother" to the enlisted men of the crew. The crew had admired Earl. These are the things that a mother would want to hear.

Ramos also wanted to tell Esther that Earl was respected within the 532nd Bomb Squadron, and that if he had completed his tour of duty, he would have attempted to advance within the Army Air Forces. Perhaps Raoul was making it clear that Earl had not been afraid to fly combat missions. He had not feared being put in harm's way. Ramos was clearly proud of the bravery that Earl had demonstrated as he attempted to better himself.

Navigator Earl Wonning.
Photo courtesy of Norman
Wonning.

With the exception of the salutation, Don Henderson's letter to Mrs. Wonning was identical to the one he had written to my grandmother. In approaching the unpleasant task of writing the next-of-kin letters, he had apparently chosen to use a form letter.

I was curious to find out how Nick DeRose had approached Mrs. Wonning. I knew he believed that Earl's death could have been prevented; so did his explanation about what happened agree with the official report on Earl's death? In the opening paragraph of his letter, he tells Mrs. Wonning that Earl "was killed in the plane while we were under fighter attack." In contrast, his letter to my grandmother said that Tony "was killed while we were under fighter attack on our last mission. . . . Anthony died in the plane." Nick did not know what had happened to Tony on the last mission. He believed that Tony was killed while they were under enemy attack.

Nick knew how Earl had met his death. Since the ME-109 was still attacking the B-17 while the men were bailing out of the plane, he was accurate when he said that Earl was killed in the plane while they were under fighter attack. By wording it thus, Nick implied that Earl had died as a direct result of the enemy attack. That was not exactly true, but the Wonning family never could have drawn any other conclusion.

The pain that Nick had suffered over the years was a direct result of his next two sentences. "I want you to know that I did all I could for him," he wrote. If he had really believed that, I doubt he would have given himself such a tough time through the years. Then he said, "he did not suffer very much and death came quickly." I think Nick wrote that for the sake of Mrs. Wonning. I don't think he believed it. Nick knew that Earl was very distressed around the time the bailout order was issued. Because Earl did not bail when he should have, Nick feared that he did suffer. All of the men must have suffered; after all, a German fighter was in the process of trying to kill them. Whether Earl rode the plane to the ground or fell to his death as a result of a botched bailout, Nick was correct in asserting that his death came quickly.

The last letter was the most interesting. If Jack Fournier wrote a letter to my family, it was lost or perhaps never sent. Thus, I was curious about what he had said to Mrs. Wonning.

I am sorry to tell you that your son Earl was killed. . . . I gave that information to the German Government so that you and your family might be spared the uncertainty of not knowing but as in so many other cases they didn't keep their word.

At a time like this I realize there is little I can say to lighten your burden but it might help to think of your son dying as a good soldier would want to die when his time comes, carrying the battle to the enemy over his own territory, ridding the world of Hitler and others who threaten our living. Earl was hit by machine gun bullets from an enemy fighter plane, he died instantly and suffered no pain.

Well Mrs. Wonning I know this letter won't make you feel any better but it will at least clear the doubt from your mind.

Earl was one of the best-liked men on the base. [He] always had a good word and a friendly smile for everyone. He was one of the best Navigators in the group it was a privilege and an honor to know and work with him.

Yours,
Lt. Jack H. Fournier

I don't know why Fournier told Esther that her son had been hit by enemy machine gun fire. Since he was the first to bail out of the plane, Fournier could not have known this. He may have gotten the information from Henderson at Camp Lucky Strike and believed it. Esther Wonning must have cherished Fournier's letter, because he told her that Earl was one of the best navigators in the group and it was an honor to work with him. In light of how Earl Wonning's family and friends felt about him, I know that he must have been deeply missed after his unfortunate death.

CHAPTER 6

Family Ties

Energized by my positive experience with Earl Wonning's brother, I set out in search of the other crewmembers' families. It took me just under a year to find them all. My method was simple: Assuming that one or both of each man's parents had passed away, I used the Social Security Death Index (SSDI) website to determine the date and place of death. I then contacted the appropriate library and requested a copy of the obituary. If other family members were named, I used switchboard.com to obtain their phone numbers. In this way I was able to find members of the Hunnicutt, Burgess, and Bartolo families. The Schilling family took a little longer.

COLONEL HUNNICUTT'S SON

Using Thomas Hunnicutt's Individual Deceased Personnel File, I searched for his mother, Eleanor, from San Antonio, Texas, in the SSDI, and found a single entry for a woman by that name who died in August 1995. The birth date for this Eleanor was January 29, 1894. Since Thomas was born in 1923, it seemed possible that she was his mother. I then conducted a web search for nearby libraries, which yielded an e-mail address for the public library in San Antonio. I sent a message requesting the obituary for Eleanor Hunnicutt and received a response from a member of the staff, who told me that the obituary had appeared in the *San Antonio Express* on August 28, 1995. A couple of days later, the library sent me a copy of the obituary in the mail.

I was pleased to see that the obituary included her full name, Eleanor J. Hunnicutt. The SSDI omits middle initials, but Thomas Hunnicutt's IDPF had included his mother's middle initial, so upon seeing the J., I knew that I was most likely on the right track. The obituary mentioned a family member named Mary F. Hunnicutt in San Antonio, so I looked up her phone number using Switchboard. I called Mary and explained my quest. She told me that Thomas had been her brother-in-law; she was married to his brother Walter. She recalled that Tommy was tall, at five feet eleven inches, slender, and a good-looking kid. He had wanted to enlist when he was seventeen, but that plan was quashed by his father, who happened to be a colonel in the Regular Army. In fact, Colonel Lee V. Hunnicutt had visited Tommy several times while both were stationed in England, his last visit being the day of his son's death.

I asked Mary whether she had any pictures of Tommy that she could send me, or any letters that he had written during the war, so that I could get a better sense of him. She said that he had not been much of a letter writer, but the family had a couple of V-mails from him that she could send me, along with some photos.

She vividly recalled the day back in 1945 when two of Tommy's crewmates visited the Hunnicutt household to tell Eleanor about his death. She told me that she felt really sorry for Tommy's mother that day as she heard her crying in the next room. Although it must have been difficult to receive firsthand information about the death of her son, Eleanor must have been relieved to know for certain that he was not coming back from Germany.

A couple of weeks later, I called Mary again, curious to know whether she had received the package I sent her. Unfortunately, I was unable to speak with her. Instead I spoke with Tommy's nephew, Lee Hunnicutt. Lee told me more about his grandfather. Colonel Hunnicutt had told him that during his last visit in February 1944, Tommy looked more exhausted than he had ever seen him. "After Tommy cleaned up from the mission, he and my grandfather went out to supper. The next day my grandfather shook hands with Tommy, watched him board his plane, and he never saw him again. Tommy's death was very, very hard on my grandfather." Because he was a colonel, Lee V. Hunnicutt enjoyed special privileges. Eight months after the plane was shot down, he went to the front and interviewed a number of Air Force men who were familiar with Don Henderson's reputation in an attempt to better understand what had happened to his son. This confirmed what Don Henderson had told me: Colonel Hunnicutt concluded that if Henderson was unable to bring Tommy back, nobody could have done it.

Colonel Lee V. Hunnicutt with son Tommy at Ridgewell Hospital, December 14, 1943. Photo courtesy of Lee B. Hunnicutt.

Several months after my conversations with Mary and Lee Hunnicutt, I e-mailed Lee to tell him that I had not heard from Mary in a while and was wondering whether she still planned to send me the letters and pictures she had promised. Lee gave me the sad news that Mary had died of cancer.

In August 1998, Lee and his wife, Eva, sent me a package containing information about Tommy. Included were three copies of V-mails that Tommy had sent his family, along with four pictures and some handwritten notes that Colonel Hunnicutt had made while investigating the loss of his son. The notes were meticulous and detailed. They said that all four of Henderson's engines were running fine when three American fighters went back to assist the B-17. Tommy's father had also noted that "Lt. Henderson was on his 25th mission and he was one of best pilots."

A HAPPY MEMORIAL DAY

On December 29, 1997, I placed a call to Jennie Bartolo Domiziano, the sister of right waist gunner Anthony J. Bartolo. The librarian in

Anthony "Sonny" Bartolo,
the right waist gunner of the
Don Henderson crew. Photo
courtesy of the Bartolo
family.

Greenwich, Connecticut, had outdone himself, providing an obituary
for Anthony's father, together with the names and addresses of several family members. Earlier that month, I had sent letters to some
members of the Bartolo family, describing the reasons for my research.
One of those recipients was Anthony Bartolo's brother-in-law Arthur.
Along with my letter I sent a packet of information, including the
German newspaper article, a copy of the 1943 crew picture, and a
description of the last mission based on my interviews with the surviving crewmates. With Arthur's help, I obtained Jennie's phone number. Soon I was talking to the sister of Tony's right waist gunner.

    I took an instant liking to Jennie. She said that she had seen the mate-
rials I'd sent her brother-in-law, Arthur, and she was more than willing
to tell me about her memories of her brother "Sonny." She still remembered the day her father received the Western Union telegram saying
that Sonny was missing in action. He had sat in a chair and cried. She
also recalled when the family received word from the Army in 1950

that Sonny's remains had been positively identified. Her father wanted his son to be buried at home. The last time the family had seen Sonny was right before her father took him to the train station in December 1942. Jennie told me that she often gets emotional when she hears the song "I'll Be Home for Christmas," because it reminds her of that day.

Inspired by my contact with her, Jennie decided to contact the Greenwich newspapers in hopes that Sonny's story could be told. In May 1998, she called to tell me that two local newspapers had each printed a Memorial Day article honoring her brother. A couple of weeks later, she sent me copies of them. In the *Greenwich Post,* reporter Alexandra Barnes wrote:

> For Jennie Bartolo Domiziano, Memorial Day has always been a time to wonder about the circumstances surrounding the death of her brother Anthony Bartolo. . . . This year she has some answers. Domiziano learned about many of the details surrounding his death just six months ago, when a stranger who had been researching the death of his own uncle contacted her with the information. "I remember when I was told Bob Korkuc was [going to contact] me, I was a little apprehensive at first but when I did talk to him it was incredible. It brought back a lot of sad memories." According to Domiziano, all surviving family members were told about Anthony's fate was that the B-17 he and nine other crewmembers were flying in was shot down on Feb. 25, 1944. He initially was listed as missing by the U.S. War Department, but it was five years before the family learned that he had not survived. "Every time a letter or telegram arrived it was horrible," Domiziano recalled. . . . The [Bartolo] family claimed the body in 1950 and Anthony was buried in Greenwich that May. But until Korkuc's [phone call], Domiziano said she wasn't even certain whether the remains which the family buried were really those of her brother's body. "We didn't even know if he'd been properly identified," she said. . . . "We always thought his plane was shot down over France," Domiziano said. "Now we know what happened."[1]

Like the Korkuc family, the Bartolos had suffered from a lack of information. The War Department's letters and telegrams had tormented them too.

In 1945, the American Graves Registration Service had a good understanding of the events that had occurred in Willmandingen. It pains

Jennie Bartolo Domiziano holds the American flag that was presented to her mother at the burial ceremony of Anthony Bartolo in Greenwich, Connecticut, on May 25, 1950. Photo by author.

me that more specific information was not made available to the families. Had the War Department been more forthright, surely the families' pain would not have been as great. With knowledge comes healing. I was the messenger who finally relayed the news that should have been delivered back in 1944–50. After all those years, Jennie Bartolo Domiziano, Norman Wonning, and my father were starting to heal.

"HOW CAN I FORGET"

Although it took me close to a year, I was finally able to track down radio operator Boyd Burgess's wife in Lexington, South Carolina. Seventy-eight-year-old Virginia Burgess Prescott told me that Boyd was her high school sweetheart, and that even though she was deeply devoted to her second husband, she still thought of Boyd. They had been married for seven years at the time of his death. Virginia told me that she never had any doubts that Boyd was killed on the last mission or that his body was buried at Arlington. Her confidence was based

Virginia and Boyd Burgess enjoy a
cool brook together in 1943. Photo
courtesy of Virginia Burgess
Prescott.

on a visit from Raoul Ramos in 1945. Prior to going to England, Boyd
and Virginia had often spent time with Raoul while the crew was stationed in Alexandria, Louisiana.

I promised Virginia that I would send her a package containing all
the information I had obtained about Boyd's last mission, and she
promised to send me copies of items from the scrapbook she had
assembled after his death. Among them was a poem that Raoul had
given her during his visit. Titled "How Can I Forget," it was written
shortly after he was sent to Stalag Luft III. Raoul signed it in memory
of his comrades: "It is my humble way of expressing my thoughts for
2nd Lt. Earl Wonning, T.Sgt. Boyd Burgess, S.Sgt. Anthony Korkuc,
S.Sgt. Thomas Hunnicutt, S.Sgt. Anthony Bartolo, and Sgt. Dale
Schilling, With whom I had the pleasure of combating the enemy."
This poem would come to haunt me as I pondered its meaning.

THE "SPARE" GUNNER

Only a week after finding Virginia Burgess Prescott, I located the
Schilling family. I was getting nowhere using obituaries, so I tried a

In Memory Of My Crew
may they rest in peace

"HOW CAN I FORGET"
That distant haunt of night and day
Reminds me of a grief,
Of men who died but not in vain,
And for a true belief.
How Can I Forget!

A pause that lingers as in dreams
My thoughts reflect their eyes,
A humble sadness stare it seems
For they knew well who died.
How Can I Forget!

The day of death arrived so soon
The Earl Kings demand,
For those who did not die in vain
They lost in blood & sand.
But even though it haunts me so
Their spirit broken not;
Forever, lives in Gold and Pride
For stars and stripes they fought.
How Can I Forget.

"How Can I Forget," written by Raoul Ramos at Stalag Luft III on March 7, 1944. Courtesy of Virginia Burgess Prescott.

different tack. According to Dale's IDPF, he had been married before joining the Air Force. In response to a query from the War Department in December 1944, Dale's mother revealed that he had married a girl named Mary, whom he had known for only four weeks. Mrs. Schilling wrote that Mary "had decided to get a divorce when [Dale] was reported missing in action. They [were] both only kids. She was sixteen when she married while Dale was just eighteen years old."[2] I was unable to trace Mary. A search for Dale's father in Illinois (Lowell, Indiana, is only ten miles from the state line) and correspondence with the *Chicago Tribune* proved equally fruitless.

As a last resort, I ran a web search on Dale Schilling's name. I got lucky and found some information about him on the Lowell Public Library website, in a section that a local historian named Richard Schmal had compiled to provide information about the World War II veterans of the town.[3] On May 28, 1998, I placed a call to Richard Schmal. It turned out that he had lived next door to the Schillings in the 1940s! The last time he had seen the family was in 1988, at the dedication ceremony for Lowell's World War II memorial. Richard told me that George and Hazel Schilling had three children—Doris, Juanita, and Dale. Both Schilling girls were married: Juanita was now Juanita Lee, while Doris was Doris Paccamonti. Hazel died in 1946. Richard promised to check the archives of the *Lowell Tribune* for any references to Dale.

A week later, I received a letter from him, with which he had enclosed copies of two articles from the *Lowell Tribune*. The first was from the February 16, 1950, edition. The Schilling family must have contacted the newspaper after they got word from the War Department that the body of their son was being returned to the United States for a military burial in Arlington National Cemetery. The article said that Dale had been a substitute on his last mission. How heartsick his parents must have been when they learned that! Tragically, twenty-year-old Dale Schilling, the youngest man to fly with the Henderson crew on February 25, was only one mission shy of returning to his family in Indiana. The second article, dated July 6, 1950, said that George Schilling and his second wife, Viola, had just completed a two-thousand-mile round trip to Washington, D.C., to attend the reburial at Arlington on June 29.

So there it was—I finally knew the date of Tony's interment at Arlington.

I next turned to switchboard.com in hopes of finding listings for Juanita Lee or Doris Paccamonti. Figuring that Paccamonti was a significantly rarer surname, I ran that search first. There were only two Paccamontis listed in the entire country; one of them was Dale Paccamonti from Louisiana. Had I found Doris Paccamonti's son? Dale's wife, Jane, answered my phone call and told me that her husband was indeed related to Dale Schilling. Unfortunately, her mother-in-law, Doris Paccamonti, had passed away, but Doris's sister Juanita Lee was alive and well and living in Florida. And living with Juanita was her father, George Schilling! No wonder I had had trouble finding George in the Social Security Death Index. He was still alive at age ninety-seven.

I had found the last family. Wasting no time, I placed a call to the father of tail gunner Dale Schilling. I briefly explained to George why I was seeking information about his son, then conveyed to him my understanding of the last mission and the treatment that Dale had received at the hands of the people of Willmandingen. George broke in to tell me that he had learned from one of the survivors that Dale's high school ring was stolen off his finger by a German guard. I assured him that the Willmandingen townsfolk had had nothing to do with the savage act of the guard. Had the villagers not argued with the Nazi officials about where the Americans should be buried, it was possible that his son's remains might never have been returned to the United States.

I asked whether George could share some memories of his son, and he kindly obliged. He said that Dale was eager to enter the armed forces. He initially tried to enlist three days before his eighteenth birthday, but George spoiled his plans. Dale eventually won out. He joined the Army Air Forces and became a gunner. According to George, Dale was a top turret gunner. On his last mission, however—a mission for which he volunteered—he flew as a tail gunner, the crew's regular tail gunner having been grounded because of severe frostbite. The February 25 mission was his twenty-fourth. As his mission count got closer to twenty-five, Dale must have been eager to substitute at any opportunity he could, because he knew that with each mission he was one step closer to going home.

George told me that he would be glad to send me a picture of his son as well as any relevant letters, and that he had taken color slides of the ceremony at Arlington on June 29, 1950. He had been deeply moved by the twenty-one-gun salute given for Dale and the three other crewmembers. Eight days later, I received a package from Danny Lee, Dale Schilling's nephew and George Schilling's grandson. He wrote, "The entire family thanks you for sharing all of the information you have gathered with us." Included in the package were two pictures. In addition, there were letters from Raoul Ramos and Don Henderson. Don's was similar to the letters he had sent Mrs. Boyd Burgess, Mrs. Wonning, and my grandmother. Raoul's read in part:

Please forgive me for not corresponding with you at an earlier date. I thought it best for my Commanding Officers to inform first of Dale's mishap. . . . I was the Engineer on the crew. Dale was flying the tail position. He was a "spare" gunner; our regular tail gunner had a bad frostbite and was grounded.

We flew to Augsburg and dropped our bomb load on the target. Immediately after this our superchargers played out. One of the engines was smoking badly. No doubt a flak burst. The Pilot and Co-pilot fought with the controls for quite a while. We fell out of our formation, losing altitude, and then fighters jumped us. We put up a good resistance; on one of the fighter sweeps the tail position received a direct hit. From my position, top turret, I could see fragments of skin torn from the tail. A few minutes later Hunnicutt, left waist gunner, shouted, "Schilling's guns are out." It is my opinion that Dale was killed or very badly wounded for I never heard his voice on the interphone again. . . .

The next day a soldier showed me Dale's ring, he was wearing it. By means of sign language, etc., he informed me that the rest of the crew were dead. . . .

I knew Dale pretty well. He was new in our Squadron. He lived with our crew in the same Nissen hut. It didn't take us long to know each other "like a book." He was a likeable kid, we attended practically the same classes and we both had the same classification although he was a spare gunner. . . .

It's hard for me to forget combat, and I'm doing my best. I realize how tough this is on you. Please take my advice and do your best to forget; have faith in God. . . . If there is any information you desire, if I can aid you in anyway, please do not hesitate.

Sincerely yours,
Raoul Ramos

Raoul sent this letter to Mrs. Schilling three days after he wrote the letter to my grandmother. In the first paragraph of both letters, he used the word "mishap." My initial reaction to my grandmother's letter was that by describing the crash as a "mishap," Raoul was implying that the downing of his Flying Fortress was an unfortunate accident that could have been prevented. But I felt differently after reading the Schilling letter. Now I was inclined to believe that Raoul simply felt that what had happened to his crew on February 25 was plain old bad luck. Because of a series of accidents or mishaps—the loss of the super-chargers, the flak hit, and then being jumped by the German fighters—the Henderson crew was doomed to lose the battle. They had simply fallen victim to some extremely unfortunate incidents. Had only one of the three mishaps occurred, they might have made it home safely. But experiencing all three had sealed the fate of the crew. Raoul had never intended to mislead my grandmother.

With his letter to Mrs. Schilling in hand, I began to better appreciate Raoul Ramos. He tended to write exactly what he knew and no more. If he felt that he knew how a crewmate had died, he stated it explicitly. Raoul knew how Dale had been killed, but it was not clear whether he was certain how the other five men had died, or even that they were all dead. I say this because of his January 11, 1945, letter to Virginia Burgess, in which he wrote, "Please have faith in God and hope that He has permitted them safety." Why was Raoul offering hope to the wife of his radio operator when he knew that the crew had all perished? Perhaps he simply wanted her to know that he prayed that God had given his fellow crewmembers a safe passage into heaven. After all, he directed Mrs. Schilling to have faith in God and to forget what he had told her about what happened to her son.

As I considered the various letters that Raoul wrote back in 1945, I knew that I would not be satisfied unless I could speak with him and ask him directly what he had believed back then and whether my interpretation of his use of the word "mishap" was correct. I wondered whether he would allow me to ask him the questions. Don Henderson hadn't; perhaps Raoul would react similarly.

Next I turned to the two photos the Schillings had sent me. Was there more to be learned about Dale from his pictures? In one photo he is wearing his dress uniform, smiling and looking too young to be serving his country. There is a ring on his left hand that looks more

Tail gunner Sergeant Dale Schilling.
Photo courtesy of George Schilling.

like a high school ring than a wedding band. Was this the ring that was
stolen from him after his death? The other photo is the more interesting of the two. Taken July 18, 1943, it shows Dale among a B-17
crew, identified in white lettering at the bottom as the Pratt crew.

By the time I found the Schilling family in June 1998, I had become
a student of the 381st Bomb Group. Knowing that another crew might
be able to tell me more about my uncle, I was very curious about the
Pratt crew. I could find no mention of a Lieutenant Pratt in Chaplain
Brown's book. I checked with the historians of the 381st, and again
found no evidence that anyone named Pratt had ever flown with the
381st. I took a closer look at the Schilling crew photo, hopeful that it
held a clue that would help me solve the mystery.

At the 381st Bomb Group Reunion in 1997, I had obtained several
black and white photos that Chaplain Brown had donated to the attendees. I noted that two of them had similar captions at the bottom: GPR-
27–18-381 and GPR-27–19-381. The last three numerals, 381, obviously
designated the bomb group. The photograph of the Pratt crew had a
similar caption at the bottom, but the last three numerals there were

Dale Schilling (standing third from the right) after a mission to Schweinfurt, Germany, on February 24, 1944. Front row, left to right: Frank Palenik (bombardier), John Howland (navigator), Bill Doherty (co-pilot), and James Tyson (pilot). Back row, left to right: Charles Churchill (waist gunner), Robert Smith (replacement waist gunner), Arnold Farmer (tail gunner), Dale Schilling (replacement ball turret gunner), Richard Jensen (flight engineer), and Henry White (radio operator). Photo courtesy of Frank Slomzenski.

303. At one time, Dale Schilling must have been with the 303rd Bomb Group. Using the information on the 303rd's website, I learned that Schilling had indeed been a member. The James N. Pratt crew had flown with the 427th Bomb Squadron out of Molesworth, England. Dale had flown on seventeen missions with the group, the first on June 11, 1943, and the last on August 24, 1943. Later, in an e-mail exchange with a 303rd historian, Lieutenant Colonel Edgar Miller, I learned that Pratt's aircraft crashed on August 4, 1943, while on a training flight, and all eight men on board that day were killed. From that time on, Dale was a replacement gunner.

Shortly thereafter, while reading Roger A. Freeman's *The American Airman in Europe*, I came across another photo of Dale Schilling. In the book, Freeman included the experiences of 381st Bomb Group navigator John Howland, as well as a photo of the Howland crew. The picture's caption reads: "A photograph taken on February 24, 1944, after the Jim Tyson crew returned from a raid on Schweinfurt." In the back row, fourth from the left, is "Sgt. Schilling (replacement ball gunner)."[4]

So Dale Schilling had flown on the February 24 raid to the ball bearing plant in Schweinfurt. My Uncle Tony and Dale had more in common than I could have imagined—they both flew the ball turret gunner position on that raid! While Dale Schilling was flying in his twenty-third combat mission, the man he would replace on the next day's mission, Don Henderson's tail gunner Butch Reeves, was suffering from the frostbite that would ground him on February 25.

After finding the photo, I contacted the historian of the 381st Bomb Group, Dave Osborne. Dave confirmed that Dale Schilling was assigned to the 381st in August 1943, but was unable to say why.

Before I closed the book on Dale Schilling, I returned to the Lowell Public Library website that had first led me to his family. There I found a reference to a letter that had been printed on page 1 of the January 20, 1944, edition of the *Lowell Tribune*. In the letter, Dale Schilling wrote,

I have been awarded the Air Medal with the Oak Leaf clusters, the Distinguished Flying Cross with one Oak Leaf cluster, the Purple Heart with one Oak Leaf cluster. . . . The Purple Heart is given when one is wounded in the line of duty against the enemy. I've only been hit twice—which is lucky. It is too bad you didn't get anything when you went hunting this year, and that shells are so hard to get. I get all I need and sometimes use two or three thousand a day.

Your son,
Dale[5]

The Henderson crew had quite a tail gunner with them on that fatal mission!

THE IMPORTANCE OF PROPER CLOSURE

It was satisfying to locate the five families who had suffered the same loss as the Korkuc family in February 1944. They had been most gracious in helping me learn more about each of the fallen men. In return, I was happy to be able to share with them my understanding of what happened to the crew on the last mission, how the men died, and how they were treated after death by the civilians of Willman-dingen. During our correspondence, I realized that each family had reacted differently to the news. Three accepted the loss without reservation, but the other three nursed doubts.

My curiosity had been fueled by my father's disbelief at hearing that his brother's body was brought back to the United States and interred at Arlington National Cemetery. With the information I was able to find, he now fully accepts that Tony Korkuc is buried at Arlington. I contrasted the information I had obtained with what the Korkuc family was told during the years 1944 to 1950. In 1945, they received three letters from the survivors of 42–37786, all of whom gently shared the sad news that Tony had perished in battle. Unfortunately, however, none of those letters provided the details that the family was yearning for. From July 1945 to February 1950, they learned nothing more about Tony from the War Department. If he was indeed dead, where was his body? Anna and Michael Korkuc clung to the slim hope that their son had somehow survived the crash. My father had clearly shared the sentiments of his parents. It was much simpler to deny death than to accept it.

In 1950, when Anna and Michael Korkuc were asked to go to Arlington National Cemetery to witness the reburial of their son's remains, they obviously were not convinced that it was Tony in the casket. My father's later behavior at Arlington was proof of that. The family was never given a definitive account of how Tony died, or where his body had been between 1944 until 1950. Without that understanding, the family was denied proper closure.

The Wonning and Bartolo families had shared similar doubts about their sons' fate. In contrast, the Hunnicutt, Burgess, and Schilling families had each accepted the death of their son. Why was this so? The latter three families had received a definitive explanation of their loved ones' deaths. The Hunnicutts were visited by two of Tommy's crewmates in 1945, and were told in person that he was dead. They had the opportunity to ask Tommy's crewmates some questions. And Tommy's father, Colonel Lee Hunnicutt, had done some investigating on his own. The Hunnicutt family thus received proper closure in 1945. Raoul Ramos visited Virginia Burgess in the summer of 1945. He told Virginia that Boyd had died that February day. The Burgess family was left in no doubt that Boyd was dead. Thus they also received proper closure in 1945. On July 5, 1945, Mr. and Mrs. George Schilling

Wearing her son's gunner's wings and holding a folded American flag, Anna Korkuc pauses at Arlington National Cemetery after Tony's funeral on June 29, 1950. Photo courtesy of the Korkuc family.

of Lowell, Indiana, received a letter from Raoul Ramos explaining the exact circumstances of their son's death. Raoul was explicit: German fighters had scored a direct hit on the tail position of the ship; that was how Dale had died. Thus the Schilling family, too, received proper closure with respect to Dale's death.

No crewmembers visited the Korkuc, Bartolo, or Wonning families after the war. Norman Wonning continued to look for his brother Earl until he was well into his fifties. Jennie Bartolo Domiziano was convinced that the remains returned to Greenwich were not those of her brother. My father was shocked to learn that his brother's body was buried at Arlington. Clearly, these three families suffered because of the lack of proper communication. Without the closure that true and convincing information can provide, the families lived in denial over the deaths of their loved ones.

The surviving crewmembers did their best to help, but the official responsibility to inform the families did not lie with them. The War Department could and should have done a better job. They could have explained what happened to the bodies after the crash. They could have explained that although sufficient evidence was not available to identify all the men individually, there was no question that six men were buried in Willmandingen in 1944. They could have explained that it took one year to find the men and another five to identify two of the six. They could have explained all this to the families, but they didn't. That lack of information in the years between 1945 and 1950 contributed to the lack of acceptance and the lack of healing on the part of the Korkuc, Wonning, and Bartolo families.

My father now knows what happened to his brother. When he first gave me Tony's letters, he could not bring himself to read them; there was too much pain associated with his memories. Because of what I learned, he is now openly proud of his brother. It is painful to know that Tony did not bail out of the plane, but at least he understands what happened on the last mission. Similarly, Jennie Bartolo Domiziano now knows, without a doubt, that her brother's remains were buried in Greenwich, Connecticut. Norman Wonning now knows what really happened to his brother. It is unfortunate that the Wonning, Bartolo, and Korkuc families did not receive sufficient closure back in 1945 from the crewmembers or from the War Department. But I am glad that I was able to help them learn the truth so that their healing could finally begin.

THE REST OF THE CREW

By now, I had gained a good understanding of Tony's last mission, and of the circumstances surrounding his death and burial. Having spoken to the surviving crewmates, I knew something of what it had been like to fly combat with my uncle. Unfortunately, neither Nick DeRose nor Don Henderson had known Tony well, and Raoul Ramos had yet to satisfy my curiosity about what it was like to have him as a friend. I knew that I had to talk to more people who had known Tony. Thus I turned my attention to locating the rest of his B-17 crew—Bill Herrington, Butch Reeves, and Jack Fournier.

Finding Bill Herrington was quite easy. Toward the end of my visit with the DeRoses in Michigan, Nick finally remembered the name of his first crew pilot. We then quickly found his address and phone number in the 381st Bomb Group Memorial Association Directory. On November 17, I placed a phone call to Bill Herrington. He was in the midst of a family get-together celebrating his eightieth birthday, but he said he would be glad to talk to me about his memories of the crew.

Bill remembered Tony, but all he would say about him was, "Korky had more guts than I ever thought was possible in flying in the ball turret." His only memory of Jack Fournier, his co-pilot, was that Jack was "morose about being assigned to the four engine bomber crew after training as a fighter pilot." He remembered tail gunner Butch Reeves, but only as a man who got into a lot of trouble. This was consistent with what I had learned about Reeves from Nick. Bill believed that he had flown about five missions with Tony's crew. When they were shot down, he was in the hospital. He mentioned that he had been having trouble breathing and had to stop flying. Bill then said it was awkward to continue talking because of his birthday party. I told him I would call him back.

About a month later, I called again, and asked Bill about his memory of the missions. He told me that during his days with the 381st Bomb Group, he flew in twenty-eight combat missions. After his early problems while flying with Tony's crew, he resumed flying combat in June 1944. He rose to the rank of captain with the 381st and later made the Air Force his career. He retired in 1965. I asked Bill about his and Reeves's reaction to the loss of their crew on February 25, 1944. Bill reiterated that he was suffering from a "minor illness" at the time, but that he and Reeves certainly mourned the loss of the men. He recalled that Reeves felt extremely lucky to have missed the mission. Bill could add no more to help me understand Tony and the crew. After this second exchange, I did not contact him again.[6]

Curious to know what Butch Reeves's memories were of Tony, I made an effort to find him. Through Joe Waddell of the 381st Bomb Group, I learned that Butch's full name was Harvey H. Reeves. Joe had a CD-ROM that contained every phone listing in the United States for 1997, and he kindly sent me the numbers for all the men named Harvey H. Reeves. There were eleven in all, from all over the country, but none of them was the one I was looking for. In June 1998, I learned from Raoul Ramos's letter to the Schillings that "H. H. Reeves" was from Orlando, Florida. I checked the Social Security Death Index and came up with a single name. This Harvey Reeves was born on October 30, 1921, and died on August 16, 1992, in Citrus Heights, California. Very possibly I had found Butch.

I renewed my search for Jack Fournier. Switchboard.com failed to yield a single Jack H. Fournier. Fearing that he too was dead, I searched for his name in the SSDI and found a Jack Fournier who had died in Sandusky, Ohio, in September 1979. That man had been born on August 28, 1915, and could very well have been the one I was looking for. In 1944, this Jack Fournier would have been twenty-eight years old. Since Nick DeRose had told me that Jack was two years older than he was, I was fairly certain that I had found the last of Tony's crewmembers.

Before I gave up on Butch Reeves and Jack Fournier, I wanted to be certain about their fate, so I requested copies of each man's Social Security application. Jack Fournier had applied for his Social Security card on February 2, 1938, when he was twenty-two years old. He had been living in Cleveland, Ohio, at the time. Given that the Jack Fournier who flew with Tony listed Cleveland as his home, I was pretty certain I had found the right Jack Howard Fournier. Harvey H. Reeves had applied for his card on May 4, 1940, giving his address as Baltimore Street, Orlando, Florida. I was now convinced that he was indeed Butch Reeves.

By September 1998, I was frequenting a number of websites dedicated to the Eighth Air Force. The United States Army Air Forces of World War II site, at www.armyairforces.com, proved to be particularly useful. One day I got a tip from a fellow user of the site, a woman who went by the user name "Little Bit." She told the HeavyBombers Forum that she had found a useful way to locate former service personnel: "I recently found out that the Veterans Administration (VA) will forward mail to living military vets for whom they have a current address. Mail should be addressed to the veteran (name and if available, the service number) care of Veterans Administration (203CI), 810 Vermont Avenue NW, Washington, DC 20420. It is recommended to call the VA first to verify that the veteran is listed in their files. The phone number is 1–800-827–1000." I wasted no time in placing a call to the VA. I learned that Harvey Reeves (Army Service Number 14076682) and

Jack Fournier (Army Serial Number 0–678850) had indeed both died, Reeves on August 16, 1992, and Fournier in September of 1979.

I asked whether there was any way that I could obtain further information so as to locate the next of kin of both men. I was told that the file on Harvey Reeves had been destroyed, but they still had Jack Fournier's file. I filed a request under the Freedom of Information Act, and while awaiting the response, I set out to learn whatever was available on Harvey Reeves. I contacted the Sacramento County Clerk's Office in California and obtained Reeves's death certificate. It revealed that he was survived by a wife, Betty. I learned that Reeves had made the military his career, serving from February 1943 until 1963. His place of burial was listed as Eternal Valley Cemetery in Newhall, California. I contacted the cemetery and learned that Reeves was buried there along with his wife. They had no children. I had reached the end of the line with Butch Reeves. But that was not the last I would hear about him. He would come back into my story.

I then turned my attention back to Jack Fournier. True to their word, the Veterans Administration sent me his ninety-two-page claims file, which listed his lifelong interactions with the VA. The file was ordered chronologically, with the most recent entries first. I learned that Jack Howard Fournier had died alone at the Ohio Veterans Home in Sandusky, Ohio, on September 4, 1979. His application for burial benefits indicated that he was a widower with no children. He was buried a week later at the Ohio Soldiers and Sailors Home cemetery in Sandusky, Ohio.[7]

Still curious, however, I continued to leaf through the file. What had life been like for Jack Fournier? And what impact had the events of February 25, 1944, had on him? When Fournier entered the service in 1942 at the age of twenty-seven, he was among the best that America had to offer. He qualified as a pilot in the United States Army Air Forces, demonstrating that he was both highly intelligent and in excellent health. But just twenty-nine years after being discharged from Stalag Luft I, Fournier applied for a total disabilities benefit. In 1961, at age forty-six, he sought medical attention for a pain he was having in his neck. According to an accompanying form, "The veteran states his neck was injured when he parachuted from a plane that was shot down over Germany during 1944. He was a POW for about eighteen months. He now complains of a dull pain in the back of the neck."

I also found Fournier's Army Separation Qualification Record, dated December 4, 1945. In the summary of his military occupation, Fournier wrote "Pilot, B-17 Heavy Bomber: piloted B-17 aircraft and commanded crew in aerial offensive operations against the enemy. Completed 12 Combat missions in the European Theater of Operations with the 8th Air Force. Has 96 combat hours, total flight time 1100 hours." Also of interest, Fournier listed that he had trained for two years as a P-47 fighter pilot with the 321st Fighter Squadron. Given that background, I could understand why DeRose, Herrington, and Henderson had each characterized him as a disgruntled bomber co-pilot.

Wondering whether his medical discharge exam mentioned any wounds, I checked the file to see if Jack Fournier had ever elaborated on what happened to him on his last bombing mission. His first post-war medical examination, in 1949 when he was thirty-four, was revealing. Jack initiated the visit because of gastrointestinal pain, but the doctor could find nothing wrong with him. Doctor E. D. Schwartz's report read:

> In February of 1944 the plane in which he was flying was shot down and he sustained minor shrapnel wounds of his left leg and right hand. He was immediately taken prisoner of war by the Germans. He was liberated in May of 1945. Veteran states that since he parachuted to the ground he has had recurrent aching in the back of his neck that occurs about once or twice a week and is frequently followed by occipital headaches lasting one-half day. . . . Veteran states that neither of his shrapnel wounds have caused him any symptoms of any kind since they were incurred. They were minor wounds and were treated by the Germans.

Jack Fournier had indeed suffered as a result of his last combat mission. He was hurt when the German anti-aircraft gunners scored a hit on the B-17's number four engine.

The doctor's final assessment of Jack Fournier was that he suffered from bouts of anxiety. To the VA's credit, they did conduct a psychiatric examination. The examiner noted that Jack had a "mild digital tremor and slightly increased knee jerks." In his final remarks, the doctor wrote, "although the veteran is showing mild anxiety reaction, it

Gravesite of co-pilot Jack Howard Fournier at Ohio Veterans Home in Sandusky, Ohio. Photo courtesy of Ohio Veterans Home.

appears that this is of rather recent origin as evidenced by the fact that it is only recently that his wife has pointed out his 'nervousness' to him." With that, Jack was given a clean bill of health and released.

It had been only four years since Jack was released from Stalag Luft I, and he was probably suffering from post-traumatic stress disorder due to his military service. Back then, very little was known about this war-related illness, and men such as Jack Fournier were left to heal themselves. All Jack knew was that he had headaches, that he was difficult to get along with, and that his wife was concerned about his irritability—all of which led him to seek medical attention. In his 1949 application for disability compensation, he wrote, "General Run down condition: nerves, stomach, loss of weight, loss of stamina, due to POW experiences of about 16 months. S.F.W. [Suffered from wound to] leg & hand. While in the POW camp, lost 35 pounds." Fournier also noted that he had married Bettie Haines in Florence, Kentucky, in 1946, and that he had a son, Jay Fournier, born on March 5 of the following year. This was the only reference in the file to his having a child.

Via switchboard.com I was able to locate Jay Fournier, and we spoke on the phone. Jay had not seen his father since 1957, and until my phone call, he did not even know that Jack had died. He had nothing good to say about his father. Jack Fournier walked out on his family when Jay was only ten years old, and he never again made contact with them. I told Jay that a little part of Jack had probably died back on February 25, 1944. I told him that his father had served his country well during the war. I could not really blame Jay for the way he felt:

Jack Fournier was never a father to him. But someday I hope that Jay will visit his father's grave and forgive him for the things he did during his life.

In the end, my efforts to learn more about Tony via Butch Reeves and Jack Fournier had ended in failure. I had gathered some information about both men, but nothing that could help me better understand my uncle. I turned my attention to the men of the 381st Bomb Group.

CHAPTER 7

With the Men of the 381st

In July and again in October of 1997, I visited with Chaplain James Good Brown in Haverhill, New Hampshire. I was thrilled to meet the author of *The Mighty Men of the 381st: Heroes All.* At ninety-six years old, he was as alert as ever, although he ruefully remarked that he had given up chopping his own firewood only a year or two earlier. During my second visit, I was accompanied by my parents. Chaplain Brown reminisced about his war years in England, and mentioned that although he was an officer, he had earned the enlisted men's medal for good conduct.

> A bomb group is entitled to have an officer as a chaplain. They don't have enlisted men as chaplains. You had to be a graduate of a university or a theological school in order to be a chaplain. So you entered as a lieutenant. Then you are promoted to a captain. There was another Roman Catholic chaplain on the base, and he was a lieutenant. Chaplain Collet was his name. The government wanted to provide a Roman Catholic for every base in the Air Force. So Chaplain Collet was assigned to a small outfit called the Air Service Group. The bomb group commander came to me and asked me to resign so that Collet could be made the chaplain of the bomb group. So they demoted me to the Air Service Group so he could become chaplain. I lost the chaplaincy of the bomb group to Captain Collet.

At this point I broke in to explain to my parents that when Tony was shot down, the Korkuc family received a letter from Martin Collet and not James Good Brown. Chaplain Brown added, "Colonel Nazzaro reversed the orders later in the war, and I once again became the chaplain of the 381st Bomb Group."

Valerie Wentworth Brown
poses with her husband,
James Good Brown, in
Haverhill, New Hampshire,
July 25, 1997. Photo by
author.

Despite my interruption, Chaplain Brown exclaimed, "I still haven't
told you how I got my good conduct medal!"

When I was in the war, I was about twenty years older than most of the
men. After the war ended, I remained in the Air Force in the Reserves.
During my years, I was promoted several times. I was promoted from
captain, to major, and then to lieutenant colonel. They would come up
to me and tell me, "Chaplain, you are entitled to your promotions." I
never made any effort to get the promotions. They did it for me. You
could not hold the rank of a lieutenant colonel after the age of sixty.
You could be an enlisted man after sixty years of age, but an officer had
to retire after reaching that age. This was mandatory. Well, I was past
sixty years old, but I had not yet made twenty years with the Air Force.
I had to retire, and thus I would be forced to miss my retirement pay. . . .
The Reserves Center commander told me there was only one way to

work this problem out. You have to retire as an officer and become an enlisted man. So I retired and they demoted me from a lieutenant colonel to a private. So in my last years, I attended the Reserves Center in New Haven, Connecticut, as a private. But as a private you can get the good conduct medal. So they gave me a good conduct medal!

At this point, Chaplain Brown let out a big laugh and said, "At the reunions, many of the enlisted men would ask me why I had the good conduct medal, and I would have to tell them that story." He added, "I stayed in for a total of twenty-three years, including my war year service." I kidded him, asking whether we should be addressing him as Private Brown instead of Colonel Brown. "No, hold on," he responded, "there is one more step to this story! The Reserves commander said there was a rule that you can retire with the highest rank you ever attained. So I retired as a lieutenant colonel and not as a private. I was forty-four when the war ended. For years after the war, on a weekly basis I went to the Reserves Center. I was very loyal and earned the right to my retirement pay."

In August 1998, I had my last visit with Chaplain Brown. As usual, we talked for hours. I brought him up to speed on my research, and he talked about his life. I have a fond and vivid memory of that evening, and am so pleased to consider him a friend. On July 17, 2001, Chaplain Brown celebrated his one-hundredth birthday with his daughters and family. Unfortunately, he had to do so without his wife, Valerie, who had passed away in February of that year. One of the chaplain's favorite axioms is "I am a part of all that I have met." I am proud to say that he is a part of me, and I am a part of him.

THE 1997 REUNION OF THE 381st BOMB GROUP
MEMORIAL ASSOCIATION

In September 1997, I attended the annual 381st Bomb Group Memorial Association reunion in Baltimore, Maryland. Every year, surviving members of the bomb group meet to socialize and exchange stories about their days with the 381st. I knew that Don Henderson, Raoul Ramos, and Nick DeRose would not be attending, but I was excited to have a chance to meet some of the men who had flown B-17 bombers out of Ridgewell. If none of the attendees had known my uncle, I at least wanted to talk to as many ball turret gunners as I could, especially any who had flown with the 532nd Bomb Squadron. My plan was to speak with as many people as possible on the day of my arrival, then drive to Washington, D.C., the following morning to visit the Washington Mall and Arlington National Cemetery. On Saturday night, I would be attending the annual banquet and dinner dance, and on Sunday morning I had signed up for the memorial breakfast.

As I drove to Baltimore, I thought about all the information I had gathered over the previous six months. During the summer, while I was corresponding with Marcus Mockler in Germany and with the three surviving crewmembers, I was also reading as many books as I could about the heavy bomber groups. One of them, *Decision over Schweinfurt* by Thomas Coffey, described the Eighth Air Force's infamous first raid deep into the heart of Nazi Germany. The objective of the daylight mission on August 17, 1943, was to annihilate the ball bearing plants that fed the Nazi war machine. During the Schweinfurt raid, the Eighth Air Force lost sixty Flying Fortresses—ten of them from the 381st Bomb Group.

I checked in at the hotel, eager to find out what the weekend had in store for me. Even though I would not know a soul at the reunion, I knew that if I wanted to learn anything, I was going to have to walk right up to the elderly airmen, introduce myself, and start talking. A large number of college students were staying at the Marriott that weekend, too, attending a convention of some kind. As I walked through the hotel to the reunion area, I felt a little out of place. I was too old to be part of the college crowd and much too young to be part of the 381st Bomb Group.

The first two former crewmembers I talked to were Burton Hill, a 532nd Bomb Squadron top turret gunner who had served at the war's end, and George Cathcart, a crew chief for the 533rd Bomb Squadron during his two-year stay at Ridgewell. As I was to learn during my weekend stay with the men of the 381st, perspectives of the war differed greatly depending on when the men had served. George and Burton had not met before talking to me. I asked George whether he remembered the Schweinfurt mission, and he responded, "It was pretty sad." He told me about one man who did not fly with his regular crew that day. "When he came back to his barracks that night, he was the only man left." I told them that my uncle's plane had lost an engine because of flak, and after being separated from the safety of the formation, it was downed by German fighters. Burton Hill nodded in confirmation: "the Germans waited for the planes to fall out, so they could pick them off one by one when they knew their firepower was limited." Burton had flown thirty-four missions between December 1944 and May 1945. He said, "Us guys that flew the last part of the missions, we knew a little bit of what it was like to almost walk on flak. But as far as the fighters were concerned, we didn't have the foggiest idea of what that was like."

After my chat with Burton, I lingered in the lounge area, hoping that someone else would come up to me. I did not have to wait long. Leonard Spivey and his companion Elizabeth Yee approached and started to talk to me. Leonard and Elizabeth were regular attendees at the reunions. They promised to help me locate members of the 532nd Bomb Squadron, and they volunteered to put me in touch with as many ball turret gunners as they could. Leonard was interested in Mockler's article in the *Reutlinger General-Anzeiger,* which I had left on a table nearby. He picked it up and began translating it into English. As luck would have it, he knew German, and in fact had served as an interpreter for the security committee during his stay at Stalag Luft III. He was also an original member of the 381st Bomb Group, having served as a navigator with the 535th Bomb Squadron. After surviving the famous first raid to Schweinfurt, he was shot down during a milk run to Gilze Rijen, Holland, on August 19, 1943.

After dinner that evening, I went back to my room to settle in for the night. But sleep eluded me, so I returned to the lobby and headed for the bar, to see what nightlife was like at the Marriott. I lasted only one beer before the music pounding in my ears forced me to seek out a quiet corner in the lounge. While I was sitting there, Elizabeth joined me, and we resumed our earlier conversation. Elizabeth had been instrumental in hooking Leonard up with the 381st Bomb Group Memorial Association, and not only had they attended reunions together, they also had visited Ridgewell, England, and the site of his plane crash in Holland. The two of them even visited the Stalag Luft III memorial in Sagan, Poland. Knowing that Elizabeth would understand my passion to learn about my uncle's mission, I told her the specifics of my research. As we said good night, I knew I had begun a

Talking to the men of the 381st in Baltimore in 1997. On my right sit Elizabeth Yee and Leonard Spivey; to my left stands George Cathcart. Photo by author.

friendship that would serve me well during that reunion and any others I might attend in the future. And I no longer felt like a lost soul.

The following morning, I drove to Washington, D.C. On this second visit to Arlington, I knew how to get to Tony's gravesite, so I walked there from the parking lot, a distance of about a mile. I moved in close to the gravestone, knelt on one knee, and said a silent prayer. Then I sat down on the ground and caught a breather. There was no one else around, and I started talking out loud to Tony. I felt foolish at first, but gradually I became more comfortable. I told him that I knew what happened to him on that winter day in 1944, and that I was glad I had gotten to know him through the letters he left behind. I said that I was inspired to learn more about him because of the love that my father still had for him. I told him I wished we could have met, that I appreciated his wry sense of humor and his love of family, and I was honored to be the second Korkuc to become an engineer. I wanted Tony to know that I would not rest until I had found out everything I could about his life, and I promised him that no family member would ever

forget his sacrifice. I would see to it that his memory was properly pre-
served. That was the least I could do for him, and for my father.

That evening at the banquet, Elizabeth and Leonard invited me to
sit at their table. As we talked, an announcement came over the public address system. Those attending the dinner were being encouraged
to meet with Bob Korkuc, the nephew of Anthony Korkuc; he was sitting at the far table and would be glad to talk with any men from the
532nd who had known his uncle or who had flown the ball turret gun
position. Elizabeth and Leonard admitted that they were responsible
for the announcement, and I thanked them for their kindness.

As the evening progressed, thanks to Elizabeth and Leonard's efforts,
I talked with many people. I was introduced to a ball turret gunner
named John Wood from the 535th Bomb Squadron who had flown during the same period as Tony. With the sounds of "In the Mood" in the
background, I interviewed my first ball turret gunner. I had wondered
whether Tony would have been able to get out of the ball turret by himself, so I asked John Wood if he could have done so. He replied:

> If the power was out, you could get out, but you had to crank yourself
> out with little hand cranks [one for the azimuth and one for the eleva-
> tion controls]. You had to crank the guns down, open the turret, and
> then find your chute, because it wouldn't fit on you while you were in
> the turret. You wore a harness; you had a little chest pack. After putting
> the chest pack parachute on, you then went out of the back hatch. If
> power was out, you could open the turret door and fall out, but with-
> out your chute that did you no good.

When I asked John about his memory of the February 25, 1944,
Augsburg mission, he recalled, "It was a long one, that's all. The one
thing I remember about the Augsburg mission, this is a pisser, we were
carrying propaganda pamphlets, could you imagine that. As we got
close to the target, we swung off a little bit, and dropped these pamphlets instead of bombs on the German population. You felt like,
'What a waste of time; we could have mailed it to them!'" I asked him
how he had felt about risking his life under those circumstances. "You
didn't think of risking your life," he said. "The funny thing is, on one
plane you could be on a milk run, but the guy in the plane next to
you, it could be hell, and he could be getting the shit shot out of him.

Cutaway drawing of a ball turret. From *Handbook of Operation and Service Instructions for Retractable Lower Ball Turret, Model A-13* (Detroit: Briggs Manufacturing Co., 1943), fig. 11, 19.

Augsburg was a long raid, but you tend to forget them as the years go by; the missions all tend to meld together."

I asked John about his impressions of flying in the ball turret.

> To me, the turret was extremely comfortable. A lot of people talked about how it was cramped. Your knees were one handspan away from your head. So you're bent up in a fetal position. The worst thing about it was your two guns were down near your head, on each side. I lost my hearing because of that. When I come back from a raid, my ears would ring for hours.

I wondered whether he had ever crossed paths with Tony while at Ridgewell.

No, I didn't know your uncle. The bomb squadrons didn't intermingle. In fact, you didn't know the guys in the next barracks. There were two crews in each barracks—a total of twelve enlisted men. The officers were in their own barracks. They had the enlisted men in one barracks and the officers in another. You knew the guys in the other end of the barracks. It was funny; you didn't purposely meet people. While I was there, we had five crews replaced in the other end of the barracks. So I didn't get to know them very well. They would last two raids or three raids and then get shot down.

I asked John his opinion on whether flying during the early raids was more dangerous. "Yes," he replied. "It wasn't until March of 1944 when we got the P-51s to escort us throughout the whole mission. Before that, the P-47s did not have the range, and the B-17s were on their own. In fact, I met a guy at these reunions who flew thirty raids, and he never saw an enemy aircraft. In 1943 and the early part of 1944, jeez, you saw them all the time! You fired at a lot of fighters." John flew his twenty-fifth and final mission on March 23, 1944, just twenty-seven days after my uncle's last mission. During his stint with the 381st, he flew as a waist gunner, as a tail gunner, and as a ball turret gunner.

At breakfast on my last day in Baltimore, I met yet another ball turret gunner. I didn't catch his name, but I did learn that he flew at the very end of the war, in 1945. I quickly learned that he saw a vastly different war than did John Wood and my uncle.

All I could hear was the rhythm of the motors; the engines would put you to sleep. I slept through most of my missions. I'd wake up as we neared the initial point of the bombing run. I turned my turret to make sure that the bomb bay doors were open and let them know if the bombs were all away, and then I would tell them when the doors were closed. I only fired my guns once in the turret. The Germans didn't have much left when I flew. Also, we had good fighter escort.

The reunion ended with a memorial ceremony honoring those who had fought and died with the 381st. The color guard presented the colors to the assembly, and the men and families of the 381st Bomb Group then stood together and recited the Pledge of Allegiance. It was many years since I had last said the pledge. I was proud to stand with those who had so valiantly served their country in its time of need more than half a century ago. It was an honor to be among them.

After the presentation of the colors, a chaplain offered an invocation prayer. As he spoke, I couldn't help but look at the faces of the veterans standing around me. I could see the sorrow in their eyes. I thought about the sacrifice made by Staff Sergeant Anthony J. Korkuc, and I felt immense pride. While the memorial choir sang "Amazing Grace," I thought about my visit to Arlington, and I started to cry. My Uncle Tony had been laid to rest some fifty years earlier, twelve years before I was born, but at that moment I felt that the assembled men and women were finally acknowledging his sacrifice.

At the close of the ceremony, LeRoy Wilcox, the 381st Bomb Group's personnel officer during the war, continued his wartime duties by reading the names of the members who had died since the last reunion. During the solemn roll call, he also mentioned the names of those who had died during the war but had never been recognized by the 381st. I knew that the 381st Bomb Group Memorial Association had never memorialized Tony Korkuc and his five crewmates, and I resolved that this should change at the next reunion. Despite being disappointed that I had met no one who had known Tony, I was pleased to have gained some new friends. I planned on staying in touch with these great Americans.

THE 1998 REUNION OF THE 381st BOMB GROUP
MEMORIAL ASSOCIATION

The 1998 reunion was held in Savannah. As the date approached, I had some solid reasons for satisfaction. I had found all of the crew's families and had gained a good understanding of what air combat was like for my uncle. But despite my best efforts, I had been unable to get any of the crewmembers' families to attend the reunion.

I arrived at the Savannah airport on a Wednesday afternoon and had a pleasant trip to the Savannah Marriott Riverfront Hotel with several members of the 381st who had arrived at the same time. George Shackley, a resident of Savannah, was hosting the reunion. During the war, Shackley had flown as the lead pilot on several missions during Tony's time with the 381st. The once mighty air commander was now frail and unsteady on his feet, but his son was helping to host the reunion and assisting him in coordinating the activities.

At one table in the reunion hospitality room, I met Frank Slomzenski, the brother of Technical Sergeant Chester Slomzenski of the 535th Bomb Squadron. Chester was killed on March 30, 1945, during a mission over Bremen. Frank was the custodian of several binders containing wartime images from Ridgewell that had been donated by Colonel George Porter of the 381st Bomb Group headquarters staff. Frank listened with interest to my account of the research I had done. He acknowledged that I had accomplished more in two years than he had in thirty. I encouraged him to use the vast resources of the Internet to learn more about his brother's last mission.

The 381st Memorial Association spent a day touring Savannah's Mighty Eighth Heritage Museum. Savannah was the birthplace of the Eighth Air Force. As our group walked through the exhibits, I struck up a conversation with a 532nd Bomb Squadron pilot named Armour Bowen, learning that he had flown thirty missions between December 1943 and April 1944. He had participated in many of the same missions as Tony. In fact, Armour flew three missions during Tony's last week.

At one point, our museum guide herded us into a Nissen hut. We were about to experience what a combat mission briefing was really like. It felt a bit strange to be sitting with Armour Bowen, knowing that he and Tony's crew had attended a similar briefing on February 22, 1944, well more than fifty years ago. After learning about our target for the day, Armour and I were told to walk to our planes. There really wasn't a plane for each of us, of course, but we moved into a dimly lit room, where we stood facing a screen that looked like the cockpit of a B-17 Flying Fortress. As the other men of the 381st and their families meandered into the room, the guide told us that we were about to experience the highlight of the museum tour—a multimedia presentation of what it was like to fly a B-17 bomber mission over Germany. A projector in back of us illuminated the screen in front of us, and before we knew it, we were staring at the backs of a pilot and co-pilot as they ran through their preflight checklists.

Even though the pilots were displayed in black and white, the presentation actually made us feel as though we were in a B-17 about to take off for Germany. As the mission wore on, we started to hear the aircrew's normal banter: "Pilot to ball turret, stay alert down there for enemy fighters." Soon the waist gunners were alerting the crew to the presence of fighters, and as the crew prepared for battle, our cockpit came alive with voices. Our ears were filled with the sounds of the four engines, the B-17 machine guns, and the enemy bullets as they made contact with our ship. Next we were surrounded by the sound of flak as we neared the target. Shortly after the bombardier took control of the plane, the bomb bays doors were opened, and we could hear the bombs whistling down toward the ground. Explosions filled the room as they struck their target. After bringing us back safely, our pilots told us that it had been a successful mission. When the lights came up, we filed out of the multimedia display room. I had found the experience exciting, and felt the museum had done a great job in helping me understand what a typical combat mission was like.

When my eyes readjusted to the light, however, I noticed that the men of the 381st looked stunned. Armour Bowen was obviously shaken. He had not been prepared for the realism of the display. He walked over to the guide and politely explained that it would be a good idea to warn future participants about the presentation's realistic content, so that they could choose to avoid it. After seeing Bowen's reaction, I realized that the men were drawn to these yearly reunions not by the memory of their missions, but rather by the camaraderie they shared with their fellow veterans. The common thread that united them was that each had endured the air war and survived; they had no desire to remember the bombing missions in detail. But at least I now knew that the presentation was close to what an actual combat mission was like.

During the weekend in Savannah, I thought about the fact that I had been unable to persuade any of Tony's crewmates, or members of the other crewmembers' families, to attend the reunion. It was now almost a year since I had spoken to Raoul Ramos, and he was proving elusive. During my last conversation with him, in October of 1997, Raoul had promised me that he would make a trip to Seekonk in 1998 so that he could pay his respects to my father and the rest of the Korkuc family. In light of Don Henderson's behavior and Armour Bowen's visceral reaction to being forced by the museum to relive a combat mission, I conjectured that Ramos had lost the desire to talk and visit with me. The past was simply too painful.

I asked a number of reunion attendees whether I should continue to pursue Raoul. One of the men I talked to was Allen Webb, a pilot from the 532nd Bomb Squadron. Webb had served with the 381st from June 1944 until his eighteenth mission to Brandenburg on August 6, 1944, when he was shot down. Like Raoul, he had been interned at Stalag Luft III for the remainder of the war. Allen admitted that Savannah was his first bomb group reunion. He had chosen to leave his memories of the war behind him; many of those who were taken prisoner felt intense guilt about having revealed information about themselves or their organizations during the week-long grilling at Dulag Luft. He had never talked about his experiences in the Army Air Forces even with his family. Recently, however, he had had a change of heart. His grandson wanted to feature him in a school essay on heroes from the war, and when Webb realized that the young boy was honoring him by taking the time to explore his past, he finally changed his mind. Had it not been for that, Allen surely would not have been speaking to me at a reunion.

Allen assured me that he understood Raoul Ramos's reticence about his memories of World War II. He was certain that every veteran who had chosen to remember was faced with the same dilemma at some point in his life. He himself had waited fifty-three years before deciding to talk to his family. Knowing the passion with which I was trying to reconstruct my uncle's wartime experiences, he encouraged me not to give up on Raoul. Without the encouragement of his grand-child, he too would have continued to withhold his past from his family. I got a boost from talking with Allen Webb, and I now felt that I had a legitimate reason for continuing to ask Raoul for information that only he could provide about Tony. Allen was convinced that with enough persistence on my part, even Raoul Ramos would be able to talk about his past.

On the last day of the reunion, I again attended the memorial breakfast. As he had done the year before, LeRoy Wilcox read the roll call of those who had died since the previous year's reunion. He then told the assembly that he was about to announce the names of several men who had not yet been memorialized. I knew that Tony was finally about to be honored. Wilcox began to read off the names of Don Henderson's fallen crewmembers. Partway through, he mentioned another name, someone from another crew who had died during the war: William Seifermann from the 532nd. I was disappointed at the time that the six members of Tony's crew were not memorialized consecutively, but later I would come to learn more about Seifermann, and in retrospect I am glad that he was announced along with Tony's crew. After announcing another unreported war death, Wilcox shared the names of association members who had died since the last reunion. Regretfully, the list contained many more than eight names.

THE 1999 REUNION OF THE 381st BOMB GROUP
MEMORIAL ASSOCIATION

The 1999 reunion was held in Houston. The major attraction that year was a visit to the Lone Star Flight Museum in Galveston, Texas, and the Wings over Houston Airshow at Ellington Field. There were two B-17s at each of those events. While at the museum, I was privileged to see an olive drab Flying Fortress with the familiar Triangle L on its tail. The *Texas Raiders* was owned and operated by the reunion's host, the Confederate Air Forces' Gulf Wing. The nose of the B-17G was adorned with the "girl next door" in the Vargas tradition, and the fuselage was stenciled with the letters "VP" in honor of the 533rd Bomb Squadron of the 381st Bomb Group.

The next day, I attended the air show. The highlight of the day's activities was a thrilling reenactment of the Japanese attack on Pearl Harbor. High over Ellington Field, Japanese Zeros dive-bombed the field, and fake fireballs erupted all around us. Within minutes, American fighters scrambled and took to the air in pursuit of the Zeros. As the men of the 381st Bomb Group watched from their special hangar, the *Texas Raiders* climbed into the air. The men cheered as the Flying Fortress proudly circled the field.

That night at the memorial dinner, I briefed Leonard Spivey on the progress I had made while researching Tony's story. Later, with big band music playing in the background, I looked over at Leonard. Because he had survived the war, I was dining with him and his family at the 381st banquet. I felt privileged. During dinner, Leonard suddenly rose from his chair and walked over to another man. They talked quietly for a while, and then Leonard gave him a full-body embrace. When Leonard returned to his seat, he told us that the man was a member of the Orlando Koenig crew—his crew. The two had not seen each other since August 19, 1943, when they both bailed out of their burning aircraft.

A REFLECTION

The reunions I attended taught me much. The aging men of the 381st took no solace in the loss of the enemy; the major theme in their stories was their desire to get through the missions as quickly as they could, so that they could go home. I never once heard a veteran talk about his hatred of the enemy. I am proud to call many of these veterans my friends, and I am grateful that they took the time to speak to me. In return, they told me that they were glad I took the time to listen to them.

Now that I have met the men, I know why they go to the reunions. They attend so that they can be with others who lived through what they experienced. The many men who were lucky enough to complete their quota of combat missions spent only six months in England. Those who had to parachute out of a burning plane spent a much shorter time at Ridgewell. But for all of the survivors, despite the passage of more than fifty years, the experiences of those few months in England left an indelible mark on their lives. In their late seventies and early eighties, they seem almost in awe of what they did when they were young. They performed their missions professionally despite the ever-present fear of death. Of course, their conversations are dominated by war stories, but they also meet to remember those who did not return. With a deep sense of honor and great reverence, the survivors pay their respects to those who paid the ultimate sacrifice. The men also attend the reunions so that they can tell their sons, daughters, grandsons, granddaughters, nephews, and nieces what they did in the war. They seem to revel in meeting the families of their comrades. They know that each of their lives has been a precious gift since they left behind the hell of war during their youths.

My experiences at all three reunions left with me a deep and profound feeling of gratitude for all those old men who as boys left the safety of their homes in America and fought to save the world from the likes of Hitler. The generations that followed them are forever in their debt.

CHAPTER 8

The Ball's-Eye View

In the spring of 1998, I was still not in communication with Raoul Ramos. Although I had left messages on his answering machine and with his wife and family, he did not appear to be interested in returning my calls. Given his initial promise to visit me and my father in 1998, I was puzzled by his strange behavior. Nick DeRose had given me all the information he could in the fall of the previous year, and he had strongly encouraged me to talk with Ramos. Knowing that Raoul had had a more personal relationship with Tony, Nick was certain that he could answer my questions.

Since Don Henderson had severed communications with me, Nick DeRose could offer no more help, and Ramos was not available, I decided to set out on another course in hopes of learning more about Tony's wartime experiences. Perhaps he had substituted with another crew or bunked with other members of the squadron. Or maybe he had gotten friendly with some men outside his crew by attending Sunday services with them or joining them at the local pub. I decided to contact the surviving members of the 532nd Bomb Squadron to see whether any of them remembered Tony "Korky" Korkuc.

With the help of Joe Waddell, I obtained a copy of the current membership directory of the 381st Bomb Group Memorial Association. Alongside each name, the directory listed which squadron the flier was with, the dates of his service, his crew position, and the crew pilot he served with. By doing an electronic search through the directory, I was able to obtain the name of every member of the 532nd Squadron who was at the base during Tony's time there. I selected names that indicated service from November of 1943 until February 25, 1944. Even if these men had arrived for duty in late February, I wanted to make contact with them. There were seventy-five men who fit my parameters.

I drafted a three-page form letter describing Tony and the men he had crewed with. I supplied as many of the crewmembers' nicknames as I knew, in case their formal names were unfamiliar. I noted when the Herrington/Henderson crew flew missions, and explained the circumstances of their last mission, including an excerpt from the Missing Aircraft Crew Report detailing the loss of Tony's B-17. I also described my contact with the German villagers of Willmandingen.

On May 31, 1998, I mailed out seventy-five copies of that letter, hopeful that someone from the 532nd Bomb Squadron would have some information to share with me. Over the next two months, I heard from twenty-five of the men. Many of them had not known Tony or the crew, but they nonetheless offered me encouragement. I also got a couple of responses from widows who had just lost their husbands. I was touched that they had taken the time to respond despite their grief.

Several respondents remembered Don Henderson, but not Tony or the other crewmembers. Marvin Fairbanks, a navigator with Edward MacNeill's crew, mentioned that he had bunked in the same Nissen hut as Henderson, whom he knew simply as "Obo." He mentioned that he'd had a great time with Obo, "Doc" Brophy, and Bernard Beckman while they were in the hut. He added, "it was an unhappy time when Obo and his crew did not arrive that afternoon of February 25, 1944. Later on we learned that some of the crew were POWs, so we all went to London and purchased 'Care Cartons' for the survivors." Henderson, DeRose, Ramos, and Fournier must have appreciated the gesture.

Dave Brophy, Bernard Beckman's navigator and a good friend of Don Henderson, also responded to my letter. He told me that he had flown on five of Tony's missions—on February 5, 11, 20, 21, and 22. He said that Henderson flew as his co-pilot on fifteen missions. He did not know any of the members of Henderson's new crew, but that was not unusual. "We had little or no contact with any of the enlisted personnel," he wrote, "except for our own crew and only those officers who lived in our hut were known to us. The rate of losses especially the new arrivals were high and we barely said hello before they were gone."

RED AND BROWNIE

A couple of days later, I heard from another member of the 532nd Bomb Squadron, Howard Van Hoozer, who called to tell me that he remembered both Korky and Ramos, and that Butch Reeves had joined his crew after Henderson's plane was lost in action. Van Hoozer had flown as a waist gunner, and his first mission was to Oschersleben on January 11, 1944, when the 381st suffered the loss of eighty men. While with the 381st, he had flown thirty-one missions, the last six in a radio relay plane piloted by none other than Tony's first crew pilot, Bill Herrington. The purpose of those missions was to fly halfway to the target and relay radio signals to the bomber formation.

Van Hoozer suggested that I contact his ball turret gunner, Richard Brown. Although Brown had not joined the 381st Memorial Association, he and Van Hoozer were still close friends. In fact, their crew had met to mark the fiftieth anniversary of their service, and he and "Brownie" had rekindled their old friendship. I placed a call to Richard O. Brown in Coldwater, Michigan. When I told him that I had gotten his phone number from his old waist gunner, he responded with a laugh and asked how "Red" was doing. I explained who I was, and I told him that Van Hoozer was sure that he would remember my uncle. Caught off guard, Brown answered yes, he did remember Korky, and later he acknowledged knowing Ramos. He also remembered Butch Reeves.

Richard told me that Reeves had joined McCrory's crew after their tail gunner, Bill Seifermann, died. In my excitement about talking to a ball turret gunner who had known Tony, I failed to recognize a key piece of information that Brown had just given me: he was the ball turret gunner who flew with pilot Dale McCrory. He was the ball turret gunner who was mentioned in the Missing Air Crew Report that McCrory filled out after the loss of my uncle's plane.

Brown told me that after Seifermann's death, Butch Reeves replaced Seifermann on McCrory's crew. At the time, I thought it was interesting that Reeves had hooked up with Brown's crew after missing the February 25 mission because of illness. I asked whether Brown remembered Bill Herrington, and he said yes. Herrington had served as his pilot during the radio relay missions. There was no need for a ball turret gunner on those missions, so he flew as the in-flight engineer.

Brown told me that he hated flying the ball turret position at first, because he couldn't wear his parachute. He also had to rely on his right waist gunner, "Red" Van Hoozer, to help him out if necessary. However, he soon grew to like the ball turret, because it was a good gun position for his five-foot-six-inch frame. He had shot down two enemy fighters. I asked him what it was like to fly during the Oschersleben mission, and he responded that the anti-aircraft guns were ferocious, and the flak was pretty scary. When a shell exploded, he would see an orange light and then an expanding black grease ball. Then all that was left was a puff of black smoke that came at him like a fog bank. The enemy fighters were also thick on that mission.

Realizing that Richard had not received my form letter, I told him that I would send him a copy on the off chance that seeing the names of Tony's crew in print might further jog his memory. Richard assured me that if he could remember anything more, he would get back to me. In mid-July, about a month after our phone call, I sent him the letter, along with a copy of my uncle's crew picture. While I was writing the cover letter, it finally dawned on me that Richard Brown was the unnamed ball turret gunner who was mentioned by Dale McCrory in MACR #02933. Brown was the man who had seen my uncle's plane leave formation. I included this new fact in my cover letter, hopeful now that he might remember Tony. More important, would he remember anything from the February 25 mission?

A couple of weeks later, I found myself once again in Indianapolis on business, having to spend another birthday away from my family. Tired from a long workday and my flight, I planned to go straight to bed when I got home. But waiting for me was a letter from Richard Brown. When I read it, I was speechless. It was the best birthday present I could have asked for. Brown wrote:

I do remember "Korky"; I did not know him very well. I knew Reeves better. I shot down a ME-109 while Reeves was flying with us. He verified this for me so I could get credit for the kill.

The dates of the missions are lost to me. I can not remember any of them. The Missing Aircraft Report by Mac our pilot, Lt. Dale McCrory, I do recall.

Lt. Henderson was our right wingman that day. On our way back to base, and with no enemy action close, his ship started to act very odd.

He was above us, then below us. He moved away then close. I told Mac on the intercom what was happening. I was then told to watch and report to Mac what happened. I carried a small camera so I took pictures of Henderson's ship. Pic #1, he was in close to us. Pic #2 he started to leave formation. I was glad to see it leave formation, I was worried he might hit one of the other planes and then two or more would be lost. I also thought somebody, not trained as a pilot, might be flying that ship.

Mac's report tells what happened, except he didn't tell of the attack of three ME-109s. They attacked head on first, then regrouped behind and attacked from the rear.

That is about all I can say. Remember 50 years has gone by since then. I do recall three days after this mission I was questioned by an officer I did not know. I knew he was not Air Force.

I wish you luck and hope I have helped you.

Please return my Photos.

Yours,

Richard O. Brown

After reading the letter, I reached for the two photographs that he had enclosed. Each was about the size of a single piece of 35mm film. When I showed them to someone later, I was told that they were small contact prints. In those days, that is what you got when you developed film. When I looked at the first photo, which Brown had labeled Pic #1, I was dumbstruck. I was holding in my hand a photo of my uncle's B-17 taken on February 25, 1944, just moments before it was attacked by the ME-109 fighters that later downed it in Willmandingen. Just below and to the left of the star, I could see the ball turret. At the moment the photograph was taken, Tony was alive and well inside.

Using a magnifying glass, I could clearly see the 381st Bomb Group tail insignia and the distinctive "VE" marking of the 532nd Bomb Squadron. Unfortunately, I could not read the tail number. I desperately tried to find some faces in the clear windows. The nose's clear Plexiglas could be seen, but Nick DeRose was not visible; nor could I see Henderson through the left cockpit window, Raoul Ramos in the top turret, Tommy Hunnicutt through the left waist gunner's window, or Dale Schilling in the tail position. Nonetheless, each of those men was in the plane at the time the photograph was taken. As I stared at the photo, I wondered what Richard Brown had witnessed during that

Ball turret gunner Richard
Brown's first snapshot of
Tony's B-17 on February 25,
1944, before it was attacked
by three ME-109 fighters.
Photo courtesy of Richard
Brown.

mission. Why was Henderson's plane flying erratically? Were the superchargers causing problems for the crew? When Raoul Ramos alluded
to a "mishap," was he referring to the event that caused them to fly so
abnormally? Did Don Henderson still shoulder guilt about the erratic
flight of his ship on that day?

Returning to Brown's letter, I wondered about the identity of the
officer who had questioned him. Only then did I recall that Colonel
Lee Hunnicutt had decided to remain at Ridgewell after his son's last
mission. It must have been the elder Hunnicutt who questioned Brown
on February 28, 1944. Certainly the colonel would have been looking
for answers from anyone who could help him understand what had
happened.

During our second telephone conversation, Richard recalled that
February 25 was a clear, sunny day with high clouds—a perfect day for
bombing. After snapping four photographs with his small camera, he
watched as Tony's plane left the 381st Bomb Group formation and
descended into no-man's land. I shared my belief that Colonel

Second snapshot taken by Richard Brown on February 25, 1944. Ball turret gunner Brown watches aircraft 42–37786 through his Plexiglas window, with the turret's .50-caliber machine gun barrel visible on the left. Photo courtesy of Richard Brown.

Hunnicutt was the man who had interrogated him. Richard said that I might very well be right. I promised to send him a picture of the colonel.

I asked whether Richard thought that any of his other surviving crewmates might remember more about Tony's last mission. He said it was doubtful given the passage of time, but he encouraged me to call them and ask nonetheless. Using the Memorial Association directory, I found Dale McCrory's number and gave him a call. Dale admitted that his memory of the war was not that good, and he had nothing to add about Tony's last mission. He told me that his was often the lead plane in the formation since his bombardier, Bill Beardon, was very good at using the Norden bombsight. So on the February 25 mission, he might have flown as the lead plane, with Henderson in the number two position, just to the right and rear of him. Dale told me that he had always wanted to fly the B-17, but after his first tour with bombers, he signed on for another and flew the P-51 fighter. He left me with the one memory that was still vivid to him about his bomber

Enlisted members of the Dale
McCrory crew stand in front
of *Mizpah*. Left to right:
Howard Van Hoozer, Jerry
Petska, Richard Brown, and
Charley Helvey. Photo cour-
tesy of Howard Van Hoozer.

missions. It was the February 24, 1944, mission to Schweinfurt in which
tail gunner Bill Seifermann was mortally wounded. He was hit by a
rocket fired from a twin-engine fighter, and died three days later.[1]

About a month after my first contact with Howard Van Hoozer, I
received a letter from him accompanied by four black and white photos. Unfortunately, none of them resembled the one that Richard
Brown had taken. There were some interesting pictures of the Dale
McCrory crew, though, including two of Butch Reeves. With the death
of Bill Seifermann, the McCrory crew had needed another member.
Given the loss of Don Henderson's crew, Butch was also in need of a
crew. The last surviving member of the Henderson crew thus found a
home with the McCrory crew. Howard said that Butch "flew as left waist
gunner and I was right waist gunner so we were back to back when flying. He flew several missions with us, sorry I don't remember how many
or which ones." Howard related, "I can see your uncle Korky just as
plain in my mind, I never got to know him real well but I liked him
very much. At that time you usually didn't get to know the men real
well other than your own crew."

First Lieutenant Dale McCrory, 532nd Bomb Squadron pilot. Photo courtesy of E. Richard Atkins of the Scouting Force Association.

Van Hoozer revealed another interesting bit of information. The Fortress they were flying on February 25, 1944, was none other than the famous *Mizpah*, tail number 42–31575. Arriving on February 20, 1944, the 532nd Bomb Squadron ship had the distinction of completing 71 missions without an abort, and it participated in a total of 102 missions before it was returned to the States.[2] According to Van Hoozer, his co-pilot, Ken Bailey, and tail gunner, Bill Seifermann, had selected the name *Mizpah.*

Just over four months later, I received a Christmas card from Richard Brown. "Hi Bob," he had written. "I guess you know I am the world's worst letter writer. I hate to write letters. Don't know why. I found picture no. 4; it is not much but I am sending it any way. I may find no. 3. If I do, I will send. You keep these pictures." At first glance, picture number 4 was not particularly interesting. It showed only clouds and the German countryside; at left were the number one and two engines of Tony's B-17. Brown must have moved at the last second, because he did not get a good view of Henderson's cockpit.

Left to right: right waist gunner Harvey "Butch" Reeves, Captain T. J. Hester, Captain Douglas Winters, and First Lieutenant Dale McCrory. Photo courtesy of Howard Van Hoozer.

Hoping that there might be more to see in the picture, I placed it on my flatbed scanner and made several high-resolution images. When I brought the photos up on my computer screen, I was surprised to see a group of eleven B-17 Fortresses flying below McCrory's and Henderson's planes. It was clear that Henderson and McCrory were indeed flying in the lead group on the mission. The formation seen in the photograph was flying in the low position.

THE PLANE WITH NO NAME

Well more than fourteen months after my letters went out to the 532nd Bomb Squadron, I was pleasantly surprised to receive a twenty-sixth response. It was from a former engineer and top turret gunner named Al Suchy, who now lived in Pennsylvania. Al explained that it had taken him a year to check his facts against his wartime records, which were now in the possession of his daughter in Virginia. He wrote:

Richard Brown took his in-flight photos of 42–37786 from within the ball turret of B-17G *Mizpah*, shown here on a hardstand at Ridgewell. Still Photo Collection, Record Group 342, FH-3A12537-A65891, NARA II.

This detailed close-up of the fourth photo taken by Richard Brown on February 25, 1944, reveals eleven Fortresses flying below Dale McCrory's ship. Photo courtesy of Richard Brown.

Enlisted men from Ed MacNeill's 532nd Bomb Squadron crew pose with another crew at Ridgewell. In the front row, second from the left (lying down), is Harry Ruth, the regular tail gunner for aircraft 42–37786; kneeling in the back row with the palms of his hands toward the camera is Robert Dearth, the plane's regular ball turret gunner. Photo courtesy of Robert Dearth.

Our crew wondered what had happened to our ship 786 and now after 55 years we finally received an answer. I often play 786, 381 and 532 in the Pennsylvania daily lottery games with not much luck. . . .

The B-17–42 37786 was assigned to our crew Pilot Edward MacNeill, an outstanding pilot. Our ground crew chief was a top-rated mechanic but very superstitious. Since his tenure with the 532nd Bomb Squadron, he had lost two other B-17's. His first plane after 6 missions over Germany, aborted on the 7th mission. The B-17 had contained the plane's name, number of aircraft destroyed, and bombing missions, painted on the front nose. On the 11th mission it was shot down over Germany. The crew chief then received his second B-17 plane. He again recorded the crew's name, number of missions, and planes destroyed on the front side of the B-17. This B-17 aborted on the 7th mission and was shot down on the 11th mission. Enter the *Hit Paraders*, my crew, with Ed MacNeill as pilot. The crew chief told us the story of his previous B-17's and he refused to add our name, the *Hit Paraders*, the number of planes destroyed, or number of missions, as we flew them. He said it was bad luck for his other two planes and he didn't want any-

Left side in-flight view of Flying Fortress 42–37786. Still Photo Collection, Record Group 342, FH-3A15775–65974A, NARA II.

more of it! He said that he was going to request that he fly on our 7th and 11th missions. So our 786 went without a name or history as it rested on the 532nd area. The crew chief was not on our 7th mission but we did abort about 1/2 way over France. Our # 3 engine malfunctioned and we were unable to "feather the prop." We barely made it back to Ridgewell for our shaking plane was falling apart. I don't have this mission recorded because I doubt it counted towards my final mission count. Even though a plane in our group that aborted several minutes after we did, was shot down by German fighters. Our B-17 was out of action and later sustained damage to the Top Turret on January 11, 1944. That was my position on the plane.

Suchy's crew did not take the ship into battle on its eleventh mission:

We were given a 3-day pass and visited London. On return to Ridgewell we were notified that our ship 786 had gone down on its 11th mission. Unbelievable another crew had borrowed it while we were in London.

Unfortunate for your uncle, but very lucky for me and the crew of Pilot Edward MacNeill. You can imagine how apprehensive I was approaching our 11th mission knowing the past history of ships assigned to our crew chief.

We finished our missions aboard the *Mizpah* and several other B-17's and returned to Ridgewell for a second tour of duty after 30 days at home.

The first time I contacted Nick DeRose, he told me that the aircraft they took into action on February 25, 1944, was not their regular plane. They had been assigned to that plane for this mission. With all the research I had done, it had never dawned on me to seek out the crew that regularly flew 42–37786. I had been disappointed that the plane was not given a name like *Memphis Belle* or *Mizpah*. But I could never have imagined that it was deliberately left unnamed in an attempt to break an apparent hex.

After reading the interesting letter from Al Suchy, I wondered whether ship 42–37786 really was doomed to go down on February 25, 1944. Had the fate of the Henderson crew been sealed even before they boarded the plane that morning? Was fate the cause of the mishap, or was the loss of the superchargers really the cause? Or was the crew chief perhaps so paranoid about the 7–11 "craps hex" that he simply could not think straight on those mornings when the plane was to head into action?

CHAPTER 9

Twelve O'Clock High

On the eve of what would have been Tony Korkuc's eightieth birthday, I received an interesting e-mail from my old friend Joe Waddell, the secretary of the 381st Bomb Group Memorial Association. He had just received a letter from a Rudi Penker of Freising, Germany, in which Penker explained that he had "worked on a chronicle over the air war on February 25, 1944, and was in search of a photo from . . . B-17, Serial Number 42–37786 and or a photo from 2nd Lieutenant Henderson's crew." Joe was asking permission to give Penker my name and address.

I was intrigued by Rudi Penker's interest, and felt that I might finally have a chance to understand the battle from the German side. I had a picture of aircraft 42–37786, as well as photos of eight of the ten members of the Don Henderson crew. I must admit, though, that given my hard work to find the materials that Penker was seeking, I was hesitant to release them to a German I did not know. Then, about three weeks after receiving Joe Waddell's e-mail, I got an unexpected e-mail from Marcus Mockler:

> Yesterday I talked to a historian in Bavaria. His name is Rudi Penker and—by accident—he is doing some research about this special day, Febr. 25th 1944.
>
> He is sure he's got the name of the pilot that shot down the B-17: It must have been Curt Clemens, a "Unteroffizer" (something like a sergeant or an airman first class). After the fight Clemens wrote a report that says that he had shot down a B-17 at 2.45 p.m. about 15 kilometers south [east] of Reutlingen.
>
> Clemens belonged to III./Jagdgeschwader 3 (name of his unit). . . . They were located in Leipheim near Ulm. On the very day they first

fighted against American planes coming from Italy. Then they landed in Echterdingen near Stuttgart to get fuel and ammunition. After that, they started to combat the American planes from England after their mission to Augsburg. Also an air defence unit on the ground ("Flak" 436) must have been involved into the shooting down of your uncle's machine—there is a report that mentions their participation. . . . Hey, Korky, isn't that interesting? What do you think about it?

Needless to say, I was thrilled by this extraordinary information. As I had been passionately researching the loss of Don Henderson's B-17 from the American side, Rudi Penker was studying it from the German perspective.

Mockler's e-mail included Penker's address, and I wrote to ask whether he could supply me with any official records that would support his assertions about Curt Clemens. While I waited for a response, I sought help once again from the Internet. I e-mailed the Bundesarchiv-Militärarchiv in Freiburg, Germany, but received no immediate response. As I had already learned in pursuing the American side of the story, patience would have to remain my friend.

On Joe Waddell's advice, I sent a letter to Ron MacKay, the author of the book *381st Bomb Group*. I told him that I was in contact with a German historian from Bavaria who was also interested in the fate of my uncle's B-17. In his response, MacKay indicated that he was very interested in learning the identity of the German, because he was in the process of doing some research on the German ME-110 aircraft. It so happened that MacKay was also in touch with a German historian who was researching the crash of 42–37786—none other than Hans Grimminger, the German enthusiast who had given the Willmandingen crash site photo to Roger Freeman. MacKay kindly enclosed his address. Wasting no time, I sent a letter to Grimminger, and soon after received this response:

> It is now 20 years back that I first came into contact with the B-17G 42–37786. In 1976, I started to search for information about the triple attack of 25/26 February 1944 against my hometown of Augsburg.
>
> In the afternoon of February 25th between 1352 and 1414 hours, the Messerschmitt aircraft factory was attacked by 199 B-17's of the 8USAAF. . . . During a visit to the Washington National Records Center

in Suitland, Maryland in 1980, I got the Missing Aircrew Report. When searching for a Bomber Command loss of a different date, I came in contact with a local historian from Reutlingen-Betzingen. He sent me a print of the photo of the crashed B-17G 42–37786. This is the same photo that you have and one that he obtained from a Willmandingen resident. The local historian told me that ME-109's fighter planes had shot down the B-17. I got all of my information from that historian.

Years later, I gave the photo to my friend Roger Freeman, which he used in his book, *The Mighty Eighth War Diary*.

He then shared one last piece of information: a German anti-aircraft battalion had also made a claim on Tony's B-17.

From a German microfilm, which shows only one line for each "shoot-down" reported by fighters and flak-units, I only learned one piece of information: "25.02.44, 1440 hours, B-17 at Willmandingen, reported shot down by . . . schw. 436 . . . but not confirmed." . . .

This is all I can tell you about your uncle's bomber. Write to the local historian, maybe he can tell you more about his research at Willmandingen. He knows about your research, last year he sent me a copy of the article in the Reutlinger General-Anzeiger.

I was amazed at the number of people who had taken an interest in the loss of this one aircraft! That circle had now closed. A local historian had obtained the photo from Hermann Möck, and he had given it to Grimminger, who in turn had given it to Roger Freeman. After seeing the photo in Freeman's book, Nick DeRose had alerted me to its existence, thus allowing me to locate Hermann Möck in Willmandingen. I got a kick out of the fact that among the papers in Grimminger's file was Marcus Mockler's *Reutlinger General-Anzeiger* article. It really is a small world! In addition to giving me a better understanding of the Allied raids on Augsburg, Hans Grimminger had shared some of his personal research on aircraft 42–37786.

VICTORY CLAIMS

After the correspondence with Hans, I badly wanted Rudi Penker to respond to me. Could Penker supply me with a copy of the official record supporting Curt Clemens's claim? In the late summer of 1998, he finally responded:

> I have a list of all the German air victories from 25.02.1944 along with the crashed planes from the USAAF Fighters and Bombers. . . . Uffz. Clemens took off at 1400 from the airfield in Stuttgart-Echterdingen and he shot down the B-17 at 1445 at Willmandingen with a Bf 109 G-6. The Flak unit 436 claims Henderson's B-17 at 1440 using 8,8 cm canons. . . . I have no reports or information to [support that Henderson's crew downed two Bf109 fighters]. Kurt Graf died without enemy action. He was a victim of high altitude sickness while Walter Kirsch crashed far away from Willmandingen. But III./JG 3 lost two Bf109s without name of pilots and place of crash.

Not wanting to sit idle while waiting for further news from Penker, I decided to find out more about the Luftwaffe organization III./Jagdgeschwader 3. I quickly learned from a web search that the English translation for *Jagdgeschwader* was "fighter wing." Further, a Luftwaffe fighter wing typically consisted of three to four fighter groups. The Roman numeral "III" preceding "Jagdgeschwader 3" implied that Curt Clemens flew with the 3rd Group of Fighter Wing number 3. Like the Army Air Forces bomb groups, the Luftwaffe fighter group was made up of three to four "squadrons"—in German, *Staffel*. A Staffel typically consisted of about twelve fighter aircraft. The organization III./Jagdgeschwader 3 was abbreviated as III./JG 3.

I stumbled onto the website for the 12 O'Clock High! Luftwaffe and Allied Air Forces Discussion Forum at http://forum.12oclock high.net/, and was impressed by the knowledge of the contributors. I posted some questions in hopes of learning more about III./JG 3, and in particular about Curt Clemens's role in downing Tony's aircraft. I did not have to wait long. "Rabe Anton" (the user name of an archivist at the Air Force Historical Records Agency at Maxwell Air Force Base in Alabama) e-mailed me directly with some information that would help me navigate through the German records. First, though, Rabe tutored me on some terminology. If Curt Clemens was responsible for downing 42–37786, he would have filed an *Abschussmeldung* (Aerial Victory Report) after the battle. "The Luftwaffe had a sophisticated and careful claims reporting system," he wrote, "at the heart of which was a one (sometimes two) page form with all particulars, including such things as time of day, type claimed, location, expenditure and type of ammunition, witnesses, and so forth. Attached to the basic form were corroborative statements from two or more witnesses, the whole package coming to five or six pages. Regrettably, very few Abschuss-meldungen survive today, either in archives or in private hands." Using his vast resources, he added, "I checked the list that I extracted from the NARA microfilm and there are approximately 25 or 30 victories recorded by I., III., and IV./JG 3, but none [are listed] for Clemens in February 1944. Ironically, there was one for Clemens on January 29, 1944."

I posted another question to the discussion group, inquiring about Rudi Penker's credibility. A user who turned out to be Don Caldwell, the author of the book *JG 26: Top Guns of the Luftwaffe*, filled me in on Penker's credentials: "Rudi Penker's name is well known to me as a German researcher (there aren't many of them). He writes only in German and I do not have any of his work. Since Jochen Prien has recently published an extensive history of III/JG 3 (have you seen it?) you need his input as well; between the two of them you should be able to confirm the responsible unit and the responsible pilot." Both Don and Rabe encouraged me to obtain the history of III./JG 3 written by Jochen Prien and Gerhard Stemmer, entitled *Messerschmitt Bf 109 im Einsatz bei der III./Jagdgeschwader 3*. Even though it was in German, I opted to buy it. Maybe it would contain a picture of interest, or a roster including Curt Clemens's name.

Two months later, the book arrived in the mail. As I had hoped, it contained many old black and white photos of the ME-109 fighter planes and the men who flew them. And to my surprise, my lack of German did not prove fatal when I attempted to decipher the text. Since the book was ordered chronologically, I was easily able to locate the pages dealing with February 25, 1944. With the help of an online translation tool, I was able to make some sense of the passage, and a friend then helped me translate it into readable English.

The 3rd Group of Jagdgeschwader 3 had indeed taken part in the battle on the day of Tony's final mission, engaging the Fifteenth Air Force based out of Foggia, Italy, and the Eighth Air Force based out of England. It became apparent that Rudi Penker had derived most of his information from Prien's book. On the morning of the 25th, twenty-seven ME-109 aircraft from III./JG 3 scrambled from their base near Leipheim and flew to the area near Passau. At around 1215 hours, the German fighters spotted thirty unescorted Fifteenth Air Force bombers at an altitude of about six thousand meters over Mühldorf am Inn. The two forces clashed in the skies south of Regensburg. By the end of the half-hour battle, III./JG 3 had claimed five kills, and had damaged another plane badly enough to separate it from its formation—an accomplishment known as a *Herausschuss*—while apparently suffering no losses.

The ME-109s then landed at the Stuttgart-Echterdingen airfield to refuel. At 1400 hours they took off again in order to intercept the Eighth Air Force B-17s that were returning from Augsburg. The third JG 3 group confronted the Eighth Air Force bombers and their P-51 escorts just south of Stuttgart. In the ensuing battle, III./JG 3 registered two more victories, the B-17 shot down by Curt Clemens and a P-51 fighter destroyed by Jürgen Hoeschelmann. Prien noted that the P-51 shot down by Hoeschelmann was the first P-51 victory ever recorded by III./JG 3. The 3rd Group of JG 3 also claimed credit for two more *Herausschussen* against B-17s.

Two III./JG 3 fighters were listed as lost during this second encounter with Allied bombers—Oberfeldwebel Kurt Gräf from the 7th Staffel and Unteroffizier Walter Kirsch from the 9th. Gräf fell to his death near Swabian Hall, apparently overcome by altitude sickness. Kirsch was shot down over Krumbach, and although he was able to eject, the parachute could not catch enough air before he fell to his death.[1]

In one of the book's appendixes, I read that III./JG 3 lost two more airplanes that same day; both pilots' names were unknown. It did note that a four-engine bomber had downed one of those fighters. In another appendix, Jochen Prien had listed all the kills claimed by III./JG 3 from 1940 to 1945—a total of 2,280 enemy aircraft. In a table titled "Abschüsse der III./JG 3 während des Einsatzes in der Reichsverteidigung, 8 August 1943 bis 6 Juni 1944," I found the entry for February 25, 1944.[2] Prien detailed the four victories claimed after the fighters left the Stuttgart-Echterdingen airfield on February 25. As Rudi Penker had related, Uffz. Curt Clemens of the 8th Staffel of III./JG 3 had downed a B-17 at 1445. There was no doubt now that the 2,039th victory of III./JG 3 took place at 1445 hours on the afternoon of February 25. As I stared at the entry for Clemens, I realized that the ME-109 fighter pilot's third victim might very well have been Don Henderson's aircraft. If I wanted to be certain, I would need to link Clemens's kill to the Willmandingen area.

Too impatient to wait for Penker, I decided to try and trace the Clemens family. I asked Rabe if he knew of any way to locate Curt Clemens's next of kin. He told me that the only resource he was aware of was the Deutsche Dienststelle (the Wehrmacht Information Office, or WASt) in Berlin, and added that my chances of finding the family were about as good as "finding a penguin in a sandstorm." I told Rabe that in the course of my research I had already found my share of penguins!

While I waited for responses from the Bundesarchiv-Militärarchiv, Rudi Penker, and the WASt, I developed a curiosity about Augsburg. What had it been like to be a resident of the city during the daylight bombing raid of February 25, 1944? I wondered about the price paid by the people on the ground. What was their perspective of the attack? Did the United States cause much damage to the Messerschmitt factories? What was the human cost? Perhaps Hans Grimminger could help me understand what the people of Augsburg had experienced during the raids. Grimminger's letter answered my questions. He had not been present during the raid, because he was not born until January 1945, but he had collected a great deal of information over the years:

> The US raid of 25 February 1944 was the first "heavy" air raid against the Messerschmitt aircraft factory in the southern parts of Augsburg. The target was the headquarters of the Messerschmitt company. In addition to the administrative complex, the site contained production lines for types: the two-engine fighter-bomber, the ME-210, the reconnaissance aircraft, the ME-410, and Hitler's ME-262 jetfighter, the ME-163 rocket fighter, and the ME-264 "American" bomber. The Messerschmitt Works employed about 17,000 people—9,000 Germans and 8,000 imprisoned foreigners.
>
> The American bombs hit all parts of the Messerschmitt Factory; causing a break in production. After the attack some of the production was moved to smaller factories outside of Augsburg. In Haunstetten and in the district along the Haunstetter-Strasse, bombs hit many civilian houses.

At least two hundred people were killed in the U.S. raid, the youngest victim just one month old. Twenty of the victims were under fourteen years of age. The oldest was seventy. . . . At the time of the raid, 195,000 people lived in Augsburg.

In writing about the history of Tony's last flight, I wanted to understand every aspect of the mission, from as many angles as possible. As the details were coming together, I was indeed getting all the necessary perspectives. The witnesses to my story would represent the viewpoints of the American and German airmen, the families of the fallen B-17 fliers, and the villagers of Willmandingen. The experiences of the citizens of Augsburg must also be taken into account.

THE ME-109 PILOT

As 1998 drifted by, there was still no response from Rudi Penker. I still needed to prove that Curt Clemens was the pilot who shot down Tony's B-17, and Penker was someone who could help me put that last puzzle piece into place. I wanted to find the record that had helped him come to his conclusions, and I wanted to locate Clemens's family and obtain photographs.

Perhaps Penker was unhappy with me. After all, I had the Don Henderson crew photos he wanted. Frustrated by his silence, I asked Marcus Mockler to give him a call. As usual, Marcus was extremely helpful. After contacting Penker, he told me that Penker had gotten his information from a friend, and had made handwritten notes—but he had not seen the documents himself. If I wanted to get copies of the original documents, I would need to contact the military archives in Freiburg, Germany.

Rabe Anton, the archivist at the Air Force Historical Records Agency, had told me that the WASt in Berlin might be able to help me find Curt Clemens's next of kin. On February 11, 1999, I finally received a letter from the WASt. Enclosed was information on a "Kurt Clemens," born November 28, 1911, in Spitzkunnersdorf, Germany. Also provided was a 1940s address for Clemens's wife, Anna, also of Spitzkunnersdorf.

I conducted a web search in hopes of finding someone in Spitzkunnersdorf who could help me locate Anna. A good Samaritan by the name of Klaus Friedrich volunteered to help. Klaus quickly made contact with eighty-eight-year-old Anna and confirmed that her husband had indeed fought for Germany during World War II. Although she was in poor health, she agreed to communicate with me via Klaus. Over the course of 1999, Klaus and I corresponded on and off via e-mail. Although I learned nothing from Anna about her husband's Luftwaffe days, Klaus did scan three images and send them to me. One was a letter describing Clemens's burial site; the others were photographs of Kurt Clemens and his gravesite. The letters referred to Kurt as having been killed on February 17, 1945, near a village called Hummersum. I was glad to have a photo of Kurt Clemens, but disappointed that it showed him in civilian clothes. He looked nothing like my mental image of a German pilot. It did not register with me at first, but according to Rudi Penker, Clemens's first name was spelled with a "C," and he had died on January 27, not on February 17. There was a serious discrepancy here.

Once again, Hermann Möck proved an invaluable ally. When he learned about my correspondence with Anna Clemens and my concerns about the inconsistencies, he offered to make some inquiries of his own. I am grateful that he did, because his research turned up a Curt Clemens who had been born on February 17, 1923. This Curt was a member of III./JG 3. It seemed evident that the WASt had inadvertently sent me on a wild goose chase. Hermann had found the real Curt Clemens.

I posted the new information on the Luftwaffe and Allied Air Forces Discussion Forum, hopeful that an interested person could confirm Hermann's data. Within a day, I received a response from John Manrho, a researcher from the Netherlands. Manrho had been studying the Luftwaffe pilot Curt Clemens for an upcoming book, and he confirmed the accuracy of the data presented by Hermann Möck. Toward the end of 1944, he told me, Clemens was the most experienced pilot within the 11th Staffel of JG 3. He also led the squadron for a time as the squadron leader (*Staffelführer*) in November of 1944. John added that in 1998 he had checked the records at the VDK, the German War Graves Committee in Kassel, but no known grave had ever been registered for Clemens. Because he was killed near Scharnikau, Poland, Manrho believed that Clemens was probably buried in an unmarked grave.

According to the JG 3 *Verlustmeldung* (Loss List), the Clemens family was living in Saarbrücken in 1945. Manrho suggested that I make an attempt to locate them. He asked me to share any information I might find with him, since he too was interested in Curt Clemens. Using a German people-search website, I retrieved the names and addresses of forty-four people in Saarbrücken with the surname Clemens. I sent each of those households a form letter, in English and in German, asking whether they were related to Luftwaffe pilot Curt Clemens. I explained that I wanted to understand the battle in which my uncle died from the German pilot's perspective. I wanted to learn more about Curt Clemens, and I was especially interested in obtaining copies of any relevant wartime letters and photographs.

Three weeks later, I received a letter from Günter Clemens—Curt's brother. He expressed a willingness to answer my questions, and he enclosed several photographs of his brother, as well as a portion of a letter from Curt dated February 25, 1944:

> In the last week, every day, we had heavy air battles. Even today, I already have two difficult patrols behind me. You can imagine how stressful this is on your nerves. In total, I now have 6 victories. Today I returned with a machine that looked like it was cut through like Swiss cheese. Yes, the Tommies aren't throwing "baked apples" at us. Well I better close now since I still need to write my reports, yes the paper war is almost worse then the four motor one.

I now had photographs of the "real" Curt Clemens, including two with his mother near his ME-109! Within a couple of weeks, I sent Günter a CD-ROM containing high-resolution scans of his three photos along with photos of Tony, aircraft 42–37786, and the crash site in Willmandingen. In the accompanying letter, I quoted the relevant excerpts about his brother from Jochen Prien's book on III./JG 3, with which he had not been familiar.

I reflected on the extract from Curt's letter. As I had already learned both from Prien's book and from Rudi Penker, III./Jagdgeschwader 3 had fought two battles on February 25, one against the Fifteenth Air Force in the morning, and another in the early afternoon against bombers returning from Augsburg. Curt mentioned that during the second battle, he shot down his sixth enemy aircraft. The enemy had

Jagdgeschwader Udet pilot
Feldwebel Curt Clemens in
April 1944. Photo courtesy of
Günter Clemens,
Saarbrücken, Germany.

fought back—shooting up his plane so that it looked like Swiss cheese!
Knowing that Tony's crew had had just such a fight with their ME-109
pursuers, I was now more determined than ever to prove that Curt
Clemens and Tony Korkuc had met in the skies above Germany.

With renewed enthusiasm, I again pursued Rudi Penker in hopes
of finding Clemens's victory claim. Yet again I received no response. I
decided to try a different approach, and posted a message on the
Luftwaffe and Allied Air Forces Discussion Forum indicating that I now
had some photographs of Curt Clemens, and was seeking help from
Rudi Penker. That afternoon, a contemporary of Penker's saw the message and contacted Rudi. Within hours, Rudi Penker e-mailed me:
clearly my newfound information had given me new leverage.

Rudi made it clear that he had never personally found a claim report
from Curt Clemens regarding the shootdown of Henderson's B-17;
he had learned the details from a good friend of Jochen Prien. That
researcher had discovered the claim on a Luftwaffe index card while

Curt Clemens poses with his mother near his ME-109 G-6 at Bad Wörishofen airfield in Germany in 1943. Photo courtesy of Günter Clemens.

Close-up of Mrs. Clemens and son Curt with his ME-109. Photo courtesy of Günter Clemens.

working in the military archives in Freiburg, but there would be no easy way to find that card again. Rudi had compiled a list of all Luftwaffe claims for February 25, 1944, and Clemens was the only pilot whose claim fit the time and location of Henderson's downed aircraft. However, it appeared that Clemens's original claim report for February 25 no longer existed. I thanked Penker for his work in establishing the association between Clemens and the plane that had crashed in Willmandingen. I knew that without his help, I would never have made the connection. I sent him the photographs he wanted in exchange for his version of the Luftwaffe Claims List.

I then called upon my friends Rabe Anton and Don Caldwell again, asking whether they knew of anyone in Germany who could help me obtain the records from Freiburg. Both referred me to Winfried Bock, a respected German researcher who was reputed to have one of the most extensive collections of Luftwaffe Victory and Loss Records of both day- and night-fighter operations. I contacted Bock, who confirmed that Clemens's claim was the only one that fit the time and place of the aircraft brought down at Willmandingen. Bock added: "Curt Clemens was a member of III./JG 3 'Udet' 8. Staffel. His victory of 25 Feb 1944 was officially confirmed by the Reichsluftfahrtministerium [German Air Ministry] or R.L.M. as the 201st victory of 8./JG3." It was clear that Penker's analysis of the available records was accurate. In the absence of the original claim form from Clemens, I now set my sights on finding the Luftwaffe Claims List issued by the RLM.

I posted a request on the Bundesarchiv-Militärarchiv (BA-MA) website in Germany in hopes of finding a researcher who could check the archives in Freiburg for the two pieces of information that Rudi Penker had linked together—the flak report and the RLM claim. I emphasized that the Abschussmeldung (victory report) no longer existed for the February 25 victory. The BA-MA gave me the names of two researchers, one of whom, Sebastian Remus, had an e-mail address. I contacted him, asking whether he could obtain copies of the two documents. I explained that although Rudi Penker had no index numbers with which to locate the reports, I knew that both were located in Freiburg. In early October, I received a copy from Remus of one of the two reports I was seeking. He had found the flak report but was having trouble finding Clemens's claim.

According to a German report, at 1440 on February 25, 1944, four batteries of Heavy Flak Battalion 436 (o) claimed a hit on a Fortress II, which then crashed in Willmandingen. The claim was filed by battery units 1, 2, 4, and 6, as shown in line numbers 4–6 of the report. Luftwaffen-Personalamt Abschuesse durch Flak U. fliegende Einheiten February 1944, Bundesarchiv-Militärarchiv, Freiburg, Germany [hereafter BA-MA], from microfilm 2026 Teil I/Film 1.

The First, Second, Fourth, and Sixth batteries of Schwere Flakabteilung 436 (o) (Stationary Heavy Flak Battalion 436) had filed a claim in reference to a B-17G model aircraft that crashed in Willmandingen at 1440 on February 25, 1944. In the winter of 1944, Schwere Flak-Abt. 436 (o) was part of the Stuttgart air defense. The anti-aircraft battalion was made up of six batteries. Each battery consisted of six 88mm cannons clustered close together. The first battery, 1./Schw. Flak Abt. 436, was located either in the Burgholzhof or the Mühlbachhof area of Stuttgart. The second battery was located in the Stuttgart–Bad Cannstatt area, while the fourth and sixth batteries were co-located close to Schmiden.

Despite twenty hours of research at a cost of $420, Remus had been unable to locate Clemens's February 25 victory claim. I was sure there must be some way to find it, so I turned my attention once again to the Internet. I ran a web search on "Luftwaffe Fighter Claims," hoping to find listings similar to those found by Penker. As has been true so many times in my research, luck was on my side. I found a JG 2 claims list compiled by British historian Tony Wood.[3] The listings included each pilot's name, his organization, the date and time of the victory, and the location of the crash.

Since Wood's list contained hundreds of entries, I concluded that he must have had access to some kind of official records. I posted a new message on the Luftwaffe and Allied Air Forces Discussion Forum, asking whether anyone knew where Wood had gotten his information. My online friend and mentor Don Caldwell, author of the JG 26 books, responded: "Tony Wood's claims list has its origin in the microfilm 'discovered' in the Bundesarchiv-Militärarchiv in the 1990's. There are a half-dozen distinctly different documents found on this microfilm, but the main file, the 'ledger,' includes locations for all claims." At last! If I could contact Tony Wood, perhaps he would lead me to the correct microfilm so that I could validate Penker's work.

By asking the question in the public forum, I made it possible for anyone who visited the 12 O'Clock High! website to see my exchange with Don Caldwell. Luckily for me, a researcher in Australia was monitoring our discussion and contacted Don. Within hours, Don sent me the following e-mail:

> Ah, the miracle of the Net! I've loaned Russell Guest in Australia two of my microfilm rolls, to see what he could decipher. Fully unprompted, he noticed our discussion on the Twelve O'Clock High board, and volunteered that one of the rolls contained the Clemens III./JG 3 claim for 25 Feb 44: 'Clemens at 1445, 15km SE Reutlingen, 5000–2000m.' Hope this answers your question satisfactorily—we've saved you big bucks, in any event.

Remarkably, Don had found my claim! I had spent four months and close to 1,000 Deutsche Marks trying to track it down, and Caldwell and an Australian researcher had found it in less than two days!

Russell Guest lacked the resources to provide me with a hard copy of the claim, but I was able to get one from Tony Wood. I finally had the elusive RLM listing that I had spent close to two years searching for. I now had proof that Curt Clemens was the pilot who had downed my uncle's aircraft. I was now fully satisfied that it was Don Henderson's crew who had turned Clemens's ME-109 into "Swiss cheese."

Line 17 shows the claim filed by Uffz. Curt Clemens for downing a Fortress II fifteen kilometers southeast of Reutlingen at 1445 on February 25, 1944. Luftwaffen-Personalamt Tageliste 1 August 1943–29 February 1944, BA-MA, from microfilm C2025N I Teil.

I wrote another letter to my new friend Günter Clemens, requesting more information about his brother. He responded eagerly, and I also received some information from a first cousin of Curt's who was living in California, Rosemarie Hunt. According to Günter, Curt "started attending gliding classes as early as the age of fourteen. Flying was his sole hobby. Yet, he was rather athletic and engaged in life saving swimming, for example." Rosemarie added, "I remember Curt very well. I was twelve when he was killed. At the end of the war, Hitler drafted young boys. Curt was a very well mannered and talented young man. He excelled in school. When he became a pilot, he excelled at that also. I am sure that in his mind he was brave by protecting his people from the enemy bombers."

To give me a better understanding of Curt's wartime exploits, Günter shared excerpts from two letters that his brother wrote home to update his mother on his progress as a young Luftwaffe pilot. After sixteen unconfirmed victories over the enemy, Curt proudly related news of his promotion to *Feldwebel,* or sergeant, on April 25, 1944, two months to the day after his air battle with the Don Henderson crew. "Today I got a delightful surprise. Perhaps you already noticed it based on the sender. When I came back from my last mission and recorded my sixteenth shootdown, I was promoted by my squadron commander, based on my bravery in the face of the enemy, to the rank of sergeant. Three shootdowns of mine are not officially recognized because I didn't have any witnesses. But thirteen is also a good number, don't you think?"

Surprisingly, Jochen Prien's history credited Clemens with only four victories by April 25. According to Prien, Curt's February 25 victory was his third. From Clemens's own perspective, by February 25 he had downed six planes, and over the next two months he registered another ten victories. But as with the Allied air forces, victories were not recognized unless there were witnesses.

A letter from Curt dated July 18, 1944, illustrates the difficulties encountered by the Luftwaffe after D-Day:

> God must have crossed his fingers for me. You don't have to worry about me for a while. I'm done with flying for a while. Maybe I'll even be lucky enough to take some vacation time. In any event, I would probably be on crutches the next time. Let me give you the details: I'm lying in a military hospital in northwestern France. On June 21, 1944, almost exactly four weeks after the last time, I was shot down here in the countryside. I was separated from my squadron and got caught in an uneven air battle, one versus eight. I struggled for over a quarter of an hour to try to get myself out of the situation as well as possible. Then I heard a crackling sound in the cabin. A fire then broke out in the cabin and my clothes burst into flames. I ejected. But as my parachute opened, it too began to burn. With a half-burned chute I came down pretty roughly and broke both legs. Other than that, I came out with minor burns on both wrists and a little on my face. I'm no longer beautiful (joking).

In less than a month, Curt Clemens had twice been shot out of the sky. His mother must have been relieved to hear that her son would not be put in harm's way for a while. But just six weeks after suffering two broken legs, he was once again flying an ME-109, as evidenced by another recorded aerial victory.

As the final year of the war dawned, Curt's days were numbered. Just eleven months after downing B-17 42–37786, Feldwebel Curt Clemens suffered the same fate as my Uncle Tony. On January 27, 1945, he was killed in an ME-109 G-14 during a low-level attack on a Russian anti-aircraft gun while northwest of Scharnikau, Poland.[4] Unlike the Korkuc family, the Clemens family was never told what had happened to Curt's remains. "We never learned any information about whether anything of Curt was found or where he was buried," Günter said. "I doubt the Russians made any effort to mark the grave location, considering how much the Russians hated the Germans. So my mother was never afforded the comfort of seeing the location of his grave or his tombstone."

I had finally proved that Curt Clemens and my Uncle Tony had met in the skies over Nazi Germany. I felt fortunate that I was able to get to know Curt Clemens a little better. I felt sorry that both men had to pay the ultimate sacrifice for their countries. Given their boyish smiles and their mutual pride in their ability as aerial combatants, I wondered whether, had the times been different, Tony Korkuc and Curt Clemens might have been friends.

CHAPTER 10

The Eagle and the Swallow

In February 1999, I got advance word that I might need to travel to Europe on business. Perhaps I could finally visit Willmandingen. Marcus Mockler assured me that he would be glad to act as my guide while I was in Germany. A few months later, however, my business trip was canceled. I was deeply disappointed; I was so busy at work that a trip to Germany on my own time did not seem possible. Rather than alert Marcus about the cancellation, I decided to simply let the matter drop. Given the length of time since our last contact, perhaps he had forgotten about my tentative travel plans. But as September approached, I received an e-mail message from Marcus: he hadn't forgotten—he wanted to help me finalize the arrangements for my trip.

Knowing that Marcus was willing to line up the Willmandingen eyewitnesses for me, and that he planned to take a couple of vacation days from work, I decided to go ahead and make the trip, and settled on the week of September 25. I was to fly first to London, then to Stuttgart. Pilot Curt Clemens used an airfield in Echterdingen, near Stuttgart, on February 25, 1944, when he started his journey to intercept Tony's Flying Fortress. It seemed fitting that I should see Stuttgart from the air and get a taste of what Clemens might have seen. Marcus told me that Herman Möck and Wilhelm Speidel were both looking forward to meeting me, but Hans Grimminger would unfortunately be away on business.

As my trip neared, I bombarded Marcus with travel-related questions. How would I get around Germany? Should I buy a Eurail pass? Would there be automatic teller machines? Where would I stay? How would I communicate with people? Marcus patiently answered each question. He assured me that he would be at the Stuttgart airport to pick me up, and he would take care of all of my lodging concerns while I was in Germany. He sent me a photo of himself so that I could identify him at the airport. All I had to do was get to Stuttgart, he said, and from then on he would take care of everything. Despite more than two years of e-mail communication, I knew little about Marcus's personal life. Since I was single, I assumed that he was, too. When I asked him, I learned that I could not have been more wrong: he was married and had six children.

Meanwhile, I sent away for some tourist literature on Willmandingen. Within a couple of days, I received a package from Sonnenbühl containing information on its four villages—Genkingen, Undingen, Erpfingen, and Willmandingen. It included an interesting booklet about the twelve-hundredth anniversary of Willmandingen in 1972. I would be visiting a village that was 1,227 years old! Even though Willmandingen had stood through more than 428,000 days of history, the event of February 25, 1944, was documented: "World War II caused little damage to Willmandingen. The village suffered no direct air raid attacks during the war. On [25] February 1944, over the Willmandingen skies, a German fighter plane downed an American four-engine bomber."[1]

On the day of the trip, Martha, my girlfriend of just over seven months, drove me to Boston's Logan Airport. During our first couple of dates, she had told me that she admired me for my passion in telling my uncle's story. Months later, she would tease me that she continued to date me in spite of it.

During the flight, sleep would not come easily. Mentally I played back everything I had learned since I began the project. I thought about the visit to Arlington with my father. I recalled the St. Patrick's Day package that began my acquaintance with the 381st Bomb Group. I remembered the exhilaration I felt when I realized that four men had survived the Augsburg bombing mission, and I recalled my conversations with them. I thought about my interactions with Marcus, and my first views of the crashed B-17. In my mind's eye, I reread the official documents and letters that had shed light on my understanding of Tony's last mission. I recalled the priceless in-flight photos taken by Richard Brown and my encounters with the crew's families. Their stories and sorrows had taught me much about the price paid by the next of kin. I recalled Raoul Ramos's poem, dedicated to his fallen crewmates.

The crash site of Flying Fortress 42–37786 can be seen in the center of the rectangular field shown in the lower left corner of this contemporary aerial view of Willmandingen. Photo courtesy of Ute Hailfinger, Gemeinde Sonnenbühl, Germany.

My plane touched down near dawn in London. A little more than three hours later, I boarded a British Airways flight for Stuttgart. As I settled into my seat, I tried to imagine what Tony had felt that Friday morning in 1944. I was about to travel on a similar path, for his aircraft had also flown through London's airspace and passed just thirty-five statute miles north of Stuttgart as it approached its target. Unlike Tony, however, I was finally overcome by exhaustion, and I slept for most of the short flight.

Disembarking at Stuttgart, I headed for the baggage claim area. As I waited for my luggage to appear, I heard a voice call out, "Korky!" Turning, I recognized the face of my friend Marcus Mockler. He smiled brightly, extended his hand to me, and welcomed me to Germany. His English was perfect. En route to Marcus's home in St. Johann, we made a side trip to Echterdingen, where I photographed a field on the outskirts of town that a local resident had said was probably the location of the 1944 ME-109 air base.

Forty-five minutes later, we pulled into a small driveway in the village of St. Johann. I was greeted by Marcus's wife, Susanne, and the Mockler children. "Hallo, Korky!" they chorused. After freshening up, I sat down to share a late lunch with the family. The children were all smiles, and I immediately felt at ease. We all laughed as the little ones at the table jibber-jabbered at each other in a language that was neither German nor English!

The next morning's drive from the Mockler home to Willmandingen was short, and before I knew it, Marcus pulled his car into a small parking lot outside a restaurant. Four men were waiting for us, two of whom I recognized. They were Hermann Möck, who had actually witnessed the crash, and Willmandingen's resident historian, Wilhelm Speidel. The others were Karl Heinz, a childhood friend of Hermann's and also an eyewitness, and a town official who was on hand to welcome me. To help make my first visit more memorable, the town official presented me with an aerial color photograph of Willmandingen encased in glass. In turn, I presented them with a copy of Richard Brown's in-flight photos, the photo of Don Henderson's crew, and a portrait of my Uncle Tony.

Hermann Möck was carrying a small cardboard box and three black and white photographs. As Marcus translated Hermann's words, I learned that the box contained artifacts removed from the crash site, including two rusted and mutilated .50-caliber gunner's shell casings and a .50-caliber bullet. There were also some unrecognizable chunks of metal that had once been pieces of Flying Fortress 42–37786. It was possible that Tony Korkuc had fired the gunner's shells that were now in my hands. I was touching a special piece of my uncle's history. Marcus then drew my attention to the three photos, explaining that they were taken in the spring of 1944. Together with the photo that I already had, these represented all the known views of the crash site. Hermann wanted me to keep the items he had brought, as a lasting memory of my visit. I was deeply moved by this special gift.

We started to talk about the events of 1944. Marcus interpreted as I conversed with the two eyewitnesses. Hermann Möck remembered that the German pilot had visited Willmandingen two days after the crash, to see the American bomber for himself. He told the villagers that he had tried his best to get the plane to make an emergency landing, but the American pilot wouldn't cooperate. Every time the ME-

109 seemed to let up on its pursuit of the bomber, the B-17 would climb. Several times the ME-109 pilot relaxed his pursuit, only to see the B-17 fly defiantly on, attempting to gain some altitude and increase its distance from the fighter. Each time this occurred, the pilot tried to force the bomber down, but he was unsuccessful. Whenever the B-17 felt free to go up, it did. Knowing that I had spoken to the Flying Fortress pilot, Marcus translated a question from Hermann: "What was the American pilot's objective as he flew over Willmandingen?" I explained that Henderson was trying to get his plane to Switzerland. I asked the eyewitnesses if they recalled seeing more than one ME-109 over the village. Both were certain that by the time the planes neared Willmandingen, there was only one ME-109.

Wilhelm Speidel suggested that we continue the discussion from the high bluff overlooking Willmandingen, which would give me a better understanding of the flight path of the two aircraft. As we stood on the ridge looking down at the village below, I wondered whether anyone had been up on that same ridge in 1944 when the two airplanes tangled. During my visit to New Hampshire's Pease Airport the previous week, I had watched a B-17G Flying Fortress take to the air. With the sight and sounds still fresh in my mind, I had little trouble visualizing Tony's airplane coming into sight over the opposite ridge.

As we collectively looked back in time, the eyewitnesses told me what they saw that February day. The B-17 had crested the ridge, with the ME-109 in hot pursuit. The planes were flying at an altitude of about 500 feet. An airman (Jack Fournier) bailed out, falling into a grove of trees. Seeing that one man had already jumped out of the plane, it appeared that the German fighter pilot was resisting the temptation to finish it off. But instead of trying to land, the bomber attempted to gain more altitude. The German then fired again at the battle-worn bomber, trying to shoot it out of the sky. As the Flying Fortress limped onward, it flew dangerously close to the village. At that moment a second airman (Nick DeRose) bailed out of the plane, followed by Henderson and Ramos. A few seconds after Henderson, the fifth and last man bailed out, but his parachute got caught on the plane and never fully opened, and he fell to his death as the plane slammed into a hill beyond the grove of trees in the distance.

As I tried to imagine the drama that took place, the trees blocked my view. I could no longer see the plane. The sound of the explosion filled my ears, and the fireball and smoke came into view. Young Hermann Möck, seeing the last moments of the battle, watched as the German fighter circled overhead. With those moments of 1944 still fresh in my mind, I emerged from my reverie and heard Marcus telling me that next we would drive over to the opposite ridge. From there, we could visualize the final approach of the Flying Fortress before it crashed into the hill outside of Willmandingen. Climbing back into the car, I felt dazed at the realization that fifty-five years earlier, Tony's four-engine bomber had flown over Willmandingen almost exactly as it had just been described to me by the two German eyewitnesses. Had I stood on that ridge in 1944, I would have experienced those last seconds of the air battle as I had just "seen" it.

After crossing to the other side of the valley, we stopped about three hundred yards from the crash site. Karl Heinz and Hermann Möck, wanting to add to the drama of my visit, told me more about the air battle that had taken place directly over our heads. As we got out of the car, Wilhelm Speidel asked me, "If it's true that the German fighter gave the Americans time to bail, why didn't the men take advantage of that opportunity?" I explained again that Henderson's objective was to reach Switzerland. Also, Henderson had told me that the plane was in rough shape. He might have felt that it would be impossible to put it down in one piece, so he was simply trying to gain enough altitude for his crew to bail safely.

Karl Heinz described his memory of the crash:

It was a winter day when the plane came down. The townsfolk were in the process of clearing the snow from the roadway to the next village when they first became aware of the approaching disturbance. They saw what looked like a big bird, something like an eagle, being followed by a little bird, something like a swallow. For a while it just looked like birds, but as they approached closer, they could tell that they were airplanes coming down. They saw one man bail out several hundred meters from our position. This man they captured, he was arrested and brought to the village. There was an explosion in the plane, before it actually crashed. That's what I saw. . . . Despite the problem of getting through the snow, the townspeople from the neighboring villages came from all over to see the burning enemy bomber.

My first view of the hill where Tony's B-17 crashed. Photo by author.

When Heinz had finished, I was startled to hear a bell ringing in the distance. According to the official American Graves Registration Service report from 1946, the ancient bells in Willmandingen's bell tower were tolling the Angelus as Tony and the five other men were buried in the town cemetery.[2] As I heard the last bell chime, a chill went up my spine.

Marcus pulled to the side of the road and parked his car next to a wooden fence. On the other side of the fence was a red barn, with horses grazing nearby. Recalling the photos I had seen in the newspaper article, I knew that I would soon be standing on the ground that once held the crumbled remains of my uncle's Flying Fortress. As I looked at the hill in the distance, I spoke emotionally into the video camera: "Dad, this is for you. In attempting to answer your question, this is where Tony's plane crashed. This is where Uncle Tony died."

When the moment at the crash site finally arrived, I was overcome with emotion. Nothing could have prepared me for what I was feeling. As I stood on the hill where my uncle took his last breath, I was moved by the historic and personal significance of the ground beneath

A front view of the site where Flying Fortress 42–37786 crashed in Willmandingen in 1944. Just to the right of center are the remains of Tony Korkuc's ball turret. Photo courtesy of Mrs. Anna Heinz Ulmer, Willmandingen, Germany. Original scanned by Ulli Semmelrock.

my feet. I walked alone on the hill for a while, and then Marcus approached and asked me a question. Although the B-17 had been traveling in a southwestward direction, it had made a last-second bank to the right, and crashed facing northeast. Many of the townsfolk at the time thought the pilot had intentionally banked his plane so that it would strike the town. Marcus wondered if I had any light to shed on that troubling subject. I pointed out that all Don Henderson wanted to do was escape from the plane with as many of his men as he could. Having talked to Don, I knew that damaging the village was the farthest thought from his mind. It seemed more likely that when he disengaged the autopilot just before bailing out, the B-17 made a lunge for the ground. The men seemed satisfied with my explanation, and willingly set aside the local belief that the American plane was deliberately aimed at the village during its death throes.

As we prepared to leave the crash site, I spoke into the video camera: "Tony, I have traveled halfway across the world to see the hill where

Right side view of the crash site showing the tail section of 42–37786. Photo courtesy of Mrs. Anna Heinz Ulmer. Original scanned by Ulli Semmelrock.

you were killed. I want to let you know that I traced you from your final resting place at Arlington to the crash site. May you rest in peace." I turned my back on the hill and returned with Marcus to his car. He said that we had one last stop to make: Hermann and Karl wanted me to see the site of Tony's first burial. Recognizing that the road we were driving on was the only way to get from the hill to the town, it dawned on me that the Germans must have used that same road when they carried the Americans' bodies into town. I was following the path my uncle's body had taken in 1944, as he too left the hill.

The drive to the cemetery was short. My first impression was that all the plots were adorned with beautiful flowers. Hermann and Karl had prepared a special surprise for my visit. Up ahead I could see a solitary wooden cross, placed to mark the location where the six American soldiers once rested. Hermann and Karl had placed a small white sign on the front of the cross that said:

Am 26. Februar 1944 wurden hier, Die sterblichen Überreste der 6 Amerikanischen Flieger beigesetzt—

Anthony Bartolo
Boyd Burgess
Thomas Hunnicutt
Anthony Korkuc
Dale Schilling
Earl Wonning

"On February 26, 1944, the mortal remains of 6 American fliers were buried here." I was moved by this simple but thoughtful gesture on the part of my German friends. On that dark winter's night in 1944, six men were laid to rest in a common grave. In 1999, two eyewitnesses saw to it that a cross would list the names of the dead.

As we stood in the Willmandingen cemetery, we talked about the Germany of 1944. I could identify with the tragedy of losing one's past. I understood how Wilhelm Speidel felt. Now seventy-six years old, he had been a member of the Hitler Youth and a pilot in the Luftwaffe. I understood why he so openly expressed his frustration about Germany's past. My visit there was important to him also. He wanted Marcus and me to understand his point of view. I am a firm believer that you can't understand your future unless you understand your past. As I stood in the cemetery that once held my uncle, I was hopeful that Germany could someday develop a proper perspective on the Third Reich. To men such as Wilhelm Speidel, it was important and necessary for the younger generations to understand their country's history.

Wilhelm spoke up. In 1944, the German populace harbored considerable animosity toward the British and American aircrews who were pummeling their country. Some of the villagers in Willmandingen resisted the idea of burying the Americans in consecrated ground, but the veterans of the First World War calmed them down. The veterans could appreciate the sacrifice that these soldiers had made for their country. Not everyone knew about the terrible crimes being perpetrated by the German government. I responded, "That's true for most wars. The common man doesn't always understand or accept why the war is being fought."

"The most important thing for many German soldiers was simply to survive and return to their loved ones," Speidel continued. That same theme had resonated again and again in my discussions with the

A temporarily placed wooden cross marks the first burial site of Anthony J. Korkuc and his five crewmates in the Willmandingen town cemetery. Photo by author.

At the first burial site of Anthony J. Korkuc with eyewitnesses Karl Heinz (left) and Hermann Möck (right). Photo by author.

Willmandingen eyewitness
Hermann Möck in 1945.
Photo courtesy of Hermann
Möck.

men of the 381st. In one instance, a ball turret gunner had mentioned that he was credited with downing a German fighter, but in the next breath he said that he was not proud of killing the enemy flier. In any case, as I could attest, the Nazis were nowhere to be seen on that dark winter's night in 1944 when the mortal remains of the six enemy soldiers were respectfully laid to rest in the historic village cemetery. As Marcus drove me back to his home, I knew that my three-hour stay in Willmandingen would leave a lasting impression.

With Marcus as my guide, I spent the next three days seeing places of interest in Munich. However, I also wanted to spend some more time in Willmandingen and visit with Hermann Möck at his house. I wanted to hold the motor that Hermann had removed from the B-17 all those years ago. I wanted to hold in my hand the almost new .50-caliber shells that he had personally pulled from the crash site. Marcus agreed to arrange this.

On the morning of Friday, October 1, I returned to Willmandingen with Marcus to visit with Hermann Möck. As we entered the village,

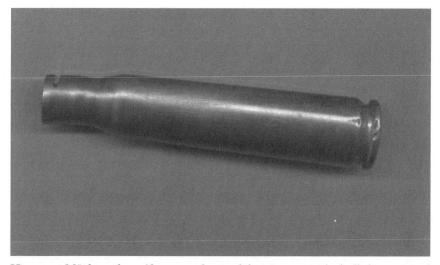

Hermann Möck made a gift to me of one of the two gunner's shells he removed from the crash site in the spring of 1944. The .50-caliber shell was made in 1943. Photo by author.

we once again drove by the hill where Tony's B-17 crashed. Hermann and his wife, Olive, greeted Marcus and me at the door and welcomed us into their home—the same house in which Hermann lived in 1944. Hermann took me into his home office, where a model of Flying Fortress 42–37786 hung from the ceiling. He allowed me to handle the motor he had salvaged from the crash site. It was like touching the plane itself.

I asked whether Hermann could tell me more about the dead American he saw outside the plane—the one who had fallen to his death when his parachute didn't open. Hermann said that the young airman appeared to be sleeping in the snow; he lay on his right side, and the left side of his face was injured. Despite now having seen pictures of the crew, Hermann was unable to determine who the young airman was.

Hermann showed me a scrapbook he had been assembling on the crash of the B-17, and I gave him an original photograph of a 381st Bomb Group B-17 at Ridgewell in 1943 that I had obtained from Chaplain Brown. Hermann left the room for a bit and returned with one of the two .50-caliber shell casings that he had removed from the crash site. He offered it to me, and I accepted the unexpected gift

Susanne and Marcus Mockler. Photo by author.

with thanks, assuring him that it would be a treasured addition to my research collection.

As we drove away from Willmandingen, I was satisfied. I had accomplished the goals I had set for my trip. On my final morning in Germany, Marcus drove me to the airport in Stuttgart, where we bade each other an emotional farewell. I had made a friend for life.

WHO WAS THE FIFTH PARACHUTIST?

Prior to my trip to Willmandingen, I had started to question whether navigator Earl Wonning really was the fifth man to bail out of aircraft 42–37786 on February 25, 1944. The only thing I knew for sure about the last man out was that his parachute got caught on the plane and he died. Another piece of information was added by an eyewitness statement in the American Graves Registration Service report: at the time of burial, one of the men could have been identified. That man was most likely the fifth parachutist.

In 1997, in the course of my phone interviews with Nick DeRose, Raoul Ramos, and Don Henderson, I learned that when Henderson issued the order to bail, Earl Wonning was alive and unhurt. Had he bailed out before DeRose, he most likely would have survived. Don also told me that at or around the time of the bailout order, he sent Ramos into the rear of the plane to check on the gunners, and Ramos reported that all the men were dead. When this was added to the evidence from the Missing Air Crew Report that each of the six men was killed at his gun position, I had concluded that Earl Wonning was the fifth parachutist.

Now, however, I was faced with mounting contradictory evidence. According to the Willmandingen gravediggers—William Möck, coroner Heinrich Möck, and Gottlo Trautmann, the leader of the fire brigade—all the men were badly burned except for one. Of the six men killed in the crash, only Thomas Hunnicutt and Anthony Bartolo were later identified by the American Graves Registration Service. If Earl Wonning was the fifth parachutist and had not been burned beyond recognition, then why hadn't they been able to determine his identity? Now it seemed that the last man out of the aircraft must have been either Hunnicutt or Bartolo. German Report KU-1022 listed the name of only one of the six men killed: Thomas Hunnicutt. On the basis of that report, it was more likely that Hunnicutt was the fifth parachutist.

There were no other strong candidates. In Ramos's letter to the Schilling family, he clearly said that Hunnicutt screamed out that Schilling had been hit. And from Ramos's letter to my grandmother, we know that a couple of minutes prior to the bailout order, Tony had some kind of trouble in the ball turret. With the aircraft power out, maybe Tony was alive but having trouble extracting himself from the turret. There was no information about Boyd Burgess.

With my thinking starting to shift, I was able to put another interesting piece of the puzzle into place. While attending the 1998 reunion of the 381st Bomb Group, I met Mark Douglas, the son of deceased 381st pilot First Lieutenant Earl Horr. On the bomb group's very first mission, on June 22, 1943, Horr's aircraft was shot down, and he spent the next twenty-two months in captivity, just over eighteen of them in the South Compound of Stalag Luft III. My ears perked up when I heard this. Raoul Ramos was also a prisoner at Stalag Luft III. Raoul's name did not ring a bell with either Mark or his mother, but Mark mentioned a book he had at home that might interest me. Titled *Behind the Wire: Stalag Luft III, South Compound,* it contained a listing of every prisoner who had spent time in the South Compound. If Ramos was listed, there might be information surrounding his crash and capture. Mark promised to check. Within a month, I received a letter from him. Not only was there a listing for Raoul, there was vital information. Raoul was entry number 1,289.

According to the book, the numbers two, three, and four superchargers in aircraft 42–37786 had failed. The plane was then attacked by ME 109s, and in the ensuing battle, three men were killed: the tail gunner, the right waist gunner, and the radio operator. This was significant evidence. At the time that he bailed, Ramos was certain only that Dale Schilling, Anthony Bartolo, and Boyd Burgess had been killed. There was no mention of Earl Wonning, Thomas Hunnicutt, or my Uncle Tony. Ramos knew that Wonning was still alive when he bailed out, but did he also believe that Hunnicutt and Tony were still alive at that time? If Bartolo was killed during the fighter attack, and neither Tony nor Wonning was identified, the evidence now strongly suggested that Thomas Hunnicutt was indeed the fifth parachutist. But why had he waited so long to bail out? Was he trying to help Tony out of the ball turret?

I wanted to understand the circumstances in which the Ramos entry had been recorded in *Behind the Wire,* so I contacted the author, Arnold A. Wright of Benton, Arkansas. Wright explained that the book was published to honor a fellow Benton citizen by the name of Ewell Ross McCright, the man responsible for compiling the names of the men who were imprisoned in the South Compound of Stalag Luft III. After McCright's death, Wright saw to it that his wartime diary and notes were published. Ewell McCright had interviewed every new prisoner who arrived at Sagan's South Compound, hoping to expose any Nazi spies. In all, he had filled four ledgers. The new prisoners usually told everything they knew in order to establish their bona fides as Allied airmen.

I learned that the McCright ledgers themselves had an interesting history. Early in 1945, with the end of the regime in sight, the Germans wanted to use the POWs as a bargaining chip with the Allies. The Stalag Luft III prisoners were moved from Sagan, and endured a 480-mile winter trek to Moosburg in southern Germany, not far from Munich. McCright smuggled the four ledgers out of the camp and kept them hidden from the German guards throughout the journey.

Arnold Wright suggested that I talk with Duane Reed, the chief archivist of Special Collections at the United States Air Force Academy in Colorado, where the original ledgers were stored. From Reed I learned that McCright was directed by Lieutenant Colonel A. P. Clark to compile the new prisoner information, in part because McCright was suffering adverse effects from his time behind the wire. Knowing that McCright needed something to do to give him purpose, Clark, the prisoners' "Head of Security," encouraged him to maintain the ledgers, which served to expose potential "stoolies." (Clark, also known as "Big S" or "Big Security," was one of the men who planned the "The Great Escape" later made famous by the movie of the same name starring Steve McQueen.)

Wanting to verify that Arnold Wright had accurately transcribed the Raoul Ramos entry for use in his book, I asked Reed to send me a copy of the handwritten notes that McCright made during his interview with Raoul. Within days, I had in my hands a copy of the original ledger entry. I immediately noted that there were several discrepancies between McCright's version and the one transcribed by Arnold Wright. Wright left out the post office box number, most likely to protect the present-day anonymity of Ramos. In addition, he omitted the fact that Ramos bailed out at 300 feet, and he misspelled the town where Ramos was captured.

Wright chose to omit several other key notations. After McCright's entry on the soldiers who were killed, Wright wrote down only that the tail gunner, the right waist gunner, and the radio operator had been killed. Reading Ewell McCright's actual notes, we see that there were other words written. The words that were omitted appeared to be "RT WING—RT/W/G." I was unable to understand the meaning of this entry, and I suspect that Wright chose to omit the words for the same reason.

The McCright ledger entry had not helped me pin down who the fifth man out of the plane was. So, hoping to find evidence for my new theory that it was Hunnicutt, I turned to the Individual Deceased Personnel Files for Bartolo and Hunnicutt to take a closer look at the reports filed by the American Graves Registration Service. The first time around, I had ignored the evidence because of my belief that Wonning had bailed out of the plane, but on this second look, I found more compelling evidence that Hunnicutt and not Bartolo was actually the

Facsimile of Ewell McCright's handwritten Stalag Luft III ledger detailing his interview with prisoner of war Raoul Ramos on March 2, 1944. Courtesy of Duane Reed, Chief Archivist, Special Collections, United States Air Force Academy, Colorado Springs, Colorado, SL3 Collections, SMS-517.

last man out. After all, with McCright's ledger entry, I knew that Ramos had reported that Bartolo was one of those killed.

Hunnicutt's IDPF contained a "Report of Investigation Area Search," filed on July 1, 1946. It stated that he was identified by his dog tag. According to the "Identification Check List" filed by the Quartermaster Corps on October 29, 1947, Hunnicutt was buried with remnants of his wool sweater, a woolen undershirt, olive drab woolen socks, and remnants of his electrically heated flying suit. Also listed were the remnants of a parachute. I concluded that Hunnicutt was most likely the fifth man to parachute out of aircraft 42–37786.. So now the question was, why had he failed to bail out when he was told to? Was he trying to get someone else out of the plane? Was that someone Earl Wonning, or perhaps Tony Korkuc?

"I DON'T LIKE TO SEE THEM BIG BIRDS DIE"

In November, a little more than a month after I got home from Germany, I received a letter from Richard Brown—the man who hated to write letters. Of all the people I had come across during my research, Richard was the most special. In his letter, he had a number of questions to ask me. Since my work was taking me to back to Indiana, I suggested that we meet. The last time I had traveled up Indiana State Route 69 North was during a trip to Grand Ledge, Michigan, to visit with Nick DeRose in November 1997. Now, two years later, I would be visiting with Dale McCrory's ball turret gunner.

I planned to give Richard a video of my trip. I was hopeful that if we watched it together, it might further jog his memory. The last man to discuss the loss of aircraft 42–37786 in any detail with Richard Brown had been none other than Colonel Lee Hunnicutt, the father of Tommy Hunnicutt. Now, more than fifty-five years after that last interview, Brown was about to debrief the nephew of the ball turret gunner of 42–37786. I hoped that this interview would be as memorable to him as the colonel's had been. We spent six hours together, in the course of which I showed him some images on my laptop computer, and he showed me his World War II scrapbook. We also watched the video of my trip to Willmandingen.

Richard had been friends with my Uncle Tony, although he had known his fellow ball turret gunner only as "Korky." During the interview, he was able to shed some light on Tony's last mission, and on aerial combat of the time. Nick DeRose had never made it clear to me that the German fighters jumped his bomber only after it left formation. I had originally thought that Tony's B-17 was still in formation when they were jumped. But Richard had earlier set me straight on that point. Now he elaborated:

> Oh, no. If they had not left the formation, I'm sure they would have got back. Because that was one of the Germans' favorite tricks—follow alongside or behind, and when a stray fell back for any reason, they would jump on them. They didn't like to attack the formation because it was risky. The formation had a lot of firepower. . . . My pilot, McCrory, was a good friend of Henderson. So when Henderson's plane started acting up, McCrory told me to watch it. While I'm sitting in that ball turret looking all around, I was watching it. I watched other things, too, because I didn't want anybody sneaking up on me. So every once and a while that plane would be way back, and then it would catch up, and then it would be up above us, and then it would drop right back down.

I asked Richard what effect losing the superchargers on three engines would have had on dropping Tony's B-17 out of formation.

Well, it could [have been] the superchargers. Because when you lost
the superchargers, you lost horsepower, and when you did that you fell
behind and there was no way out. Losing three superchargers would be
rare but very possible, very possible. Only once we lost one, and once
we had a runaway engine, where it spun so fast it blew itself all to
pieces. . . . The more I think about it, I think that supercharger thing
sounds like a very plausible reason why they fell behind.

Richard shared his memories of my uncle's crew pilot:

Henderson was an excellent pilot. No doubt his mind was on cor-
recting the problem instead of on the level and true and straight flight.
Truthfully, I just couldn't figure out, nor could my pilot, what in the
world was going on over there. You didn't dare break radio silence; that
was unheard of on the missions. So you just watched them, and we
watched them. Finally, when they fell back, they turned to the left toward
Switzerland. After they dropped down and they made the turn, I kept
on watching them because McCrory told me to. They were getting out
there quite a bit.

Richard's memory of the mission was remarkable. He recalled with
clarity the attack by the enemy fighters:

The first pass the 109s made was a head-on pass, which was their normal tactic. Then I couldn't watch, and it didn't go down. Not on that
first pass, I know it didn't. But I was watching something else, or something else drew my attention away. The next time I looked, I saw two of
them lined up on their tail. Now, the Germans never attacked on the
tail unless that plane was in bad shape. That was almost suicide for the
Germans to come in from the tail. A head-on attack was their best
approach, because the old B-17 just didn't have the firepower up front
that it had in the back. So when the Germans made that tail-on attack,
it had to be because a lot of the guns weren't manned. The men were
dead or getting ready to bail out or something. . . .
[But]when they made that tail attack, that gunner was still alive,
because he was shooting. At least, if the tail gunner were wounded he
would have let the guns drop down when he let go of the handle. But the
guns were up, and I swear they were firing during the tail attack. However,

I did not see the top turret gunner doing anything . . . at that time. I never saw more than two [fighters] on the tail-on attack. There were three on that head on attack that I'm sure of, that was on the first attack. . . .

The last time I saw them, I watched that front-on attack. Then I took my eyes off and then I watched them again. When I looked back, there were two fighters coming in from the rear. After that, I got busy with other things, and I never saw them again. . . . It wasn't on fire or nothing; it was being shot up, though. Three to one, the B-17 didn't have a chance. So I just quit watching. I don't like to see them big birds die. You get so attached to them things. I remember [the attack] well. . . . I felt sorry for the people in it because I knew them. I felt sorry for them because they were so close to Switzerland; another ten minutes would have put them out of reach, and the Germans couldn't have touched them. That part is like watching your own home team losing. You just feel bad. I saw too many of our planes go down.

Richard also recalled the rumors that were spread around the base after the mission:

After Henderson's crew was lost, I heard remarks from the other crews that made me very angry, it made me quite upset. But they figured that [Henderson's] crew was trying to skip out and go to Switzerland. But why would a pilot with just one mission left, why would he do that? I heard this, and I was upset with it. I couldn't say if it were true or false; as I say, we'll never know.

Another thing that comes to my mind. I never thought about it until, well, just today, I was seeing that picture in my mind, and that B-17 was taking no evasive action. If two ME-109s were on my tail, if I was flying that thing, I'd be all over the sky with it. Everything that big bird would do, I'd be trying to do it. Unless she was so sick she couldn't. I mean, she could have been heading down, and down is the only way she could go.

I reminded Richard that Henderson and Ramos were both preoccupied with trying to fix the in-flight engine problems. "If that bird was that sick," he replied, "then that's a good reason why they weren't taking evasive action."

Lost in thought, Richard continued to ponder why Tony's plane had flown so erratically.

Ball turret gunner Staff
Sergeant Richard Oliver
Brown. Photo courtesy of
Richard Brown.

You know, that's odd I never thought about the superchargers causing
them to fly erratically. . . . It's rare that all three of them went out instead
of one or two. Well, when you think about it, if one or two could go out,
why not three. . . . If there had been a close anti-aircraft burst, sometimes the shrapnel would turn to powder and make small holes every-
where. That could have got one side of the plane and the third
supercharger. The [superchargers] also have an oil line that lubricates
them. In fact, that line could have got ruptured and the superchargers
could seize up due to lack of oil. We lost one once on an inboard engine
on the way home. They feathered it; they didn't even to try to run it at
all on the way home on that mission.

Richard questioned the actions of the enemy pilot: "I don't know
how I would have taken it had I been that German pilot and I knew
that plane was going to be interned in Switzerland with the crew on
it. I don't think I would have shot it down." He described a mission in
which he was credited with downing a ME-109:

You know that when I shot that German plane down, I said a little prayer,
I hope he gets out of it, knowing the next day that he could be in another

plane shooting at me again, but still, I never wanted to kill nobody. I still don't. That's one of the reasons that I went into the Air Force instead of the Army. I didn't want to have to look at another human being by sight. When we saw another fighter coming in, I thought that a human being was not there. This was just a machine. There was a man there and I knew it, but I just never thought of it in that sense. Maybe he did. Maybe he just saw a B-17 and wanted to shoot it down.

I asked whether the photographs that Richard had taken of Tony's plane helped him remember the incident.

Oh, yeah, definitely, sure. Course, I remember the incident so well. My pilot was so concerned as I say he was a good friend with the other pilot. He told me, he says, watch him, and I watched him for a long time. Then I got interested in something else that was going on, maybe enemy fighters coming in close or flak or some reason, I took my eyes off of it. Then I looked back and then I took my eyes off. When it was under attack, I watched it but I didn't want to. They must have been firing on the tail on attack but I couldn't tell so much. You see a little trail of smoke that comes over the wing when they're firing their guns. But when they made that head-on attack, my plane was at such an angle that I could see the German fighter right down the barrel, I could see the flash. It's like a neon sign blinking at you. When they made that initial attack, I watched it, then I took my eyes off of it, and I don't know what happened after that for a while. But when I looked back, then they were attacking from the tail. It was all over. That airplane was done. . . . I didn't want to see it go down. When they came in from the rear, I was so sure that nobody was shooting at them. Because them ME-109s just didn't attack from the rear knowing that the tail gunner, the top turret sometimes, and the bottom turret sometimes, could fire back at them. You can get all those guns on the fighter at once. The waist gunners can't reach it because they'd shoot off their own tail off if they tried to get back there.

He reflected on flying as a ball turret gunner: "I'll tell you what, you had to have some guts, because that was one awful scary feeling. You're laying on your back with your feet up here, and you're looking between your heels, out there aiming with two .50-caliber machine guns. It was something else."

Richard Brown, while
training in Amarillo, Texas,
in 1943. Photo courtesy of
Richard Brown.

Richard also talked about the job done by the B-17 pilots.
"Henderson was an excellent pilot. You get a lot of good feelings
toward that pilot; he works hard. Flying in formation was hard work.
I'd see McCrory after the mission; he'd be soaking wet from the per-
spiration. He could hardly hold his arms up. Tight formation is what
saves you." He recalled a mission that demonstrated this key defensive
tactic:

> The fighters did not like to attack a tight formation. I'll never forget
> [one mission], it was a real bright sun shiny day and we were cruising
> along. We could see up ahead of us [one bomb] group and behind us
> another group. All of sudden out there on the horizon there were 250
> German fighters, 190s and 109s. And they come up right alongside of
> us. Well, I figured they were going to make that loop and come in from
> the front, which they always did. But for some reason, and the only rea-
> son I can possibly believe was because our group was so tight, we actu-
> ally had airplanes lapping wings. We were scared. We tucked her in.
> They made their U-turn and went in behind us and hit that group
> behind us. When they went out the other side, there were only six

With ball turret gunner
Richard Brown at his home
in Coldwater, Michigan, in
November 1999. Photo by
author.

B-17s left; the rest of them were going down. Them Germans shot down
the whole bomb group except for those six airplanes. That group lost
about thirty planes.

Richard recalled the bravado of his adversaries: "Those Germans made
great sport in coming right through the formation. I have seen them
come so close I could look over and see their faces. I wouldn't recognize them if they came through again, but you know what I mean. You
could see the man, especially if the sun was shining on his face."
He talked about his favorite crew position:

The position I liked the best was the top turret. . . . In that ball turret,
I felt trapped. . . . [In the top turret] I could stand up and I wasn't so
confined. Even though it was small, but from your shoulders up, your
body stuck out above the airplane. You could look out the Plexiglas and
see pretty well. [If the] servo-motors that turn the ball turret [were
turned off], you [couldn't] get that door open and get up out of there,
you're just stuck down there. There's nothing you could do. If there
was somebody outside, they could shift it into neutral and it turns by
itself. If you turn it to neutral, the weight of the ball turret is such that
the barrels will move straight down, and then you could come out. But
somebody would have had to go back there and grab that lever and
shove it into neutral for the ball turret gunner.

Richard explained that he and his waist gunner, Howard Van Hoozer, had an understanding that if Brown needed help, Hoozer would perform that task for him.

I had learned much from my interview with Richard Brown. He had solved the fifty-five-year mystery of why aircraft 42–33786 had behaved so erratically. As I drove away from Coldwater, Michigan, on that November night, I was more determined than ever to complete my book project. I also wondered what the new year would bring for the both of us.

CHAPTER 11

The Earl King's Demand

As the year 2000 rolled in, my "Uncle Tony research" was almost complete. I had achieved most of my goals, but one last objective was still nagging at me: I wanted to meet and talk with Raoul Ramos. During our last conversation, in October 1997, Raoul had said that he intended to travel across the country to pay his respects to my father. I was touched by his offer, and I patiently waited for him to contact us. But he never made good on that promise. I attempted to contact him several times the following year, but he was never available to talk, and he didn't return my calls.

Over the more than two years since our last conversation, I had come to believe that Raoul simply did not want to meet with me. On those occasions when I was out in California, he was nowhere to be found. On one of my trips west, I was told that he was in Nebraska, and another time, no one in the Ramos household could tell me when he would return. Raoul had been forthcoming when we'd spoken earlier, but now I sensed that he no longer wanted to talk about the war. Nevertheless, I could not give up on him. Only if, like Don Henderson, he sent me a letter requesting that I sever communication with him would I lose hope of someday hearing his side of the story. And now, after hearing Richard Brown's detailed description of the last moments of aircraft 42–37786, I was even more eager to talk to Raoul, the crew's engineer, about the problems the plane was experiencing on that mission. I also wanted to ask him why he wasn't manning his guns during the attacks by the ME-109 fighters.

As my research progressed, I mailed Raoul periodic updates on my findings. I let him know that I had made contact with his wartime friend Virginia Burgess, and that she had given me a copy of his poem

"How Can I Forget." Not once did I receive the slightest acknowledgment from him. In one letter I even pleaded with him to respond, childishly asking whether he had chosen to forget Tony despite his assertion to the contrary in his 1944 poem.

I knew more about the Raoul Ramos of 1944–45 than about the present-day man. Much of the information that I had on the crew had come from the young man he once was. One thing that had always impressed me about Raoul was that he wrote unique letters to each family. The letter that he sent to my grandmother was heartfelt, and has been greatly cherished by the Korkuc family. Raoul Ramos was clearly a very sensitive man. I also valued his willingness to tell the truth, regardless of its impact on the families. With total candor, he told Dale Schilling's father that after the crash, a German soldier was walking around wearing Dale's high school ring. By relaying this fact to the grieving father, Ramos was telling all he knew. He held nothing back.

Fearing that Raoul would never communicate with me again, I decided to look more closely at his poem. I had a sense that it was saying more than met the eye. If I could only understand it, perhaps I could solve the enigma that was Raoul Ramos. I reread the haunting verses:

> That distant haunt of night and day
> Reminds me of a grief,
> Of men who died but not in vain
> And for a true belief
> How Can I Forget!

> A pause that lingers as in dreams
> My thoughts reflect their eyes.
> A humble sadness stare it seems
> For they knew well who dies
> How Can I Forget!

> The day of death arrived so soon
> The Earl Kings demand,
> For those who did not die in vain
> They lost in blood and sand.
> But even though it haunts me so
> Their spirit broken not

Forever lives in Gold and Pride
For Stars and Stripes they fought.
How Can I Forget!

It was clear that Raoul was deeply affected by the loss of his crew. While I was at work one day, I showed the poem to a friend who had spent some time in Germany. He commented that the line "The Earl Kings Demand" reminded him of the poem "The Erl-King" by the eighteenth century German author Johann Wolfgang von Goethe. I located a copy of "The Erl-King" and read it with great interest. In Ramos's poetic tribute to the deceased members of the Henderson crew, was he making reference to Goethe's poem? Was the reference intentional, and if so, might it shed some light on what he was feeling?

In "The Erl-King," a father and his young son are traveling on horseback on a cold night. The father has his arm around the child to keep him safe and warm. While they ride, the father asks the son why he is hiding his face so timidly. The child responds that the Erl-King is nearby. When the son asks why the father can't see what he sees, the father says reassuringly that the boy is simply being fooled by the mist rising along the trail they are riding on. The child listens as the Erl-King attempts to lure him away, promising that they will play games together, surrounded by beautiful flowers. The child questions the father yet again: can he not hear the Erl-King's whispered promises? The father again comforts his child, reassuring him that the sound he hears is only the wind in the trees. The Erl-King then says that his daughters are waiting for the boy to come with them, so that they can tend to him "with sisterly care." When the boy asks why his father cannot see the Erl-King's daughters there waiting for him, the father says that he is only seeing the willows in the night. Frustrated by the child's unwillingness to come with him, the Erl-King finally takes the little boy by force. The boy screams that the Erl-King is hurting him; he cannot free himself from his forceful grip. In a panic, the father spurs his horse to a gallop and races toward home, only to find his son dead in his arms.

I subsequently learned that the Erl-King was the mythical King of the Elves in German folklore who often lured children to their deaths. Said to haunt Germany's Black Forest region, he would also use deception to seduce grown men to come with him. Since Willmandingen is located not far from Germany's Black Forest, I was now fascinated by Ramos's use of the Erl-King in his poem.

There were obvious parallels between the two poems. Both deal with death. The crewmembers who died can be seen collectively as the child in Goethe's poem, and Ramos as the father. Ramos had been sent by Don Henderson to check on the gunners, and he had found them dead or badly wounded and unable to bail out. Just as the father was unable to save his son from the clutches of the Erl-King, Raoul was unable to save his crew. He was haunted by that fact. The second stanza strongly suggests that some of the men in the rear of the plane were not dead but only wounded when Ramos first saw them. They knew that death was coming for them, and there was nothing he could do to alter that fact. As the plane neared the end of its journey, the trapped men accepted death, and silently let Raoul know that it was all right for him to go on living.

Like the father in Goethe's poem, Raoul could not understand why his crewmates were so easily enticed by death. Why were they choosing what the Erl-King offered over life? Why were they so accepting of their fate? Just as the father could not comfort his son, Raoul was unable to reassure his crewmates that they would not be harmed. Whatever attempts he might make to help them, he could not protect them from their inevitable deaths. Perhaps, like Goethe's father, Raoul felt betrayed. Why hadn't the men listened to him and bailed out, choosing life over death? Did they not know that in the end, the Erl-King would only make them suffer?

When Don Henderson instructed Raoul to go back and check on the crew, it is doubtful that the twenty-one-year-old engineer did so in a calm and deliberate manner. He must have been scared; his mind must have been racing. In those few short moments, he found out that the five men in the back of the plane would not survive. Minutes later, he had to force open the bomb bay doors so that he could escape death himself. I believe that he questioned why he survived when others did not. Did he feel guilt because he lived and they died? Had he betrayed them by living? Or had his crewmates betrayed him by dying?

When I first contacted Don Henderson, Nick DeRose, and Raoul Ramos in 1997, I was at the beginning of my journey of discovery. With no appreciation for the physical and mental trauma that each had endured, I lacked the sensitivity to deal with them appropriately. And yet they responded to me out of respect for Tony Korkuc. I now understood that each man had carried away from that last mission a traumatic memory that would haunt him forever. Henderson had lost six members of his new crew. DeRose had failed to save Earl Wonning. Ramos had looked into the eyes of comrades who were doomed to die. By contacting them, I had revived the guilt and trauma from the mission.

Now that I had a better understanding of Raoul Ramos's poem, I could appreciate his reluctance to talk to me further. But I also knew that he was the only one who could help me grasp what had really happened on that last mission. I made up my mind to meet and talk with him—if he would let me.

To prepare myself for approaching Raoul, I studied a report titled "Psychiatric Experiences of the Eighth Air Force: First Year of Combat (July 4, 1942–July 4, 1943)," which had been published in 1944. It gave me further insight into what the crew of aircraft 42–37786 had experienced, and why the survivors were reluctant to resurrect memories of the war. A particularly interesting section covered the cost of "flying fatigue," which occurred when an airman had been exposed to multiple missions too close together—for example, four missions on consecutive days, high-altitude missions, and insufficient sleep. Those conditions certainly applied to the Henderson crew during the last week of February 1944. That week they suited up for combat on six consecutive days—and flew on five of them. Several of the raids took them deep into Germany. Despite their competence as a fighting unit, the lack of sleep must have worked to counteract their coolness under pressure. When their superchargers forced them out of formation, they most likely worked as a team to fix the problem. When their plane was hit by flak and attacked by the three ME-109s, the crew may well have reached their breaking point.

On January 31, 2000, I placed another call to the Ramos residence. Raoul's wife answered the phone. I asked whether Raoul was available to talk, and she said no. I asked whether he had received the information I had been sending him—had he received any of the wartime photos or a copy of his 1944 poem? She said she didn't think he had gotten any of it. I found this hard to believe. Was she censoring her husband's mail? Did Raoul even know about my previous attempts to reach him? My mind was racing with questions and accusations.

Mrs. Ramos politely explained that Raoul had no interest in talking to me. In my frustration, I said that when we had talked on those earlier occasions, he had spoken freely and candidly. Meaning no disrespect toward Mrs. Ramos, I explained that if Raoul truly wanted to sever communications, I needed to hear that directly from him. I delicately expressed my opinion that she was protecting him from me. In response, she attempted to give me some insight into how her husband of more than fifty years dealt with grief. She told me that when Raoul's father passed away, he remained completely stoic; she never saw him cry. I got the impression that Raoul had a tendency to tuck his pain away and not talk about it.

Despite her requests, I asked her to tell Raoul that I had called, and further that I wanted to set up a meeting with him. "I'll tell him that you called," was all she said. Frustrated, I asked whether she was going to tell him *why* I had called. She said no. My frustration level quadrupled with that response. I now believed that Raoul was not being reticent; he did not even know I was trying to reach him. I believed that his wife was ensuring that the two of us would never talk again. If I called back later that night, would Raoul be at home? She said yes.

Later that night, I did call again. As before, Mrs. Ramos answered the phone. Yes, Raoul was at home. No, he would not come to the phone. She had told him that I would be calling, and he had said that he did not want to talk to me. She then politely asked me to respect her husband's wishes and never contact him again. I told her that I would leave him alone. After I hung up the phone, however, I had to wonder: Whose wish was I granting—Raoul's or his wife's? Was Mrs. Ramos protecting Raoul from further hurt?

Despite my promise, I could not shake my desire to speak with Raoul. In May 2000 I contacted Virginia Burgess Prescott by mail and described my recent exchange with Mrs. Ramos. Knowing her enthusiasm for my project, I asked whether she would plead my case to Raoul. She agreed to try, but told me not to hold out much hope; her second husband had served in the Navy in World War II, and he would never talk about the war.

Weeks went by, and I began to resign myself to the likelihood that I would never again talk to Raoul Ramos. Then, a couple of days after the Fourth of July, a letter arrived. It was from Coldwater, Michigan, the home of Richard Brown. It read:

I'm writing to inform you Richard passed away June 21 at home at 10:00 o'clock in the evening. I am sure he would like for me to inform you as he sure enjoyed his talks & his visit with you and admired you so for what you are doing for your uncle. He suffered no pain. Just dropped dead of a heart attack. The doctor said he was dead when he hit the floor. . . .

As ever,

Jean Brown

I was stunned. The man who had sent me the in-flight photos of Tony's plane, the man who hated to write letters but had so generously shared his experiences with me, was dead. I was grateful that his wife had taken the time to let me know. Of all the men of the Greatest Generation that I had had the pleasure and privilege to meet and talk to, Richard was the first I had to mourn.

A couple of weeks later, I found out that I would have to travel to San Diego on business. I struggled with my conscience. I had promised Mrs. Ramos that I would never contact her husband again, yet I still wanted to meet him. Death had denied me further conversations with Richard Brown, and now I feared that death would take Raoul away from me before we could meet. I knew that I had to make one more attempt to talk to him. I would have to go back on my word to Mrs. Ramos. I would have to drive up to his house, knock on his door, and ask to speak with him—with no prior notice.

As the days ticked by, I struggled with my selfish need to speak with Raoul. I felt that it was essential for me to meet him, but I knew that he did not want to meet me. I feared that the meeting might be traumatic for him. I feared that he would be angry with me. The words of Don Henderson's last letter rang in my head: "I don't believe you are aware of the cost to others."

I put together eleven sets of questions that I wanted to ask Raoul. The first group dealt simply with his memory of Tony. I would then ask about the crew and their relationships with one another. My next questions involved the missions in late January and early February after Bill Herrington was forced to step down. If Raoul was still talking to me by the sixth set of questions, I planned to ask him about the last mission. Did he know the identity of the fifth parachutist? Was it Tommy Hunnicutt? Did he recall meeting with Colonel Lee Hunnicutt that morning?

My tenth set of questions focused on specifics about the last mission. What was the crew's demeanor? What happened to the superchargers? How were the engines lost? Was he troubleshooting the engine problems when the three ME-109s attacked? Did he ever get to man his guns during the fight? Did he know what really happened to Tony? Did he know what Tony's last words were? I was hopeful that Raoul would allow me to ask my final question about the relationship between his 1944 poem and Goethe's "The Erl-King." I knew that this final question would bring out his deepest feelings about his crew—if he responded.

When I boarded the plane bound for San Diego at dawn on the morning of July 31, I was nervous. What would the day bring? Would my visit hurt Raoul in any way? Would he open up to me? If so, I knew that I would learn much about Tony and the last mission. I took with me several gifts that I hoped he would accept. One was a gray baseball hat with the Triangle L insignia that I had bought at the Houston reunion. Another was a video of my trip to Willmandingen; I was hopeful that we could watch it together. I had one more gift that I considered giving to Raoul, which I put in my pocket. It was a valuable item, and one I was not certain I could part with. But I took it with me anyway, prepared to offer it to him if I felt the need.

The plane touched down in the late morning. I picked up my rental car and headed north on California Route 5. Within two hours, I pulled into Raoul's street. I parked my car on the opposite side, about three houses from his home. In those last moments before I opened the car door and prepared myself for the final part of my journey, my conscience pressed heavily on me. I was about to break a promise I had made. Did my feelings about Richard Brown's death truly justify my unannounced visit to Raoul Ramos?

I had brought a camera, a microcassette recorder, a notebook containing my questions, and a photo album. Included among the photos was a single black and white image: the 1943 photo of Raoul with his B-17 crew. Finding it hard to hold everything, I decided to leave the baseball cap and the video in the car. If the interview went well, I could always retrieve those items later.

As I walked to the house, I fidgeted with the item that rested in my left front pocket. With each step I took, I wondered what meeting Raoul Ramos would be like. When I approached the house, I was relieved to see that the front door was ajar. I could see inside through the screen door. I rang the doorbell a couple of times, but there was no answer. I walked around the property trying to decide what to do next. I called out, but there was no answer. After waiting about five minutes, I rang the bell again.

An older man, in good physical shape, came to the door. He was dressed in a casual button-up shirt with green shorts. He was wearing sandals with no socks, and his California tan was quite a contrast to his gray hair. Because of his youthful look, I was uncertain whether this was Raoul. As the man looked back at me through the screen door, I asked for Raoul Ramos. He confirmed that I was speaking to him. I stared back at the seventy-seven-year-old man who had flown with my uncle on February 25, 1944, and then I introduced myself.

Raoul opened the door, shook my hand, and graciously welcomed me into his house. When his wife, Edwina, came into the room and asked who was at the door, he responded that it was "that young man," the nephew of one of his wartime crewmates. Raoul invited me to sit down on the couch, then sat down beside me just to my right. I told him that I had some things I wanted to ask him about the war and about what happened on February 25, 1944. He initially said that he preferred not to answer any of my questions. The memory of Tony and the crew was something he wanted to put behind him. He wanted me to respect the fact that he had trouble dealing with his war memories. He explained that the first time I called him, in 1997, he answered my unexpected questions to the best of his ability. But as I continued to press him for answers over the next few months, he became uncomfortable. He found my questioning technique disturbing—not unlike the interrogations he had been subjected to at Dulag Luft just after his capture. During our last conversation in 1997, he had fully intended to travel to Seekonk and pay his respects to my father. But then he became nervous, and he decided that he didn't want to talk to me anymore, because when he remembered the war, his hands began to shake and he got cold sweats.

I didn't know what to say to him. It was painful to hear that I had been the cause of such a reaction. Not wanting to hurt him further, I told him it was best for me to leave, and I started to get up from the couch. Surprised by my abrupt reaction, he gently grasped my arm. "Please don't leave," he said. "You came so far to visit me, and I know you're well-intentioned. I don't think Korky would have done that to my nephew had the circumstances been different. Please stay." I sat back down.

Feeling a little uncomfortable, I told him that in coming to meet him, I had wanted to ask him some questions about Tony, the war, and the last mission. He again said that he did not want to answer them. I asked him whether I could record our conversation, and he quietly said no. Next he respectfully denied my request to have a photograph taken with him. My only image of him would have to remain that crew photo from 1943.

Not certain how to proceed or what to talk about, I began asking him my prepared questions. When he wouldn't respond, I responded for him, telling him what I thought the answers were. When I couldn't answer my own question, I simply went on to the next one. He seemed to accept this approach. I told him how I felt about his wife, that I had wrongly blamed her for denying me access to her husband. He said no, he was intentionally avoiding me. He truly did not want to talk to me. He was afraid of the sensations that had begun surging through his body as the memories came back. He made up his mind that not remembering was the best way for him to deal with his past.

I could see no physical signs of discomfort on his part as he sat beside me, so I began to go through my list of questions. I asked him what he had thought of Tony. Raoul replied that he had the utmost admiration for Tony. Tony had a lot of guts; he was a strong, rugged kid, and had a lot of upper-body strength. I asked whether he knew why Tony was assigned to the ball turret despite being a qualified flight engineer. Raoul replied that when he himself was assigned to the crew by Bill Herrington, it was as the top turret gunner. That left the ball turret for Tony. I guessed that Herrington had probably used height as the determining factor. At five foot six, Tony was two inches shorter than Raoul.

Raoul said that Tony had good morals, and that Tony, Raoul, and Nick DeRose often attended Catholic Mass together. He told me that Nick was not the reason that Tony went to church; each man went of his own accord. He seemed to be clarifying Nick's statement in his letter to my grandmother that Nick was the reason Tony went to church. That was my first indication that Raoul had indeed been reading the letters I was sending him.

Raoul Ramos rests his hand on Tony Korkuc's shoulder, August 1943, Alexandria, Louisiana. Detail close-up from photo courtesy of Nick DeRose.

As we continued to talk, I could tell that Raoul was beginning to like me. Meeting me in person was not as bad as he had thought it would be, based on my intimidating "phone self" of 1997. I told Raoul that I was sure not a day went by when he didn't think about his crew. He looked me straight in the eyes with an expression that seemed to convey agreement. It was as if he were doing the speaking and I were doing the listening. It was as if I were interpreting what was in his heart.

I started to tell Raoul about my research and my proposed book. I told him about all the people who had helped me understand the past—my encounters with members of the other families: Norman Wonning, George Schilling, Jennie Bartolo Domiziano, and Mary Hunnicutt. I talked about the Hunnicutt family's memory that Colonel Hunnicutt had met with the crew on the day of their last mission. I told him of my interactions with Virginia Burgess Prescott, and our recent conversation in which she had described an unexpected snowstorm in South Carolina with youthful enthusiasm. Raoul's eyes lit up when he heard about his old friend. I explained that if he had received a letter from her recently, it was written at my request. He wouldn't acknowledge having gotten it, but I knew that she had kept her word and sent it. At some level, I'm sure that Raoul enjoyed hearing from Boyd Burgess's wife again, even though he wouldn't acknowledge it to me.

I told him about my visit with Nick DeRose and my phone conversations with Don Henderson. Then I started to talk about Richard Brown and the photographs he had taken from the ball turret of

McCrory's plane. I described my daylong visit with Richard, and his recollections of the last mission. At that point I said that Richard Brown's death had been the catalyst for my meeting with Raoul. I knew that it was selfish of me to visit him unannounced, but I felt that I had to meet him. Raoul listened quietly.

I apologized for pursuing him in the way that I had. Because of his pledge to meet my father, I had assumed that he felt comfortable recalling the events of 1944. I also apologized for the way I had questioned him back in 1997; at the time I did not yet understand the trauma the crew had experienced. He graciously accepted my apology, and in turn apologized for his inability to talk about the war. I told him that I understood.

We had reached a sort of balance: he spoke when he felt comfortable, and I talked about my research. When he listened, he looked me straight in the eyes. I could tell that he was not offended by any of the information I was sharing with him. On those occasions when I answered my own questions, I focused on his facial expressions. His eyes often seemed to be signaling agreement with my conclusions. As I talked about the crewmembers from the families' point of view, I could tell that he had respected the hell out of his crew.

I continued to ask my prepared list of questions. Raoul told me that to the best of his recollection, his crew stayed intact after Bill Herrington left and until Don Henderson took over. When I asked him what he'd thought of the crew, he said that he had the utmost respect for every single man. He admitted that he didn't understand the process that the Air Force used to assemble the crews, but he felt privileged to have served with that particular group. They all were good men.

I told him that over the course of my research, I had concluded that my father, Norman Wonning, and Jennie Bartolo Domiziano had all suffered from a lack of proper closure after the loss of their loved ones. Despite the official notices from the Army, the letters from the crewmates, and the funerals that were held, the families were dissatisfied with the answers they received. In contrast, the Hunnicutt, Schilling, and Burgess families had accepted that their loved ones died in combat. I told Raoul that he was a major factor in providing closure for the Burgess and Schilling families. His visit to Virginia Burgess and his very candid letter to George Schilling had made it happen. I mentioned that Nick DeRose's visit to the Hunnicutt family in San Antonio had helped Tommy Hunnicutt's mother accept the death of her son. Only now, with the facts that I had accumulated, were Norman Wonning, Jennie Bartolo Domiziano, and my father finally coming to terms with their loss.

At one point as he listened, Raoul told me that my blue eyes reminded him of Tony's. I was no longer a "Nazi interrogator," but simply Tony Korkuc's curious nephew. It was obvious that he had never forgotten Tony and the other members of the crew. I told Raoul that I was happy to learn about the time when he and Tony cranked down the gears so that the plane could land safely. Raoul elaborated on his memory of that day. He said that Tony was very composed during the incident. With the bomb bay doors open as they flew miles above the earth, the two of them stood on the catwalk together and cranked down the landing gear, then manually closed the doors.

As we sat shoulder to shoulder on the couch, I could feel a strong emotional bond developing between us. Over the course of the talk, I shook his hand several times, and on one occasion as I brought my hand toward him to make a point, he misinterpreted the gesture and grasped my hand to shake it again.

I talked about my correspondence with Günter Clemens, the brother of the German pilot who shot down the B-17. I described my visit to Willmandingen and emphasized that without the villagers' kindness in 1944, Tony's body might never have been returned to the States. I mentioned the video I had taken of the hill in Willmandingen, and offered him the videotape of my trip to Germany, but he respectfully declined. I mentioned the mutilated .50-caliber gunner's shell casings that I had been given. As I was telling him about them, I reached into my left pocket and handed Raoul one of those rusted old shells. He recognized what it was immediately, and as he held it in his hand, fidgeting with it, he was silent for about thirty seconds, his eyes elsewhere. Perhaps for that brief time he allowed himself to be back in that plane again. As he stared at the shell, I told him that I would be honored if he would keep it, and he nodded acceptance. I knew that I had chosen wisely in deciding to give him this gift. For the rest of my visit, that shell never left his hands.

I told Raoul how much I admired him and the rest of his crew, and that I was proud to be telling him about my research. Raoul told me he was sorry that he was not like the others I had spoken to. "I can't give anything back," he said, "at least not in the way you want me to." I told him that was all right—I was pleased that he was sharing with me what he could. Throughout the interview, as he considered telling me more information, all he could say was, "It was very sad." He must have used that phrase five times.

I finally moved into the questions that dealt with his last mission. I shared Richard Brown's observations that Henderson's ship was flying erratically during its last moments in formation. Richard had concluded that malfunctioning superchargers might well have been the cause. That would also explain why the top turret gunner wasn't firing, and why Don Henderson was not able to take evasive action: pilot and engineer were both preoccupied with trying to fix the mechanical problem. I assumed that if this was an inaccurate account, Raoul would react negatively. But he didn't. It seemed that I was on the right track.

I told him that five men parachuted from the plane in its dying moments, and that I thought it was Tommy Hunnicutt who was killed in the process. Perhaps Tommy had been trying to get others out of the plane before he jumped. Might he have been trying to get my Uncle Tony out? Raoul had no comment; he simply listened. I don't think he knew the answers either.

I stared at the last question that I had planned on asking. It was the question I most wanted answered, but it was one that I suspected Raoul would never answer. Nonetheless, I broached the subject. I told him that Virginia Burgess had given me the copy of his poem that he had given her during his visit to South Carolina in 1945. I was uncertain whether Raoul would acknowledge that he understood this last line of questioning. After all, according to his wife, he had never received the poem I sent. But he seemed to know exactly what I was referring to.

As I shared my thoughts about the poem, Raoul seemed to get a chuckle out of my frustrations in trying to decipher it. I confessed that my engineer's mind often lacked the ability to understand the abstractions of poetry, and he seemed a little amused. I told him that I knew he had written the poem to express what he felt in his soul about the loss of Tony and his other crewmates. Raoul's eyes softened as he began to see me as an interested student, seeking information about those verses he had written more than half a century ago. I explained that despite my initial trouble in understanding the poem, I felt that I had unlocked one of its hidden meanings.

I asked whether the line about the "Earl Kings" was an intentional reference to Goethe's poem "The Erl-King." As the question hung in the air, Raoul's eyes signaled that I had finally asked the right question—a question that he was willing to answer. Slowly he nodded his head affirmatively, and he grasped my hand. It was a very special moment. Someone had taken the trouble to gaze across more than fifty years into his soul. In doing so, I had gained an intimate understanding of Raoul Ramos.

I told him what I felt the poem was really trying to say. I thought that he represented the father in Goethe's poem, while his crew collectively stood in for the child. I told him how sorry I was that he was forced to look his dying crewmembers in their eyes, knowing there was nothing he could do to alter their fate. I understood why he could say only that the last mission was "so sad." Knowing that their efforts to battle the ME-109 fighters had helped to save his life, it is no wonder that Raoul maintained such a high regard for the crewmates he left behind. In their dying moments, they were able to let him move on with his life, because they knew full well who was supposed to die that day.

Rather than refute my interpretation, Raoul said simply that the poem was not well written. The stanzas weren't balanced, and he wasn't satisfied with the way the lines rhymed. I disagreed with him. I told him that the poem was an impressive accomplishment for a twenty-one-year-old survivor of an air battle that had killed six of his crewmates, and that it was a haunting and beautiful tribute to the fallen men.

After I had asked my last question, I pulled out my photo album. I showed Raoul the pictures of the ball turret and the crew, and said that because he had his arm around Tony, I could tell that they had been good friends. As he gazed at the crew picture, his eyes were in a distant place.

I knew that it was time to leave, and I thanked Raoul for allowing me to spend some time with him. It had helped me greatly. As I was about to go, Edwina approached the screen door and finally spoke to me. With a strained smile on her face, she said she was surprised to see me after the promise I had made to her earlier that year. I briefly told her about the death of Richard Brown, and my consequent decision to meet Raoul. She nodded. She then told me that the war was many years ago, and she felt that it was best left in the past.

While I stood outside the front door, I thanked Raoul again for allowing me to talk with him. I sensed that he would never again speak with anyone in such depth about the loss of his crew. I was grateful that he had allowed me to stay long enough to have the talk we did. Those two hours with one of Tony's best friends will last me a lifetime. I told Raoul at his front stoop that Nick DeRose had begun to heal after learning that he was not the only crewmember who could have persuaded Earl Wonning to bail out. By sharing that information, Raoul had helped start the healing process for Nick. So it was that I tried to convince Raoul Ramos that good could come out of talking about the war.

Despite the painful sweats and shakes that I feared Raoul would experience as a result of my visit, I was pleased that he had allowed me to sit with him and recall his crew. I sensed that he still had not forgiven himself for leaving his men on board the doomed aircraft. But I had hope that he could come to terms with his memories. Finally, I thanked him for being Tony's friend. At the last moment, he looked me in the eye and said, "I want you to tell your father that I truly respected Tony, and I respect him." Raoul Ramos had given me a gift that I needed: an acceptance of the research that I had spent the last five years of my life pursuing.

CHAPTER 12

Coming Full Circle

The first time we stood together in Arlington National Cemetery at the grave of my Uncle Tony, my father and I were equally ignorant of what actually happened on his brother's last mission. Since that time, I have been privileged to unearth the facts, and with each new discovery, my joy has been heightened by sharing the information with my dad. He may not have understood his role in fueling my passion, but whenever he sat quietly and listened to what I had to say, my desire to uncover the past increased.

On Labor Day 2000, I gave an early draft of this book to my father. I knew that reading it would give him an understanding of what his brother had experienced in World War II. I wanted him to appreciate what Tony's combat missions were really like. And to that end, I told him how badly I wanted to fly with him in a B-17. On two previous occasions, in the fall of 1997, we had been denied trips on the Collings Foundation's *Nine-O-Nine* B-17 Flying Fortress because of mechanical difficulties. We were about to have another chance. One week prior to my father's seventy-third birthday, the *Nine-O-Nine* was scheduled to appear at an air show sponsored by Daniel Webster College in Nashua, New Hampshire. For $350, civilians could take a flight in the vintage bomber.

Dad eagerly accepted my offer to fly. The only day we could both make it was Sunday, the last day of the show. The previous day, he would be attending his East Providence High School class of 1945 reunion in Rhode Island. I reserved two seats on Sunday's dawn flight, although I was warned there was no guarantee that it would take place. A minimum of six passengers would have to reserve seats on that same flight, so that the $2,000 per flight hour expense could be covered. At the time of my call, Dad and I were the only ones signed up.

On Saturday, September 16, my fiancée and I attended the air show. As Martha roamed around the grounds, I anchored myself near the Collings Foundation booth so that I could monitor the status of the Sunday dawn flight. As of mid-afternoon, there were still not enough people signed up. If the flight was going to happen, we had to be ready by 7:30 A.M. Dad would have to travel up from Rhode Island in the hope that we would get our chance.

Meanwhile, Martha had befriended a father and his son, and excitedly told them that her future father-in-law and her husband-to-be would be going up in the Flying Fortress the next day. As her new friends shared her excitement, the father offered Martha a free pass on the B-17, courtesy of Daniel Webster College. She happily accepted, although she had no plans to use it herself. As the afternoon wore on, the dawn trip finally filled up. When Martha and I met up again later, I told her that as long as the weather cooperated, I would finally get to ride in a Flying Fortress! With a huge grin, she told me that she wanted to contribute to our experience: instead of paying $700, we would be getting two seats for the price of one!

That night I was restless and couldn't sleep. Two members of the Korkuc family were finally going to return to the air in a Flying Fortress. The last time a Korkuc had flown in a B-17 was on February 25, 1944, more than fifty-six years earlier. I thought that our trip would be all the more memorable if we each carried something special from my research. My father would carry Tony's Purple Heart and the unfired .50-caliber bullet retrieved from the Willmandingen crash site, while I would take Hermann's spent .50-caliber shell casing and wear Tony's aerial gunner wings, just as my grandmother had on June 29, 1950, at Arlington National Cemetery. In this way, three generations of the Korkuc family would be bonded together.

The next morning, we were finally on board the B-17. The Collings Foundation aircraft was painted to resemble ship 42–31909 from the 91st Bomb Group. Strangely enough, the real *Nine-O-Nine* saw its first combat action on February 25, 1944, the same day Curt Clemens ushered aircraft 42–37786 out of action. It went on to fly a total of 140 combat missions without an abort or the loss of a crewman. It was as if the *Nine-O-Nine* had been destined to replace 42–37786 and keep taking the fight to the Germans. It was the perfect plane for our memorial flight.[1]

Sitting a few feet from the ball turret, my father, Edmund Korkuc, patiently awaits our flight on the *Nine-O-Nine*. Photo by author.

My father was the "Old Man of the Crew" on our flight, while at thirty-eight years old, I was the youngest. Dad and I would be flying in the waist section with Dave Abramo and his girlfriend, Megan—the only female "gunner" on the "mission." Coincidentally, it turned out that Dave and I were both descendants of 381st Bomb Group ball turret gunners.

Before we knew it, the number one left outboard engine's propeller began spinning through the still air. Within minutes, the left inboard engine added to the noise, and vibrations resonated in the cabin. As we waited for our mission to get under way, nervous chatter helped occupy our time. I sat ready for my first B-17 flight, and wondered whether Tony had felt the same kind of nervous energy as he prepared to go up for the first time. Next we heard the sound of the number three engine. The full noise of the engines did not invade our senses for some time, because the pilot was having trouble getting the number four engine running. Each time the right outboard engine seemed to be gaining momentum, it would sputter to a stop. But finally it fired. We were on our way!

Held tightly in place by my seatbelt, I had trouble seeing out the window. I lifted my head up just long enough to see Boire Field passing by me outside the right waist window at about ten miles per hour. While the plane groaned and squeaked as it made its way down the taxiway, we were comforted by the constant drone of the engines. Martha videotaped the Fortress while it was taxiing, exclaiming as she did so, "Uncle Tony got that last engine started for you; now he'd better get you back safely on the ground!"

Soon we were up and away. As I stood in the waist area just behind the ball turret, an emotional wave hit me. I started to yell out the roll call of 42–37786 on February 25, 1944. I was screaming at the top of my lungs, but I could hardly hear my own voice over the roar of the engines. I knew that my father couldn't hear me, but I sensed that the deceased members of the Henderson crew were listening as I acknowledged their presence. As I screamed out each name, I thought about the price paid by each of the boys on that mission: Dale Schilling . . . Tony Bartolo . . . Tommy Hunnicutt . . . Tony Korkuc . . . Boyd Burgess . . . Nick DeRose . . . Earl Wonning . . . Raoul Ramos . . . Don Henderson . . . Jack Fournier. Only six of the men had died on the mission, but the other four had been scarred for life.

During the flight, we were able to move around, and my father and I ventured into the radio room, the bomb bay, the cockpit, and the navigator's compartment. I stood on the top turret gunner's pedestal and got a 360-degree look around me. From my perch, I could see the blades of the four engines spinning in the wind as they pulled us through the skies. I tried to imagine what Raoul Ramos experienced during his combat missions as he looked out the windows of his B-17 and scanned the sky for enemy fighters. Unfortunately, the ball turret was off limits for our special flight.

All too soon, we were told to strap ourselves back into our seats. As we touched down, I was pleased to see my father let out an infectious grin. We had symbolically helped Tony complete his fifty-six-year journey back to earth.

I was first out of the plane, and looked back to see my father jump energetically from the old bomber. It was as if for that one moment, time had been erased. As we walked side by side, I felt that I knew a little of what Tony's combat missions were like. I strolled to the car, my thoughts reverting back to Tony's final mission aboard 42–37786.

FINISHING AT THE BEGINNING

During Memorial Day weekend of 2002, I felt compelled to spend some moments remembering my Uncle Tony. I could think of no better place to do so than Arlington National Cemetery, so that I could finish my journey where it began in 1995 when my father and I stood side by side on that hot July afternoon. Dad remained behind in Rhode Island, fully satisfied by the answers I had found for him concerning the death of his brother.

During Memorial Day ceremonies at Arlington, American flags are placed on each of the more than 270,000 graves. It is the only time of year that the graves are so adorned. It was humbling to see the red, white, and blue flags waving in silent respect for all those Americans who served their country in its time of need. A single flag was posted in front of Tony Korkuc's etched granite gravestone.

As I stood there, the memories of my years of research flooded over me. I knew that I had done everything humanly possible to learn the true details of Tony's journey to Arlington. The battle that took Tony's life is long since over. As I stared at the names of four of the six men who died on February 25, 1944, I was pleased that I had gotten to know something of their lives and their families. The men had become real to me. My research had brought them alive again.

I was not alone that day at Tony's grave. Alongside me was my wife, Martha. Together we spent a few solitary moments paying our respects to Tony Korkuc. We prayed for him and honored his memory with some tears.

Soon my mind was transported back to a brick-floored porch in Long Beach, California, where I had said good-bye to one of Tony's dearest friends. Before I left Raoul Ramos's house that day, I explained that I was approaching the end of my journey. With my upcoming marriage and plans to start a family, it was necessary for me to complete the story so that I could put that part of my life behind me. Raoul nodded his head and told me that he understood the importance of moving on with one's life. Then, after a slight pause, he looked me in the eyes, and with a serious tone, counseled me that it was important

Tony Korkuc's grave on Memorial Day of 2002. Photo by author.

to leave a special place in my heart for Tony throughout my life. As I listened to the advice of that sensitive and loving man, I realized that Raoul Ramos was telling me where he held the memories of his crew. He had kept them safely in his heart.

CHAPTER **13**

The Last Day of the Big Week

Tony Korkuc and the rest of the Don Henderson crew participated in each and every bombing mission from February 20 to 25, 1944. The historians of the Army Air Forces later referred to these five missions as "The Big Week." Superb weather over Germany allowed the United States Strategic Air Forces to finally realize their desire to wreak havoc on Germany's aircraft industry. As a result, the Allied leaders were now confident that the skies over German-occupied France offered little threat to those who would participate in the invasion of France in the late spring of 1944.

In order to feel closer to my uncle, I wanted to bring him and his crew to life once again. "The Last Day of the Big Week" is my dramatic portrayal of Tony Korkuc's last day on this earth. Although I had to take some creative license in re-creating conversations and filling in missing details, the following events have been reconstructed from my research with as much historical accuracy as possible. The timeline was derived from Missing Air Crew Report #02933 and the German victory claims.

Endnotes are offered to help the reader separate fact from fiction. Where such notes are lacking, the astute reader should be able to locate the appropriate references in the preceding twelve chapters or by using the index and searching for specific names.

On the early morning of Friday, February 25, 1944, a tired but satisfied Major General Jimmy Doolittle, commander of the Eighth Air Force, prepared himself for another day of bombing attacks against Nazi Germany's aircraft factories. Operation ARGUMENT was nearing completion.

In launching the Friday attack, Doolittle was on the verge of achieving Army Air Forces Commanding General Henry "Hap" Arnold's directive of December 27, 1943: "It is a concluded fact that [the Allied invasion of Europe] will not be possible unless the German Air Force is destroyed. Therefore my personal message to you—this is a MUST— is to, 'Destroy the Enemy Air Forces whenever you find them, in the air, on the ground, and in the factories.'"[1]

The last week of February saw favorable weather over both England and central and southern Germany. Much of Jimmy Doolittle's satisfaction that Friday morning stemmed from the fact that since Sunday, his Eighth Air Force bombers had taken full advantage of the good weather and launched four daylight missions in five days against Germany's aircraft factories. On Sunday the 20th, for the first time in the war, the Eighth Air Force had been able to send more than one thousand bombers and eight hundred fighters deep into Germany. The targets for the daylight raids were the factories in Leipzig, Oschersleben, Bernburg, Magdeburg, Brunswick, Gotha, Tutow, and Rostock.[2] As a result of the heavy bomber attack, in Leipzig alone, four twin-engine Ju-88 assembly plants sustained heavy damage. The Eighth Air Force suffered the loss of only twenty-one planes.[3]

Monday the 21st saw further successful raids, with the Eighth Air Force now joined by the Fifteenth Air Force based in Italy. Poor weather on Tuesday prevented many aircraft from finding their targets, and forty-one of the Eighth Air Force bombers failed to return. Bad weather on Wednesday accorded the Eighth Air Force crews a much-needed day of rest. On Thursday, they struck again in force. Five combat wings were sent to bomb the Schweinfurt ball bearing plant, while three wings targeted the ME-110 twin-engine fighter factory in Gotha. The raids caused considerable damage, and in the Schweinfurt raid alone, Allied fighters claimed 37 enemy fighters shot down, and the bombers claimed the destruction of a further 108.[4]

The all-out attack by the United States Strategic Air Forces was demonstrating to the Germans that the Army Air Forces could do whatever they pleased against the once mighty Luftwaffe. Adding insult to injury, each night during the week, the British Royal Air Force wreaked havoc on the same targets. The number of bombs dropped by the Eighth Air Force during that week equaled the total number of bombs it had dropped during its entire first year of operations![5] The air war over Europe had finally turned in favor of the Allies. With the successes of the "Big Week," the Allied planners could now commit themselves to Operation OVERLORD—the invasion of France.

As dawn neared on Friday morning, the weather reports indicated that all of Germany was free of clouds, and the prospects for visual bombing were excellent. It was decided to launch yet another coordinated attack by the Eighth and Fifteenth air forces against the remaining high-priority targets in southern Germany. The Fifteenth would attack the Messerschmitt component plants at Regensburg, and the Eighth would concentrate its efforts against the Messerschmitt parent plant in Augsburg, the ball bearing plant in Stuttgart, and the ME-110 plant in Furth. A contingent of Eighth Air Force bombers would be sent to Regensburg to assist the Fifteenth, in the hope that attacking from two different directions would further confuse the Germans.[6]

During the early morning hours, Colonel Harry Leber, the commanding officer of the 381st Bomb Group, was busy preparing his bombers for their role in the day's action. The 381st would be attacking the Messerschmitt fighter assembly plant located about two miles south of Augsburg. As Colonel Leber assessed his group's flight readiness for the mission, he determined that he would send thirty-two bombers to Augsburg. Twelve would fly as part of a composite bomb group with the 91st Bomb Group, while the remainder would fly in a separate formation.

While Leber was preparing the 381st for its seventy-second combat mission in the European Theater of Operations, on the flight lines his crew chiefs were readying their aircraft. Apprehensively, a 532nd Bomb Squadron crew chief was preparing Flying Fortress 42–37786. The bomber was about to embark on its eleventh combat mission. As the crew chief surveyed the olive drab–painted aircraft, devoid of any nose art, he wondered whether this plane would suffer the fate of his previous two.[7]

At 0500, the aircrews slated to fly in the day's mission were awakened by the Charge of Quarters (CQ) assigned to their respective Nissen huts. Tony "Korky" Korkuc was already half awake, but it took a while for his eyes to adjust to the beam of the CQ's flashlight. He suppressed his desire to remain in the warm sack and reluctantly planted his feet on the cold floor of the hut. This was to be his fifth mission in six days, and his crew was about to enjoy the distinction of being the only 532nd crew to fly every mission during the week.[8] Physically exhausted, he nevertheless dressed quickly so that he could get his morning coffee and grab a smoke. As he finished dressing, he wondered where the day's mission would take him.

Meanwhile, Raoul Ramos was busy waking up the rest of the enlisted men in his crew. Boyd Burgess gave Ramos a bit of a fight before succumbing to the inevitability that he would be flying yet again. The waist gunners, Tommy Hunnicutt and Sonny Bartolo, yawned while they stretched their arms in an attempt to accelerate the wake-up process. Since Butch Reeves had spent the night in the hospital recovering from frostbite suffered on the previous day's mission to Schweinfurt, Ramos did not have to worry about getting Reeves up on this cold Friday morning.

As the five enlisted men made their way to the mess hall, Tommy Hunnicutt excitedly told them about the previous evening's dinner. Although no member of the crew asked, they were all curious where Hunnicutt had disappeared to on the previous night. After hearing that he had spent the evening with his father, Korky felt a brief pang of envy. Hunnicutt's father was a colonel in the Regular Army, and also stationed in England. As the five men trudged onward in the dark toward the smell of coffee, Tommy promised to introduce each of them to his dad.[9]

While Henderson's enlisted men were in the process of waking up, another CQ was entering the Nissen hut of Earl Wonning, Nick DeRose, and Jack Fournier. Earl, still in the grips of his Indiana farm boy habits, was already awake. He tapped the co-pilot's shoulder, and soon Jack Fournier was awake also. Hearing the commotion, Nick DeRose was abruptly wrenched from a dream about his wife, Charlotte, in Hillsdale, Michigan.

A couple of huts away from Nick DeRose, Bernard Beckman watched while his former co-pilot, Don "Obo" Henderson, was awakened for his final mission. Beckman still missed flying with Obo. Not wanting to jinx the mission, he had not let on that Don's former crewmates were going to throw a big party for him on his return. Beckman's crew had had the utmost admiration for Don Henderson ever since the February 11 mission, during which he had risked his life to escort them back to Ridgewell after they dropped out of formation.[10]

As Henderson's enlisted men entered the mess hall, Sergeant Dale Schilling called out to Raoul Ramos; he would be flying as their tail gunner. Ramos was pleased to learn that Reeves's replacement gunner was the seasoned veteran of twenty-three missions, as well as a friend.

At 0540, while the four officers of Henderson's crew were entering the mission briefing hall, the enlisted men were eating breakfast after being introduced to Colonel Lee Hunnicutt. After eating, the enlisted men dressed for their subzero flight. Then Korky and the rest of the gunners made their way to the armament shack to pick up their guns, before being trucked to aircraft 42–37786.

In the mission briefing hall, the officers patiently waited for the briefing officer to reveal the day's mission. A collective groan could be heard as he uncovered the target map. Today's mission would be a 1,380-mile round trip to bomb the Messerschmitt plant in Augsburg. Silently, Don Henderson contemplated that his last mission was going to be his toughest yet, but knowing that his crewmates were watching, he did not let his feelings show. Jack Fournier, seated to Henderson's right, scanned the room in search of another 532nd Bomb Squadron pilot. George Darrow was about to fly his twenty-fifth and final mission, and Fournier was hopeful that he would be taking over as pilot of either Darrow's crew or Henderson's after the mission.

The pilots were handed a formation list indicating the positions in which they would be flying. The briefing officer explained that for today's mission, the 1st Combat Wing would consist entirely of 381st and 91st Bomb Group planes—fifty-seven ships, thirty-two from the 381st and twenty-five from the 91st. The main group of the 91st Bomb Group, consisting of eighteen aircraft, would be flying as the lead group, the main group of the 381st as the low group. The remaining nineteen planes would form a "composite group" that would fly in the high group position. Henderson noted that his was one of six 532nd aircraft that would be flying in the lead squadron of the composite group, and that 42–37786 would be flying in the number two position of the first element, behind Captain Charles Wood. In bombing Augsburg, the briefing officer explained that the 1st Combat Wing would be the third wing from the Eighth Air Force's 1st Air Division to strike the target. After the briefing, as the morning light filtered

A typical 381st Bomb Group mission briefing, September 12, 1943. Still Photo Collection, Record Group 342, FH-3A13944-A66140, NARA II.

through the clouds, the four officers of the Henderson crew hopped into a jeep and headed for their waiting aircraft.[11]

While Henderson's crew was readying for their mission, Curt Clemens of the Eighth Staffel of the Third Group of Jagdgeschwader III was just waking up in Leipheim, Germany.[12] The recent efforts of the Eighth and Fifteenth air forces had left him exhausted. He had flown combat missions on each of the past five days. As Curt drank his coffee, he cautiously eyed the new morning. The sky was clear, and he knew that today the Allied Air Forces would again strike deep into Germany.

By the time Curt finished his second cup of coffee, the Schwenkreis household at Jahnstrasse 9 in Haunstetten, just south of Augsburg, was getting into the rhythm of the new day. While Maria was busily cleaning up after the family's breakfast, her husband, Josef, was out shoveling snow away from their front stoop. He wanted to make sure that his father, Kreszentia, would not fall on the ice. Maria was relieved

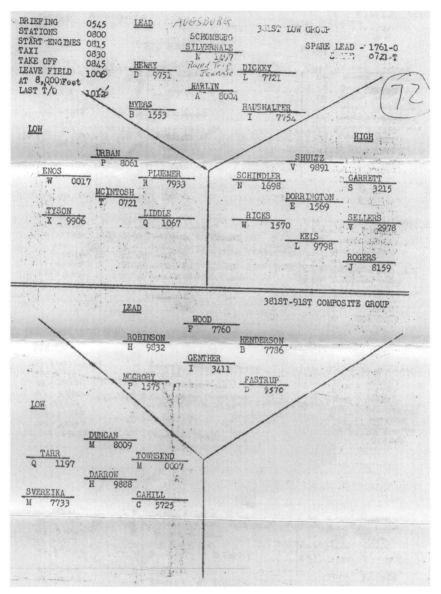

381st Bomb Group formation sheet for the Augsburg bombing mission on
February 25, 1944. Courtesy of Dave Osborne, unofficial historian of the 381st
Bomb Group.

Curt Clemens of the Eighth
Staffel of the Fighter Wing
UDET, III./JG 3. Photo
courtesy of Günter Clemens.

to finally have her older children, Marianne and Elfriede, out of the
house and off to school. In the living room, young Fritz was sitting on
his grandfather's lap as the old man read the morning paper.

Just one house over, Johanna Bock was busy taking care of her one-
year-old baby, Heinrich, while her husband, Alfred, was outside smoking a cigarette. Alfred was worried about his family. Living so close to
the Messerschmitt factory, he knew it was just a matter of time before
"child killers" bombed his neighborhood. Alfred was glad that Josef
Schwenkreis had offered the Bocks a safe haven in his shelter in the
event of a raid.[13]

In Willmandingen, it was a normal morning for young Hermann
Möck. His father had gotten up early again, and Hermann had missed
his departure. Hermann's mother fixed breakfast for him before herd-
ing him off to school. As he walked up Lauchertstrasse, she called out
that she would need him home right after school to help with some
errands. Hermann yelled back that he would be home by two o'clock.

The 381st Bomb Group planes line up in preparation for takeoff on January 12, 1944. Still Photo Collection, Record Group 342, FH-3A5897–66026AC, NARA II.

By 0800 hours, Don Henderson and Jack Fournier were sitting in the cockpit of 42–37786 going over the preflight check. In the nose, Earl Wonning was studying his navigation charts and updating a map to show the expected locations of the German flak batteries. For today's mission, the bombardier, Nick DeRose, would fly as a togglier, since his ship was not fitted with a Norden bombsight. DeRose would be ready when the time came to release the bombs on the Messerschmitt plant. Raoul Ramos was running some last-minute equipment checks; the other enlisted men checked their guns. The ship was fueled and ready for its long mission. At 0815, Henderson started the number one engine. Engines two, three, and four also started without incident.

Fifteen minutes later, Captain Wood rolled his B-17 *Avenger* onto the runway. Trailing Wood were the other eleven 532nd Bomb Squadron planes that would fly with the 91st Bomb Group that day. Following closely behind Wood was Second Lieutenant Don Henderson's name-less plane. Third in line was Lieutenant Richard Robinson's *Our Mom,* tail number 42–29832.[14]

In the second element of Wood's lead squadron, Henry Genther, commanding *Jomo,* moved out onto the taxiway behind the first ele-ment planes. Next came *Big Time Operator II,* with Milton Fastrup at the helm. The last of the six planes flying with Henderson was a new one that had arrived in Ridgewell only five days earlier. With its nose freshly painted with the Hebrew word signifying "God watch over us while we are apart from each other," the olive drab *Mizpah* confidently took its place. Hoping that the ship would live up to its name, pilot Dale McCrory sat in the left seat of *Mizpah* as it taxied onto the con-crete runway. In tenth position, George Darrow, flying in *The Joker,* was calmly waiting for his turn in line. He liked his chances on his twenty-fifth mission. In contrast to the earlier days of flying combat, for today's mission the 381st Bomb Group would be escorted by plenty of fighter aircraft. Among the "little friends" would be the P-47 Thunderbolt and the new P-51 Mustang.

As 42–37786 taxied into position, Korkuc, Hunnicutt, Bartolo, and Schilling each sat patiently in the waist section. DeRose and Wonning were manning their nose positions, and engineer Raoul Ramos stood behind pilots Henderson and Fournier, carefully checking the cock-pit instruments. Sitting alone in the radio room was Boyd Burgess. Meanwhile, in *Mizpah,* ball turret gunner Richard "Brownie" Brown sat with Howard "Red" Van Hoozer and the other gunners in the radio room. Red and Brownie were both praying that their tail gunner, Bill Seifermann, would recover from the neck wound he had suffered on the previous mission.

Don Henderson was finally given clearance to take off. Once air-borne, he formed up on Wood's right wing and waited for the other planes to form up behind him. While Henderson flew high above Station 167 in a racetrack pattern, Korky looked at the airfield down below. Despite all the times he'd flown, he was still in awe of the view from such a height. While watching the other planes take to the sky, Korky stretched his legs in preparation for his descent into the turret. He would be spending upwards of ten hours curled up in the belly of the plane.

The 532nd Bomb Squadron's B-17 hardstands are visible in the lower half of this wartime view of Ridgewell Airfield, Station 167. Still Photo Collection, Record Group 342, FH-3A13092-66105A, NARA II.

As Henderson's 42–37786 ascended to 8,000 feet, Korky climbed into his ball turret. Dale Schilling crawled past the rear wheel and knelt down in the tail gunner's position. Tommy Hunnicutt took his position in the left waist, and Bartolo moved over to the right waist guns. The crew hunkered down for a very long mission.

Despite the 10/10ths cloud cover over England, the assembly of the two bomb groups went flawlessly.[15] The 1st Combat Wing left the coast at Selsey Bill right on schedule at 1030 hours and headed toward Germany. As the planes droned over the English Channel, they climbed to 15,000 feet. When they crossed the enemy coast just before noon, they were met by friendly fighters. As Korky twirled around in his turret, constantly searching for the enemy, he was relieved to see the "little friends" join up with the massive bomber armada. Just the appearance of the fighter escorts boosted the confidence of the bomber crews.

Co-pilot's view of the bomber formation, looking through a feathered number four engine. Still Photo Collection, Record Group 342, FH-3A15598–26795A, NARA II.

At 1230, the 1st Combat Wing found themselves near Bar-le-Duc, France, as they continued to inch closer to Germany. Curt Clemens and his twenty-six comrades from III./JG 3 were doing battle with the bombers of the Fifteenth Air Force just south of Regensburg. A little more than forty minutes later, Clemens, having completed his first sortie of the day, was landing at a fighter field just outside Stuttgart. Having just missed the formation of Eighth Air Force bombers heading deep into southern Germany, Clemens refueled his ME-109 in preparation for intercepting the bombers as they returned.

While Clemens was catching a much-needed breather in Echterdingen, the 91st–381st Composite Group was approximately sixty miles northwest of Augsburg. As Henderson continued to fly off Wood's right wing, Korky was pleased to see the friendly fighters still with them. Standing on the top turret gunner's pedestal, Raoul Ramos was also glad to see P-51 fighters nearby. So far, the flight had gone smoothly.

Ten minutes before 2:00 P.M. in Willmandingen, young Hermann Möck was walking home from school with his friend Karl Heinz. As Möck neared his house, he saw his mother out front waiting for him. Hermann said goodbye to Karl and jogged over to her. Mrs. Möck swiftly put her son to work, and while Hermann was outside completing his errand, Curt Clemens was airborne once again, heading toward Augsburg to greet his second bomber formation of the day.

At 1356, the composite bomb group found itself about forty miles west of Regensburg and fifty miles northeast of Munich. At that point the formation made a seventy degree turn and headed due south. Far below, Korky could see the winding Danube. Eight minutes later, the planes turned due west at the initial point of the bomb run, approaching Augsburg from the east.

As they neared Augsburg's Messerschmitt factory, DeRose waited patiently for Wood's bombardier to give the signal to open the bomb bay doors. With the target in perfect view and no more than two minutes left before dropping their bombs, a flak burst just under the right outboard engine rocked Henderson's plane. Co-pilot Fournier let out a loud gasp as he was hit by shrapnel—one piece striking his left shin, the other his right middle finger. Warm blood dripped from his hand and leg, and Henderson's Fortress lost its position in the formation. Both Genther's *Jomo* and Fastrup's *Big Time Operator II* followed. Perhaps, Don surmised, the two planes were trying to protect him, much as he had protected Beckman two weeks before.

Henderson quickly regained control of his ship and guided it back toward the formation. As they jockeyed for position once again in preparation for the bomb drop, Genther took over Henderson's former position off Wood's right wing. Dale McCrory's *Mizpah* closed up behind Genther, taking up the lead position of the second element, and Fastrup formed up on McCrory's left wing. Seeing the vacancy, Don Henderson closed up just behind *Mizpah* on its right wing. His ball turret had been spared damage from the flak burst, but the ninety seconds of chaos during which the three lead planes had broken formation and re-formed had given Korky and *Mizpah*'s ball turret gunner, Richard Brown, an adrenaline rush.

At 1410, while the composite group crossed over the Lech River just east of snow-covered Augsburg, the bombardier of Wood's *Avenger* released its bombs over the target. A few seconds later, Nick DeRose

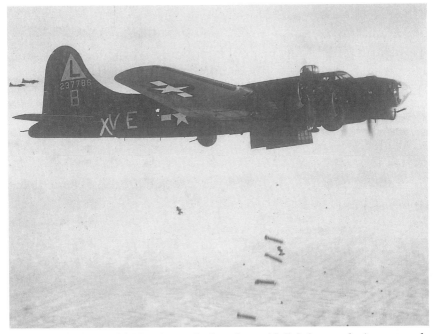

Flying Fortress 42–37786 releases its bombs amid flak bursts during an early February 1944 mission. Photo courtesy of 381st Bomb Group pilot Edward Carr.

toggled the bomb release switch in 42–37786, and it also jettisoned its bombs toward the earth below. From his perch in the belly of the B-17, Korky watched as the bombs plummeted down and exploded all around the Messerschmitt factories. Despite having seen that same scene unfold many times before, he was transfixed by the sight.

As Korky left the bomb drop zone behind him, the planes following bombed the target. One of the bombs missed its mark and fell on a small house in Haunstetten. The ten members of the Bock and Schwenkreis families died instantly as the house at Jahnstrasse 9 disintegrated.[16]

After leaving Augsburg, the huge bomber formation headed in a southwesterly direction. At 1417, just after the planes had turned once again to the northwest, trouble hit: 42–37786's number four engine started to malfunction. Looking to his right, Fournier concluded that flak must have struck the underside of the engine. Over the interphone, engineer Ramos asked Korky whether he could see any visible damage. Korky responded that he could see oil leaking. As the oil

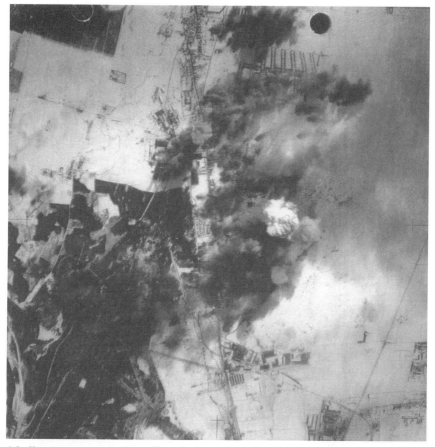

A ball turret gunner's view of bombs impacting the Augsburg target at 1409 hours on February 25, 1944, from B-17G *Dame Satan II* of the 91st Bomb Group, 322nd Bomb Squadron, tail number 42–31070, flown by Second Lieutenant Bryce M. Evertson. Combat Mission Reports for 91st Bomb Group, February 25, 1944, SAV-91–237-6 Composite Group, Record Group 18, NARA II.

sprayed out from under the damaged engine, it became difficult to maintain level flight. Henderson was having difficulty keeping 42–37786 in the bomber formation. In the co-pilot's seat, Jack Fournier also fought with the controls, trying to help Henderson feather the propellers on the number four engine. Meanwhile, engineer Ramos was trying to cut off the fuel to the damaged engine.

As 42–37786 was tossed around in the sky, *Mizpah*'s ball turret gunner, Brown, alerted pilot Dale McCrory to the fact that it was flying dangerously close to them. McCrory ordered Brown to keep a close eye on Henderson's plane. Brown remembered the small camera he was carrying, and swiftly snapped a photograph of the distressed B-17.

At 1420 hours, about 8,000 feet beneath the formation, a swarm of thirty ME-109s were milling around near Ulm, Germany.[17] Unaware of the threat they posed, Henderson, Fournier, and Ramos struggled to fix the problem created by the damaged engine. Kneeling behind Henderson with his back to the cockpit, Ramos suddenly detected a difference in the sound of the engines while working on the control panels. The superchargers were no longer giving off their familiar high-pitched whine. The superchargers for engines two, three, and four were failing. Over in *Mizpah*, Richard Brown watched as 42–37786 left formation and began to drop back. He continued to snap photographs of the Fortress.

Down below in the belly of 42–37786, Korky was relieved that the ship was no longer in danger of colliding with other aircraft. Outside the formation, however, 42–37786 would be vulnerable if enemy fighters should happen upon them.

As McCrory's ball turret gunner watched, 42–37786 began to lose altitude. Within minutes, Henderson's plane was flying 4,000 feet below the formation at 16,000 feet.[18] On board the stricken aircraft, the crewmembers offered up silent prayers for deliverance from enemy fighters. But 4,000 feet below, Curt Clemens and two of his fellow ME-109 pilots from III./JG 3 had caught sight of the straggling B-17 above them. Like wolves zeroing in on an injured animal, they began to climb.

As the minutes ticked away, Ramos was frustrated by his inability to figure out what was wrong with the superchargers. Intermittently they kept cutting out and coming back on line. Each time 42–37786 regained power, it would quickly lose it again. Adding to the tension, Henderson and Fournier could not control the number four engine. Between the loss of the superchargers and the loss of the right outboard engine, the pilots knew that their ship would not be able to rejoin the safety of the formation.

At 1429 hours, the ME-109 fighters, flying three abreast at an altitude of 16,000 feet, closed on the crippled B-17. Curt Clemens, flying slightly ahead of the other two fighters, approached head-on at a closing speed of about 450 miles per hour. Earl Wonning shouted a warning: three fighters were about to attack from the left front. Korky and the rest of the gunners swiveled their guns, seeking a target.

In-flight photo of two ME-109 fighters of III./JG 3, the top one from the 8th Staffel. Reproduced by permission of Jochen Prien, *III./Jagdgeschwader 3*, bottom photo 340.

From five hundred yards, the ME-109 unleashed a stream of 20mm bullets at the lone Fortress. Then, as the fighters snap-rolled away from the bomber, the ball turret and right waist gunners fired at one of the ME-109s emerging from under the right wing. Both scored a direct hit, and the ME-109 rolled over and fell earthward.

Knowing that the other two ME-109s would attack again, Korky hastily turned his ball turret toward the rear of the plane. Over the intercom, Dale Schilling issued a shrill warning: the two ME-109 fighters were attacking from the rear. Watching from *Mizpah*, Brown could see 42–37786's tail gunner firing. When would the top turret gunner open fire also?

As the fighters came in for the second attack, engineer Ramos stopped troubleshooting the supercharger problem and quickly stepped up to the top turret pedestal to help defend the plane. As the two fighters bore down on the Fortress, the tail gunner, veteran Dale Schilling, defiantly fired his two .50-caliber guns. Korky too was firing, when he heard bullets rip through the airframe. Up in the top turret, Ramos saw that skin fragments were being torn off the tail. Before he could get off any rounds at the enemy, the planes streaked past. But radio operator Boyd Burgess was ready at his guns, and as one of the ME-109s flashed by, he opened fire. The German aircraft exploded in midair.[19]

Tommy Hunnicutt screamed over the interphone that Dale Schilling's guns were out.[20] With his tail gunner perhaps dead, Henderson knew that another attack could be disastrous. He banked the plane to the left and entered a shallow dive, picking up momentum as he started down toward the deck. From above, Richard Brown watched as 42–37786 finally gave up the attempt to reach home and headed in a southwesterly direction. He put his camera away and said a silent prayer for Korky and the other crewmembers.

Henderson brought the plane ever closer to the ground. Over the interphone, he assured his crew that he would get them safely to Switzerland. For the time being, there was no need to bail. Now that he was flying at a low altitude, Henderson was relieved to note that the supercharger problem was no longer a concern. From his perch in the top turret, Ramos could see that Henderson might just succeed; the Swiss Alps loomed ahead in the distance. Then he was startled to hear Korky shouting that the remaining ME-109 was trailing them. The surviving gunners braced themselves for another attack.

On the ground, the soldiers of Heavy Flak Battalion 436 (o) defending Stuttgart eyed the lone Fortress, their guns tracking the tempting target. Facing only one ME-109, the B-17's gunners had begun to think they might make it. But as the lone fighter approached, the B-17 was unexpectedly rocked by flak. The First, Second, Fourth, and Sixth batteries of Flak Battalion 436 had unleashed a wall of shrapnel at the plane, striking it under both wings.[21] Radio operator Boyd Burgess was mortally wounded by flying shrapnel, which also badly wounded Tony Korkuc and Tony Bartolo.

With the plane now severely damaged, Don Henderson doubted that his ship could reach Switzerland. Over the interphone, he issued the order to bail out. As the firing subsided, Henderson once again ordered his men to bail, but there was no acknowledgment. Was the interphone still working? Below Henderson, in the nose of the plane, despite the confusion of the air battle, navigator Earl Wonning was still attempting to determine their course and position. His best estimate was that they were still about forty miles from Switzerland.

A typical 88mm heavy flak cannon, 1944, located near Schweinfurt, Germany. Photo courtesy of Edmund Scheckenbach.

Henderson decided to hug the ground even closer, hoping that the German fighter pilot would not be able to spot the B-17 against the surrounding terrain. With luck, could he reach the Swiss Alps? Unfortunately, as he approached higher ground, Henderson knew that the ME-109 pilot would have little trouble spotting his olive drab plane. When the ME-109's 20mm fire raked his plane yet again, Don Henderson finally abandoned all hope of reaching Switzerland.

Preparing to bail out, Henderson switched from manual control to autopilot. He was exhausted from trying to keep the B-17 flying level. With Fournier wounded, the task of controlling the plane was left to him alone. As they approached a small cluster of houses, Henderson attempted to open the bomb bay doors, but with his control panel shot up, he could not determine whether they had opened. He instructed Fournier and Ramos to check on the doors. They found them firmly closed. As Ramos surveyed the situation, he recalled another time when Korky and he had been forced to crank up the bomb bay doors. Ramos grabbed the manual crank and started cranking the doors down. Over his right shoulder, he saw Burgess lying face down in the radio room. Telling Fournier to continue cranking the doors, Ramos negotiated the shaky catwalk and jumped into the radio room. There was so much blood! Boyd was still alive, but he waved Ramos off. "Go check on the others!" he managed to hoarsely whisper. With pleading eyes, Ramos looked at his friend for a few more seconds, and then he glanced into the waist section.

Both Hunnicutt and Bartolo were lying down just behind the ball turret, surrounded by thousands of spent .50-caliber shells. As shells from the ME-109 once more reached the B-17, Bartolo raised his head just long enough to lock eyes with Ramos. Ramos could see that Bartolo was badly wounded. In that moment, Ramos knew that Bartolo's only chance of survival was for Henderson to bring the plane down safely. Bartolo seemed to know this, too: both knew that the odds of a safe landing were close to nil. Raoul was disturbed at the calm look in Bartolo's eyes. In that moment, he knew that Sonny lacked the strength to bail out of the plane. Over the roar of the engines, Ramos once more heard machine gun fire coming from the front of the plane. Reluctantly he made his way back, resigning himself to the fact that he could do nothing more for his crewmates.

Tommy Hunnicutt watched as Ramos left the waist area. Although thrown to the floor and stunned during the battle with the ME-109s, Tommy was miraculously unhurt. He went back to check on Korky in the ball turret. He could hear Korky pounding on the turret's inner shell. Something was obviously wrong.

Suddenly Tommy realized that spent shells were jamming the turret. He started to slap shells away from the azimuth ring, and when he thought he had cleared enough away, he slammed his palm down to signal Korky to try and move the turret again. But the turret still didn't move. Why wasn't Korky making any effort to get out? "Come on, Korky, get out!" Hunnicutt screamed at the metal bubble.

Hunnicutt remembered one more thing to try. He reached for the switch that forced the turret motor into neutral. As it disengaged, the ball turret spun downward, and the ball turret door spun into view. Hunnicutt reached down and opened it.[22]

Inside, Korky lifted his head and looked upward at his left waist gunner, his face filled with relief. But when he attempted to extricate himself from the sitting position, he could not move his injured body.

With knowledge that the ground was rising up to meet him and that he was too badly wounded to bail out, he waved Hunnicutt away. Accepting that he could do nothing more for his friend, Hunnicutt reluctantly made his way toward the waist section door.

Meanwhile, Ramos had reached the bomb bay catwalk again, and noted that Fournier had succeeded in opening the bomb bay doors. The drag of the open doors was further buffeting the plane. As Ramos entered the bomb bay, Fournier bailed out. Ramos continued on to check on Henderson, who said that he could no longer control the plane; Ramos was surprised to see that Don was smoking a cigarette.[23]

Down below in the nose section, Wonning was poring over his navigation charts. Frantically, he tried to figure out the plane's location. He wanted to help Henderson navigate to Switzerland. But fear was preventing him from thinking clearly. Were they heading west or south? Another hail of machine gun fire struck the plane.

As the ME-109 emerged from under the nose of the B-17, Nick DeRose raked it with a long burst of fire. A second burst missed, and as the fighter barreled away, DeRose was startled to catch a glimpse of the young pilot's face. DeRose could see that his B-17 was fast approaching the ground.

As Clemens swung away from the B-17, satisfied that the plane was doomed, he noted that the time was 1445. The four-engine bomber would never again terrorize German cities. But his victory was bittersweet, for he must now mourn the loss of his two comrades.[24]

As the ME-109 flew nearby, Don Henderson rang the bailout alarm bell. Nick DeRose, the image of his wife flashing through his mind, got up from his seat and moved toward the nose hatch. Wonning was sitting at his navigation table, seemingly lost in thought. DeRose screamed that it was time to bail, but Wonning wouldn't listen. DeRose pleaded with him, but to no avail. Wonning left his seat and headed toward the cockpit area.

DeRose was confused. Why wasn't Wonning bailing? What the hell was he doing? Why was he heading up to the cockpit? As Nick thought of Charlotte and his unborn baby, he punched the nose hatch open and toppled out into the wind. He hit the slipstream, and his harness tugged violently at his body. Descending by parachute, Nick watched as the olive drab Flying Fortress hurtled itself through free space toward a small village below.

Not fully understanding Nick's urgency, Wonning crawled up to the flight deck hoping to get verbal directions from Henderson. Within seconds after issuing the final order to bail, Henderson saw a red-faced Wonning coming out of the nose section. "Earl, what the hell are you doing? I ordered you to bail! Didn't you hear the bailout alarm?"[25] Wonning looked back at Henderson with shock. Had he lost valuable time coming up to the cockpit? Henderson waved him back toward the nose. Wonning headed swiftly back the way he had come. Henderson yelled at Ramos to bail out of the bomb bay, and Ramos leaped instantly into the cold air only 300 feet above the snow-covered ground. After disengaging the autopilot, Henderson followed Ramos into the slipstream.

On the ground, young Hermann Möck looked up at the sky and saw what looked like a swallow circling an eagle. Quickly realizing that it was a Luftwaffe fighter trying to down an enemy plane, Hermann ventured out in front of his house to watch the aerial battle.

With great haste, Hunnicutt made his way toward the rear waist door. He grabbed hold of the door hatch and flung it open. At that moment, 42–37786 made a lunge over its right wing. As the ground came at him, Hunnicutt leapt from the plane, reluctantly leaving behind his fellow gunners. He had done all he could for them. As the cold air struck his face, he was jerked back toward the plane. Looking back, he could see that his parachute had caught in the wing. As he sailed toward the ground, he thought of his father and was thankful he had been able to say goodbye to him earlier in the day.

When Wonning was within a couple of feet of the nose hatch once again, the plane seemed to turn over. Earl was stunned as he slammed into the window of the nose section. Dazed by the plane's last movement, Earl looked forward just in time to see a small hill come into view. In that moment, he knew he had run out of time.

In those last moments, Korky also knew his fate. He was grateful that Hunnicutt had kept his promise and tried to get him out. But he had no more strength. That last flak burst had sprayed his ball turret with shrapnel, and his body was injured beyond repair. As the plane surged to the right in its final death swoon, Korky closed his eyes and thought one last time of Seekonk. Then he looked up, put out his hand, and touched the face of God.[26]

Notes

PREFACE

1. Elma Dean, "Letter to Saint Peter," *The American Mercury* 55, no. 227 (November 1942): 592. This beautiful poem by Oakland housewife Elma Grace Dean helped people from all over the country cope with the loss of their loved ones in combat during World War II. More than sixty years later, it continues to bring comfort to the families of the fallen.

CHAPTER 1

Some of the information and quotations in chapter 1 are drawn from the National Personnel Records Center website, http://www.archives.gov/st-louis/military-personnel/; a letter to the author from the American Battlefield Monuments Commission dated June 24, 1996; a letter to the author from the U.S. Total Army Personnel Command in Alexandria, Virginia, dated March 10, 1997; an e-mail message to the author from Joe Waddell dated March 19, 1997; letters to Michael Korkuc from the Memorial Division of the Quartermaster Corps dated February 8, 1950, and October 28, 1952; and a letter to the author from James Good Brown dated April 2, 1997.

1. "Batcha" was our affectionate Americanization of *babcia,* a Polish word for "grandmother."

2. James Good Brown, *The Mighty Men of the 381st: Heroes All,* 2nd ed. (Salt Lake City: Publishers Press, 1989), 9.

CHAPTER 2

Some of the information and quotations in chapter 2 are drawn from e-mail exchanges between the author and Ted Darcy dated April 21, 22, and 23, 1997; a telephone conversation between the author and Ted Darcy on April 23, 1997; a telephone conversation between the author and Nick DeRose on April 23, 1997; a telephone conversation between the author and

Raoul Ramos on April 24, 1997; and a telephone conversation between the author and Don Henderson on June 30, 1997.

1. Missing Air Crew Report 02933, Record Group 92, National Archives and Records Administration II, College Park, Md. [hereafter NARA II].

2. Camp Lucky Strike, located in Le Havre, France, was the collection depot for all of the newly released prisoners of war. Lucky Strike was a brand of cigarettes.

CHAPTER 3

Some of the information and quotations in chapter 3 are drawn from e-mail exchanges between the author and Sigrid Kellenter dated May 3, May 10, and June 4, 1997; e-mail exchanges between the author and Jens Boysen dated June 4 and 9, 1997; e-mail exchanges between the author and Marcus Mockler dated June 10, 11, and 12, 1997, and July 9, 1997; and telephone conversations between the author and Nick DeRose on June 12 and 13, 1997.

1. Excerpt from Thomas R. Hunnicutt's Individual Deceased Personnel File, 293 File, Total Army Personnel Command, Alexandria, Va. [hereafter TAPC]. The statement of Mayor Heinz was dated June 12, 1946. The original AGRS English translation was incorrect. With the help of Michael D. Smith, corrections were added to overcome the awkward sentence structure.

2. Excerpt from Anthony J. Bartolo's Individual Deceased Personnel File, 293 File, TAPC. The statements were made on June 12, 1946, by William Möck, gravedigger; Heinrich Möck, coroner; and Gottlo Trautmann, leader of the fire brigade.

CHAPTER 4

Some of the information and quotations in chapter 4 are drawn from a letter to the author from Nick DeRose dated July 10, 1997; letters from Tony Korkuc to his family dated March 15, September 23, and May 24, 1942, and January 3, February 11, March 18, May 2, and September 22, 1943; a letter from Helen Korkuc to Tony Korkuc dated December 23, 1943; a letter from Chaplain Martin J. Collet to Anna Korkuc dated March 5, 1944; a letter from Helen Korkuc to Chaplain Martin J. Collet dated April 27, 1944; a letter from Major E. A. Bradunas to Anna Korkuc dated May 20, 1944; a form letter from Helen Korkuc to the crews' families dated May 24, 1944; a letter from Mrs. Boyd Burgess to Anna Korkuc dated May 26, 1944; a letter from Mrs. Don Henderson to Anna Korkuc dated May 27, 1944; a letter from

Virginia Burgess to Anna Korkuc dated June 3, 1944; letters from Major General J. A. Ulio to Anna Korkuc dated October 20, 1944, and February 6 and May 11, 1945; a letter from Mrs. Gertrude Fournier to Anna Korkuc dated June 4, 1945; a letter from Don Henderson to Anna Korkuc dated July 1, 1945; a letter from Nick DeRose to Anna Korkuc dated July 2, 1945; and a letter from Raoul Ramos to Anna Korkuc dated July 2, 1945.

1. "Seekonk Veterans: In Memoriam," *Seekonk (Mass.) Sentinel*, Wednesday edition, May 8, 1974.

CHAPTER 5

Some of the information and quotations in chapter 5 are drawn from a letter to the author from Don Henderson dated September 11, 1997; an interview with Nick DeRose at his home in Grand Ledge, Michigan, on November 14, 1997; an interview with Norman Wonning in Indianapolis, Indiana, on January 16, 1998; a letter from Raoul Ramos to Esther Wonning dated June 19, 1945; and a letter from Jack Fournier to Esther Wonning dated July 9, 1945.

1. Henderson was in error when he told me that *Baby Dumplin*, tail number 42–30676, was the plane he escorted back to base. *Baby Dumplin* was shot down on January 5, 1944. Bill Lofton's newspaper clipping makes it clear that *Baby Dumplin* had been flown by the Bernard Beckman crew in their earlier days. According to the *532nd Bomb Squadron War Diary, February 1944* (Air Force Historical Research Agency, Maxwell Air Force Base, Alabama), Don Henderson did not fly as pilot until February 5, 1944, a full month after *Baby Dumplin* was lost in action. The records show that Henderson and Bernard Beckman flew only four missions together as lead pilots—on February 11, 20, 21, and 24, 1944. I am doubtful that the mission occurred during the "Big Week"; I believe that it took place on February 11, 1944. According to the formation sheet for the February 11 mission, obtained from 381st Bomb Group historian Dave Osborne, Henderson was flying in 42–37786, while Bernard Beckman was flying in *Bar Fly*, tail number 42–40008.

2. "Lt. Don Henderson Praised for Heroic Action." *Red Cloud [Neb.] Commercial Advertiser*, May 12, 1944.

3. Donald G. Henderson passed away on October 13, 2001, in Wichita, Kansas, at the age of eighty-three. He was born on December 4, 1917. Ironically, Tony's first pilot, Bill Herrington, had died just eleven days earlier. Social Security Death Index, http://ssdi.rootsweb.com/.

4. Roger A. Freeman with Alan Crouchman and Vic Maslen, *The Mighty Eighth War Diary* (London: Arms & Armour Press, 1990), 188.

CHAPTER 6

Some of the information and quotations in chapter 6 are drawn from a telephone conversation between the author and Lee B. Hunnicutt in December 1998; an e-mail message to the author from Lee B. Hunnicutt dated September 2, 2001; handwritten notes of Colonel Lee V. Hunnicutt about the loss of his son's aircraft on February 25, 1944; a letter from Raoul Ramos to Mrs. George Schilling dated July 5, 1945; a letter from Raoul Ramos to Virginia Burgess dated January 11, 1945; an e-mail message to the author from Edgar Miller dated August 20, 2001; an e-mail message to the author from Dave Osborne dated December 2, 1998; telephone conversations between the author and William Herrington on November 17, 1997, and in December 1997; postings on the HeavyBombers Forum, http://www.armyairforces.com; and XC-15–032-261, Veterans Administration Claims Folder for Fournier, Jack H., Federal Records Center, Dayton, Ohio, NARA..

1. Alexandra Barnes, "A Happy Memorial Day: Mystery of Dead Brother Revealed by Stranger," *Greenwich [Conn.] Post*, May 15, 1998, 6.

2. Dale E. Schilling, Individual Deceased Personnel File, 293 File, TAPC.

3. The Lowell, Indiana, Public Library website lists Dale Schilling in its World War II Veterans section, http://www.lowellpl.lib.in.us/schillin.htm.

4. Roger A. Freeman, *The American Airman in Europe* (Osceola, Wis.: Motorbooks International, 1991), 64–65, photo 22.

5. *Lowell [Ind.] Tribune*, January 20, 1944, 1, col. 5, http://www.lowellpl.lib .in.us/schillin.htm.

6. William C. Herrington died on October 2, 2001, in Melbourne, Florida, at the age of eighty-three. He was born on November 14, 1917. Social Security Death Index, http://ssdi.rootsweb.com/.

7. The enclosed death certificate indicates that the date of death was September 4, 1979. The gravestone incorrectly states the date as September 5.

CHAPTER 7

Some of the information and quotations in chapter 7 are drawn from an interview with Chaplain James Good Brown at his home in Haverhill, New Hampshire, in October 1997; and audiotaped interviews with Burton Hill, George Cathcart, Leonard Spivey, John Wood, and an unnamed ball turret gunner at the 381st Bomb Group reunion in Baltimore, Maryland, on September 5–6, 1997.

CHAPTER 8

Some of the information and quotations in chapter 8 are drawn from a letter to the author from Marvin Fairbanks dated June 7, 1998; a letter to the author from Dave Brophy dated June 24, 1998; telephone interviews with Richard Brown on June 6, 1998, and in August 1998; a letter to the author from Richard O. Brown dated July 30, 1998; a telephone interview with Dale McCrory in August 1998; a letter to the author from Howard Van Hoozer dated August 24, 1998; e-mail messages to the author from Howard Van Hoozer dated July 9, 2000, and January 10, 1999; and a letter to the author from Al Suchy dated June 10, 1999.

1. Bill Seifermann died on February 27, 1944. *532nd Bomb Squadron War Diary, February 1944*, microfilm A0638, frames 1800–1804.

2. Roger A. Freeman and David R. Osborne, *The B-17 Flying Fortress Story: Design—Production—History* (London: Arms & Armour Press, 1998), 164; *532nd Bomb Squadron War Diary, 1 Apr 45–30 Apr 45* (Air Force Historical Research Agency, Maxwell Air Force Base, Alabama), microfilm A0638, frame 1719.

CHAPTER 9

Some of the information and quotations in chapter 9 are drawn from an e-mail message to the author from Joe Waddell dated December 24, 1997; an e-mail message to the author from Marcus Mockler dated January 13, 1998; letters to the author from Hans Grimminger dated July 19, 1998, and January 1, 1999; a letter to the author from Rudi Penker dated September 20, 1998; an e-mail message to the author from Rabe Anton (pseudonym) dated October 8, 1998; e-mail messages to the author from Don Caldwell dated October 22, 1998, and November 29, 2000; an e-mail message to the author from John Manrho dated January 6, 2000; a letter to the author from Günter Clemens dated March 27, 2000, quoting from a letter from Curt Clemens to his family dated February 25, 1944; a letter to the author from Winfried Bock dated May 1, 2000; an e-mail message to the author from Uwe Kühnapfel dated December 10, 2006; a posting to the author by Don Caldwell on http://forum.12oclock high.net/ on November 28, 2000; e-mail messages to the author from Günter Clemens via Hans-Bernd Wibbelt on March 6 and April 5, 2002; a letter to the author from Rosemarie Zander Hunt dated May 9, 2000; and letters from Curt Clemens to his family dated April 25 and July 18, 1944.

1. Jochen Prien and Gerhard Stemmer, *Messerschmitt Bf 109 im Einsatz bei der III./Jagdgeschwader 3, 1940–1945* (Eutin, Germany: Struve-Druck, 1995), 285–87. English translation courtesy of Michael D. Smith.

2. Ibid., 458, 502.

3. Tony Wood's Combat Claims & Casualties Lists can be found at http://www.lesbutler.ip3.co.uk/tony/tonywood.htm.

4. According to the III./JG 3 (Loss List) Namentliche Verlustmeldung for January 27, 1945, Feldwebel Curt Clemens was flying in a Bf 109 G-14, with Werknummber (Wing Number) 64156, and a plane identification number of Gelbe 15. During his last mission, he was flying for 11./J.G. Udet. Deutsche Dienststelle (WASt), Berlin, Germany, http://www.dd-wast.de/.

CHAPTER 10

Some of the information and quotations in chapter 10 are drawn from a videotaped conversation between the author, Hermann Möck, and Karl Heinz in Willmandingen, Germany, on September 26, 1999, as interpreted by Marcus Mockler; a videotaped conversation with Hermann Möck at Möck's home in Willmandingen, Germany, on October 1, 1999, as interpreted by Marcus Mockler; and an interview with Richard Brown at Brown's home in Coldwater, Michigan, on November 13, 1999.

1. *1200 Jahre Gemeinde Willmandingen* (Willmandingen, Germany: Local Printer, 1972), 62. The text incorrectly stated that the American four-engine bomber crashed on February 23, 1944. In quoting from the anniversary booklet, I corrected the date.

2. Statement of William Möck, gravedigger, June 12, 1946, from Anthony J. Bartolo's Individual Deceased Personnel File.

CHAPTER 11

Some of the information and quotations in chapter 11 are drawn from a telephone conversation between the author and Edwina Ramos on January 31, 2000; a letter to the author from Jean Brown dated July 4, 2000; and an interview with Raoul Ramos at his home in Long Beach, California, on July 31, 2000.

CHAPTER 12

1. My information was obtained from the Collings Foundation literature distributed prior to the flight. More information is available at http://www.collingsfoundation.org/.

CHAPTER 13

1. Wesley F. Craven and James L. Cate, eds., *The Army Air Forces in World War II*, vol. 3: *Europe: Argument to V-E Day, January 1944 to May 1945* (Chicago: University of Chicago Press, 1951), 8.

2. Glenn B. Infield, *Big Week: The Classic Story of the Crucial Air Battle of WWII* (New York: Brassey's, 1993), 52.

3. Craven and Cate, *The Army Air Forces in World War II*, vol. 3, 34.

4. Ibid., 39.

5. Ibid., 43.

6. Ibid., 41.

7. Al Suchy, letter to author, June 10, 1999.

8. *532nd Bomb Squadron War Diary, February 1944.*

9. Lee B. Hunnicutt, e-mail to author, September 2, 2001.

10. "Lt. Don Henderson Praised for Heroic Action."

11. Report of Operations Officer, 91st Bombardment Group, Mission of 25 February 1944, Record Group 18, NARA II.

12. Prien and Stemmer, *Messerschmitt Bf 109 im Einsatz bei der III./Jagdgeschwader 3*, 286.

13. Hans Grimminger, letter to author, January 1, 1999.

14. The tail numbers and names of all the B-17s from the 381st Bomb Group mentioned in this chapter were derived from the Formation Sheet for February 25, 1944, supplied by 381st Bomb Group historian Dave Osborne.

15. 10/10ths cloud cover meant that there was 100 percent cloud cover over England. Had there been no cloud cover, it would have been referred to as 0/10th cloud cover. This cloud characterization was derived from the February 25, 1944, Combat Mission Reports of the 91st Bomb Group, Record Group 18, NARA II.

16. Hans Grimminger, letter to author, January 1, 1999.

17. The ME-109s were seen near 48 degrees 23 minutes north latitude, and 10 degrees 8 minutes east longitude. Operational Report of Mission, 25 February 1944, to Headquarters 1st Combat Bomb Wing from the 381st Bomb Group, Record Group 18, NARA II.

18. The altitude of 42–37786 was obtained from the Casualty Questionnaire of Donald Guy Henderson, Missing Air Crew Report 02933, 10, and from Richard Brown, interview with author, November 13, 1999.

19. My description of Clemens's battle tactics was derived from his first aerial victory with 8./Jagdgeschwader 3, Abschussmeldung, January 29, 1944, Curt Clemens, RL 10/583 Einsatz SU und Reichsluftverteidigung, Bundesarchiv-Militärarchiv [hereafter BA-MA]. The report was translated

courtesy of Michael D. Smith. In describing the air battle, I assumed that Clemens used similar tactics when downing aircraft 42–37786 less than a month later. The claim that Flying Fortress 42–37786 downed two of its attackers was derived from Don Henderson, letter to Anna Korkuc, July 1, 1945.

20. Raoul Ramos, letter to Mrs. George Schilling, July 5, 1945.

21. Luftwaffen-Personalamt Abschuesse durch Flak U. fliegende Einheiten February 1944, BA-MA, from microfilm 2026 Teil I/Film 1.

22. During my interview with Richard Brown on November 13, 1999, he told me that he and waist gunner Howard Van Hoozer had a pact that should Richard have trouble getting out of the ball turret, Howard would switch the turret motor into neutral. My idea to have Tommy Hunnicutt do the same for Tony was derived from this conversation.

23. Yolanda Henderson, phone interview, July 10, 1997. Don had told Mrs. Henderson that just prior to bailing out, he was smoking a cigarette.

24. For February 25, 1944, Curt Clemens recorded his victory at 1445; Luftwaffen-Personalamt Tageliste 1 August 1943–29 February 1944, BA-MA, from microfilm C2025N I Teil. At that time in the war, the German and British times were the same. This information was obtained from Robert de Bruin, "Time Calculation 1940–1945," *Bulletin Airwar 1939–1945* 11, no. 99 (January 1985): 26–27.

25. Don Henderson, phone interview with author, June 30, 1997.

26. John Gillespie Magee, Jr., "High Flight," in Rose N. Cohen, ed., *Flying High: An Anthology of Aviation Literature for Junior High School Students* (New York: Macmillan, 1942), 181.

Bibliography

Armstrong, Roger W. *U.S.A. the Hard Way: An Autobiography of a B-17 Crew Member.* Orange County, Calif.: Quail House Publishing Co., 1991.

Bigler, Philip. *In Honored Glory: Arlington National Cemetery Final Post.* Arlington, Va.: Vandamere Press, 1997.

Brown, James Good. *Gems for Living.* Madison, Wis.: 381st Bomb Group Memorial Association, 1993.

———. *The Mighty Men of the 381st: Heroes All.* 2nd ed. Salt Lake City: Publishers Press, 1989.

Bruin, Robert de. "Time Calculation 1940–1945." *Bulletin Airwar 1939–1945* 11, no. 99 (Dutch Airwar Study Group 1939–1945, January 1985): 26–27.

Caldwell, Donald L. *JG 26: Top Guns of the Luftwaffe.* New York: Ivy Books, 1991.

Carr, Edward C. *On Final Approach: Recollections of a World War II B-17 Air Crew.* Oak Harbor, Wash.: Whidbey Printers, 2002.

Childers, Thomas. *Wings of Morning: The Story of the Last American Bomber Shot Down over Germany in World War II.* Reading, Mass.: Addison-Wesley, 1995.

Coffey, Thomas M. *Decision over Schweinfurt.* New York: David McKay Co., 1977.

Cohen, Rose N., ed. *Flying High: An Anthology of Aviation Literature for Junior High School Students.* New York: Macmillan, 1942.

Comer, John. *Combat Crew: A True Story of Flying and Fighting in World War II.* New York: William Morrow and Co., 1988.

Craven, Wesley F., and James L. Cate, eds. *The Army Air Forces in World War II.* Vol. 3: *Europe: Argument to V-E Day, January 1944 to May 1945.* Chicago: University of Chicago Press, 1951.

Darcy, Ted, and Ray Emory. "Finding America's Missing." *After the Battle,* no. 122 (2003): 30–35.

Durand, Arthur A. *Stalag Luft III.* New York: Simon & Schuster, 1989.

Fletcher, Eugene. *The Lucky Bastard Club: A B-17 Pilot in Training and in Combat, 1943–45.* Seattle: University of Washington Press, 1992.

Freeman, Roger A. *The American Airman in Europe.* Osceola, Wis.: Motorbooks International, 1991.

———. *The Mighty Eighth: A History of the Units, Men, and Machines of the US 8th Air Force.* New York: Orion Books, 1970.

————. *Mighty Eighth War Manual.* London: Jane's Publishing Co., 1984.

Freeman, Roger A., with Alan Crouchman and Vic Maslen. *The Mighty Eighth War Diary.* London: Arms & Armour Press, 1990.

Freeman, Roger A., and David R. Osborne. *The B-17 Flying Fortress Story: Design—Production—History.* London: Arms & Armour Press, 1998.

Gawne, Jonathan. *Finding Your Father's War: A Practical Guide to Researching and Understanding Service in the World War II US Army.* Drexel Hill, Pa.: Casemate, 2006.

Greene, Bob. *Duty: A Father, His Son, and the Man Who Won the War.* New York: Harper Collins, 2000.

Harding, Steve. *Gray Ghost: The R.M.S. Queen Mary at War.* Missoula, Mont.: Pictorial Histories Publishing Co., 1982.

Hastings, Donald W., David G. Wright, and Bernard C. Glueck. *Psychiatric Experiences of the Eighth Air Force.* New York: Army Air Forces, 1944.

Havelaar, Marion H., and William N. Hess. *The Ragged Irregulars of Bassingbourn: The 91st Bombardment Group in World War II.* Atglen, Pa.: Schiffer Publishing, 1995.

Infield, Glenn B. *Big Week: The Classic Story of the Crucial Air Battle of WWII.* New York: Brassey's, 1993.

Jablonski, Edward. *Flying Fortress: The Illustrated Biography of the B-17's and the Men Who Flew Them.* New York: Doubleday and Co., 1965.

Kaplan, Philip, and Jack Currie. *Round the Clock.* New York: Random House, 1993.

Kaplan, Philip, and Alan Rex Smith. *One Last Look.* New York: Artabras Publishers, 1983.

Linderman, Gerald F. *The World within War: America's Combat Experience in World War II.* New York: Simon & Schuster, 1997.

Mackay, Ron. *381st Bomb Group.* Carrollton, Tex.: Squadron/Signal Publications, 1994.

————. *Ridgewell's Flying Fortresses: The 381st Bombardment Group in World War II.* Atglen, Pa.: Schiffer Publishing, 2000.

McGuire, Melvin W., and Robert Hadley. *Bloody Skies: A 15th AAF B-17 Combat Crew—How They Lived and Died.* Las Cruces, N.Mex.: Yucca Tree Press, 1993.

McGuire, William C., II. *After the Liberators: A Father's Last Mission, a Son's Lifelong Journey.* Boone, N.C.: Parkway Publishers, 1999.

McManus, John C. *Deadly Sky: The American Combat Airman in World War II.* Novato, Calif.: Presidio Press, 2002.

Miller, Donald L. *Masters of the Air: America's Bomber Boys Who Fought the Air War against Nazi Germany.* New York: Simon & Schuster, 2006.

Moriarty, Ernest T. *One Day into Twenty Three.* Self-published, 1987. ISBN 0962013900.

Novey, Jack. *The Cold Blue Sky: A B-17 Gunner in World War Two.* Charlottesville, Va.: Howell Press, 1997.

O'Leary, Michael. *Boeing B-17 Flying Fortress.* Oxford: Osprey Aviation, 1998.

O'Neill, Brian D. *Half a Wing, Three Engines and a Prayer: B-17s over Germany.* Blue Ridge Summit, Pa.: TAB/Aero Books, 1989.

Osborne, David R. *They Came from Over the Pond.* Madison, Wis.: 381st Bomb Group Memorial Association, 1999.

Prien, Jochen, and Peter Rodeike. *Messerschmitt Bf 109 F, G, & K Series: An Illustrated Study.* Atglen, Pa.: Schiffer Publishing, 1995.

Prien, Jochen, and Gerhard Stemmer. *Messerschmitt Bf 109 im Einsatz bei der III./Jagdgeschwader 3, 1940–1945.* Eutin, Germany: Struve-Druck, 1995.

Sledge, Michael. *Soldier Dead: How We Recover, Identify, Bury, and Honor Our Military Fallen.* New York: Columbia University Press, 2005.

Smith, Starr. *Jimmy Stewart: Bomber Pilot.* St. Paul, Minn.: Zenith Press, 2005.

Spivey, Delmar T. *POW Odyssey: Recollections of Center Compound Stalag Luft III and the Secret German Peace Mission in World War II.* Attleboro, Mass.: Colonial Lithograph, 1984.

Steinbeck, John. *Bombs Away: The Story of a Bomber Team.* New York: Paragon House, 1990.

———. *Once There Was a War.* New York: Penguin Books, 1994.

Stiles, Bert. *Serenade to the Big Bird.* Carthage, Tex.: Howland Associates, 1998.

Stone, Ken, ed. *Triumphant We Fly: A 381st Bomb Group Anthology, 1943–1945.* Paducah, Ky.: Turner Publishing Co., 1994.

Watry, Charles A., and Duane L. Hall. *Aerial Gunners: The Unknown Aces of World War II.* Carlsbad, Calif.: California Aero Press, 1986.

Welch, John F. *Dead Engine Kids: World War II Diary of John J. Briol, B-17 Ball Turret Gunner.* Rapid City, S.D.: Silver Wings Aviation, 1993.

Wood, Tony, and Bill Gunston. *Hitler's Luftwaffe.* London: Salamander Books, 1997.

Wright, Arnold A. *Behind the Wire: Stalag Luft III South Compound.* Benton, Ark.: Arnold A. Wright, 1993.

Web Resources

GENERAL RESOURCES

Babel Fish translation tool
   http://babelfish.altavista.digital.com/babelfish/tr
Directory assistance websites
   http://www.switchboard.com/
   http://www.infospace.com
   http://www.whitepages.com/
   http://www.411.com/
Search engines
   http://www.ask.com/
   http://www.google.com
Social Security Death Index Interactive Search
   http://ssdi.rootsweb.com/

U.S. RESOURCES

Air Force Historical Research Agency at Maxwell AFB, Alabama
   http://afhra.maxwell.af.mil/
National Archives and Records Administration
   http://www.archives.gov/
National Archives Archival Database Search Tool for Finding World War II Enlisted Men
   http://aad.archives.gov/aad/fielded-search.jsp?dt=893&tf=F&cat=all
National Archives Archival Database Search Tool for Finding World War II Prisoners of War
   http://aad.archives.gov/aad/fielded-search.jsp?dt=466&tf=F&cat=GP24&bc=sl

National Archives Military Resources: Archives Surviving from World
War II
  http://www.archives.gov/research/alic/reference/military/ww2-
records-in-archives-globally.html
National Personnel Records Center
  http://www.archives.gov/st-louis/military-personnel/
National World War II Memorial Search Registry
  http://www.wwiimemorial.com/default.asp?page=registry.asp&
subpage=intro
United States Army Air Forces of World War II
  http://www.armyairforces.com/
  http://www.armyairforces.com/help.asp (a useful summary of
research help)
United States Department of Veterans Affairs
  http://www.va.gov/
  Toll-free telephone number: 1-800-827-1000

ONLINE DISCUSSION FORUMS

United States Army Air Forces of World War II (various forums)
  http://www.armyairforces.com/forum/
12 O'Clock High! Luftwaffe and Allied Air Forces Discussion Forum
  http://forum.12oclockhigh.net/
381st Bombardment Group (Heavy), Ridgewell, England
  http://www.381st.org/

GERMAN RESOURCES

German Military Archives
  http://www.bundesarchiv.de/aufgaben_organisation/
dienstorte/freiburg/
Tony Wood's Luftwaffe Combat Claims & Casualties Lists
  http://www.lesbutler.ip3.co.uk/tony/tonywood.htm
World War II German Soldier War Losses and Prisoners of War
Information Office (Deutsche Dienstselle [WASt])
  http://www.dd-wast.de/

TIPS FOR FINDING WAR DEAD

To obtain an Individual Deceased Personnel File, send your request to:

   U.S. Army Personnel Command, Public Affairs Office (FOIA)
   200 Stovall Street
   Alexandria VA 22332-0404

To obtain a Missing Air Crew Report,

   (1) Search the Army Air Forces MACR Database page at http://www.armyairforces.com/dbmacr.asp to obtain the MACR number, then

   (2) Contact the National Archives at the following address to request a microfiche of the Missing Air Crew Report:

   National Archives, Record Group 92
   National Archives at College Park
   8601 Adelphi Road
   College Park MD 20740–6001

Index

References to illustrations are in italic type.

"How Can I Forget", 99–100, *101*, 192–93
.50-caliber, 45, 57, *139*, 168, 176, *177*, 187, 203, 208, 229, 232
1st Air Division, 217
1st Combat Wing, 217, 223, 224
20mm bullets, 229, 231
293 File, 6, 236n1, 236n2, 238n2
303rd Bomb Group, 107
321st Fighter Squadron, 115
322nd Bomb Squadron, 227
381st Bomb Group, 6, 8–10, 13–18, 21–22, 28, *30*, 33, 35, 41, 44, 64, 66, 106–108, 112, 117–18, 121–22, 126–28, 131, 137, 209, 215, *218–19, 221*, 222
381st Bomb Group Memorial Association, 112, 120, 122, 127–28, 131, 133, 135, 139, 147
42-37786 (B17G), 18, 25, 41, *51*, 52, *76*, 86, 109, *139*, 144, *145*, 146–50, 156, 163, *167*, 168, *173*, 177–78, 180, 182–83, 191, 195, 208, 210–11, 215, 217, 221–23, 226–30, 234, 237n1, 241n18
532nd Bomb Squadron, 6, 8–10, 21, 28, 32, 90, 121–22, 128, 130, 133–35, 137, 141–42, 144, 215, 217, 221, 237n1, 239n1, 239n2, 241n8

533rd Bomb Squadron, 8, 121, 131
534th Bomb Squadron, 8, 16
535th Bomb Squadron, 8, 122, 124, 128
91st Bomb Group, 208, 215, 217, 221, 224, *227*, 241n11, 241n15

Abramo, Dave, 209
Abschussmeldung (victory report), 150, 159, 241n19
Air Force Historical Records Agency, 10, 150, 154
Alexandria, Louisiana, 24, 43, *59*, 63, *81*, 100, *201*
Alliance, Nebraska, 26
Amarillo, Texas, 63, *188*
American Battle Monuments Commission (ABMC), 5
American Graves Registration Service, 9, 11, 49, 52, 98, 171, 178–79, 181
Anton, Rabe (pseudonym), 150–51, 153–54, 159
Arlington National Cemetery, 3–5, 7–10, 12, 46, 49, 59, 65–66, 77, 99, 102–103, 109, *110*, 121, 123, 127, 166, *173*, 207–208, 211
Army Air Forces, 3, 17, 26, 29, 63, 66, 90, 103, 113–14, 130, 213, 214, 241n1, 247